The Story of Westminster Abbey

Violet Brooke-Hunt

Alpha Editions

This edition published in 2024

ISBN : 9789362996855

Design and Setting By
Alpha Editions
www.alphaedis.com
Email - info@alphaedis.com

As per information held with us this book is in Public Domain.
This book is a reproduction of an important historical work. Alpha Editions uses the best technology to reproduce historical work in the same manner it was first published to preserve its original nature. Any marks or number seen are left intentionally to preserve its true form.

Contents

INTRODUCTION .... - 1 -

PART I WITH KINGS AND QUEENS IN
THE ABBEY .... - 5 -

CHAPTER I IN THE MISTY PAST .... - 7 -

CHAPTER II THE HALLOWING OF THE
ABBEY .... - 15 -

CHAPTER III SAXONS AND NORMANS
AT WESTMINSTER .... - 25 -

CHAPTER IV THROUGH SEVEN REIGNS .... - 32 -

CHAPTER V WITH KINGS AND QUEENS
IN EDWARD'S SHRINE .... - 42 -

CHAPTER VI EDWARD III. AND QUEEN
PHILIPPA .... - 52 -

CHAPTER VII RICHARD II. AND QUEEN
ANNE .... - 58 -

CHAPTER VIII HENRY V. AND HIS
CHANTRY .... - 67 -

CHAPTER IX THE WARS OF THE ROSES
AND THE THIRD ROYAL BUILDER .... - 79 -

CHAPTER X THE ABBEY AND THE
REFORMATION .... - 89 -

CHAPTER XI IN THE CHAPEL OF
HENRY VII. ....- 97 -

CHAPTER XII FROM THE STUARTS TO
OUR OWN TIMES...- 109 -

PART II AMONG THE MONUMENTS ....- 119 -

CHAPTER XIII PURITANS AND
CAVALIERS IN THE ABBEY ....- 121 -

CHAPTER XIV CHAUCER ....- 131 -

CHAPTER XV SPENSER, ADDISON, AND
THE POETS' CORNER..- 140 -

CHAPTER XVI GARRICK, JOHNSON,
AND SHERIDAN..- 154 -

CHAPTER XVII THE MUSICIANS IN THE
ABBEY ....- 165 -

CHAPTER XVIII WILBERFORCE AND
HIS FELLOW-WORKERS ....- 173 -

CHAPTER XIX PITT AND THE
STATESMEN'S CORNER ....- 186 -

CHAPTER XX INDIAN STATESMEN
AND SOLDIERS: LAWRENCE AND THE
HEROES OF THE MUTINY ....- 198 -

CHAPTER XXI DICKENS, BROWNING,
AND TENNYSON ....- 208 -

CHAPTER XXII A LAST WANDER
AROUND...- 221 -

INTRODUCTION

Geoffrey's father had gone to be the representative of the Mother Country in one of the distant Colonies, and as the boy had "more brains than body," to quote his house-master, his parents had taken him with them for a time, making a long journey first. When he came home to go to Eton, I found him a much-travelled person, brimming over with a host of new ideas and impressions, though otherwise the same original dreamy boy as ever. The inches he had added to his height and his chest testified to the success of the experiment on that score, while it was evident that his active little brain and his big eyes had made the most of their opportunities.

"I seemed to be doing lessons all day," he confided to me, "only they weren't lessons out of a book, and they seemed so much easier to remember. I wish I could always learn things by seeing them!" As the Christmas holidays had to be spent in London, I took Geoffrey at his word, and one morning we wandered down to Westminster Abbey for the ostensible purpose of seeing the Coronation Chair. Of course we saw a great deal more, and one visit led to another.

"It's not a bit like a churchyard, though it is full of monuments," was Geoffrey's criticism one morning. "It is just a book about English history right from the very beginning; and please I want you to write it all down; because now I've seen the places and the monuments and the figures, I shall understand reading about them."

I demurred, but Geoffrey had answers for most of my objections, and here is his view of the matter, imparted to me in fragments and at intervals during the day.

"It's not only what I want," he said, "but I know some of the boys and girls where father is would like it too, especially if you put in plenty of pictures. You see though lots of them have never been over here at all, they always call England home, and they all mean to come some day. And of course when they do come they will go to Westminster Abbey, because it partly belongs to them. I am afraid I can't explain it very well, but what I mean is that now I have learned so many new things about the Abbey, I feel as if I understood ever so much more about history; not the dates and the Acts of Parliament and the dull parts, but the kings and the queens, and the important men who really lived and did things. And all those people must belong to every one who is English, no matter where they live, mustn't they? So if you put them all into a book, every one who reads it will know what to go and look for in the Abbey, and they won't feel quite strange when they get inside the doors, because they will see old friends all around them."

Geoffrey's remarks were suggestive, to say the least of them, and as he spoke I could not help feeling that there were other boys and girls besides those across the seas, and possibly some grown-up people too, who would learn to better know and love the Abbey, with its eight hundred years of unbroken traditions, if they could read its story written in simple language and told in a simple way.

That is at once my excuse and my justification for a book which does not aspire to be technical, exhaustive, or very erudite. Critics will find plenty to criticise, especially in the latter part, for I am well aware that with such a mass of material to draw from, much has been left unsaid that is nevertheless full of interest. Many events have of necessity been crowded into a few lines, when a few chapters would not have done them justice, while I plead guilty to having dwelt at greater length on some names than is perhaps warranted by their actual position in history. Broadly speaking, my desire has been, firstly, to consider the Abbey as including the Palace of Westminster, and to weave men and events connected with both into the story; secondly, to try and make clear how wonderfully representative, how all-embracing, is this glorious old Church, with its continual reminder to us that though former things may pass away, new things for ever spring up to fill the empty places.

Then Geoffrey had his favourites and I had mine, for both of us in our different ways are hero-worshippers, and thus has our selection been made.

For the rest, I can only feel that, despite its shortcomings, the book will not altogether fail in its object if it makes the Abbey a more familiar place to the boys and girls of the Empire, if it helps, in the words of Matthew of Paris, "to keep alive the memory of the good in the past generations, for the which all sacred historians have striven, from Moses down to the deep-souled chroniclers of the years in which we ourselves are living."

Many are the books to which I am deeply indebted, but especially would I mention, among other works, Dart's "History of the Abbey Church" (1723), Widmore's "History of the Church of St. Peter" (1750), Neale and Brayley on "The History and Antiquities of the Abbey" (1818), and portions of the Chronicles, Matthew of Paris, Froissard, and Stowe. Among modern works Dean Stanley's "Memorials" easily takes the first place, as much for the charm of its style as for its general value and admirable classification; and I am especially obliged to Mr. John Murray, the publisher, for allowing me to use two of the copyright plans from this book. Stanley's "Sermons on Special Occasions" are also so closely connected with Westminster Abbey that I have found them very suggestive.

The Deanery Guide is invaluable, and contains a storehouse of information concisely and correctly tabulated. No one should go round the Abbey for the first time without this excellent little work, and I gratefully acknowledge the assistance it has been to me. I must also include the "Annals of Westminster Abbey," by Mrs. Murray Smith; "Westminster Abbey," by W. J. Loftie; "Westminster," by Sir Walter Besant, and "A Little Guide to Westminster," by E. M. Troutbeck.

For more general information and for biography I have turned to the standard histories, especially to Freeman's "Norman Conquest," and to those most useful lists of authorities given in the "Dictionary of National Biography."

VIOLET BROOKE-HUNT.

45 ALBERT GATE, S.W.
February 1902.

PART I
WITH KINGS AND QUEENS IN THE ABBEY

VAULTING IN HENRY VII.'s CHAPEL.

CHAPTER I
IN THE MISTY PAST

"Without the walles of London, uppon the river Thames, there was in Times past, a little monasterie, builded to the honour of God and St. Peter, with a few Benedict monkes in it, under an Abbote serving Christe. Very poore they were, and little was given them for their reliefe. Here the king intended, for that it was near to the famous citie of London, and the river of Thames, that brought in all kinds of merchandizes, from all partes of the worlde, to make his sepulchre: he commanded that of the renters of all his rentes the work should be begunne, in such a sorte, as should become the Prince of the Apostles."

These are the words which gather up the early story of Westminster Abbey.

Try to forget for a few moments that pile of splendid and richly decorated buildings, majestic and dignified in its beauty, which to-day stands out so clearly against the grey of London skies as if conscious of its right to be regarded as the most wondrous treasure belonging to London City, and come back with me a journey of many hundred years, to make the acquaintance of the Abbey as it appeared to the boys and girls who lived under Saxon and Danish, English and Norman, Plantagenet and Tudor kings. For only so will you come to understand how the history of the Abbey has been interwoven with the history of England; how, in days gone by, kings and nobles, commons and people gathered beneath its shadow, making it not only the centre of the nation's life and activity, but also the starting-point from which set out every English sovereign called to the throne, the resting-place to which so many of them were borne back, when they had received their summons to the high court of the Great King.

Then you will feel something more than a sense of wonder as your eyes rest on its beauties. It will speak to you in a language of its own, as it tells you of that past which you must learn to know aright if you are to play your part nobly in present or in future days. It will open your ears so that you will catch echoes of the melodies which float down the ages. It will bring to your heart a thrill of reverence and a thrill of pride, as you realise that this treasure-house of memories is a national inheritance in which you have a share. It will make you familiar with that company of men and women who, by reason of their goodness or their greatness, or their many gifts, so won the respect of their fellows, that in death they were deemed worthy to lie within walls "paved with princes and a royal race." And it will teach you, as no book can teach you, the story of the land we love, the land which all the great men of history—kings, soldiers, statesmen, poets, workers, and thinkers have helped to build up, that it might be ours to inherit and then to pass on to coming generations in unsullied greatness.

Now if we wish to trace back to its first commencement that "little monasterie without the walles of London," we must frankly admit that concerning its earliest history any information we possess is of a very shadowy character. Certain it is that for some centuries a religious building had existed on Thorn-ea, one of those many little islands standing above the reach of the floods which rose at high tide in that part of the Thames where it broadened out into a great marsh. Possibly the Romans had a station at Thorn-ea, as Roman bricks and pieces of mosaic and such remains as a fine Roman coffin have been discovered from time to time, and Bede, our first English historian, states that Lucius, king of Britain, himself a Christian, built a church on Thorney Island about the year A.D. 178. For nearly four hundred years England had remained the conquered province of the Roman Empire. Then the greatness of that power began to wane; Rome was threatened at her own doors by the Goths, and to defend herself she had to call back her legions from Britain and leave the island to its fate. Picts, Scots, and Saxons bore down on it, and the Saxons, "fierce beyond other foes, cunning as they are fierce, the sea-wolves that live on the pillage of the world, to whom the sea is their school of war and the storm their friend," swept all before them. Wherever they went on their victorious way they slaughtered and shattered, and whatever Christian church existed on Thornea they razed to the ground. For awhile the curtain falls, then it rises to show us Sebert, a Christian king of the East Saxons, who lived at the beginning of the seventh century. He was converted and baptized by Mellitus, the Bishop of London, and founded the Minster of St. Paul on the east side of London. But in years to come, when Thornea was no longer a desolate "Isle of Thorns overrun and wild," but the spot above which there towered the Abbey, the Palace and the Monastery all grouped together under the name of the West Minster Foundation, the monks declared that King Sebert had raised a second church in this very place, dedicated to St. Peter, the Prince of the Apostles. Furthermore they told how one dark and stormy Sunday night, the eve of the day set apart by Bishop Mellitus for the consecration of the new church, Edric, a fisherman busy at his craft, heard a voice calling him from the opposite side of the river. He went across in his boat, and found there a stranger, who begged to be rowed over to the island. This Edric did with some difficulty, as the waters were rough, and raised with "prodigious rains," and the stranger, landed safely on the island, at once went towards the newly builded church. "Watch well this night, Edric," he said as he left the astonished fisherman. So Edric waited and watched, and in the space of a few moments he saw the empty church ablaze with light, standing out without darkness or shadow in the wild night. Voices, such as he had never heard before, sang chants and hymns:—

"Yonder swelled that strain,

And still the Bride of God, that Church late dark,

Glad of her saintly sponsors laughed and shone,

The radiance ever freshening....

The fisher knew that hour

That with vast concourse of the sons of God

That Church was thronged."—AUBREY DE VERE.

Then the lights faded, the music died away, and once more the stranger stood at Edric's side.

"Give me to eat," he asked of him.

But Edric had as yet caught nothing.

"Cast forth thy nets, for the Fisherman of Galilee hath blessed thee," said the stranger, and then he added, "Tell Mellitus on the morrow what you have seen, and show him the token that I, Peter, have consecrated mine own church at Westminster. For yourself, go out into the river; of fish you shall catch plenty, and many salmon. But the tenth of all you take, you shall pay to my church, and never again shall you seek to catch fish on any Sunday."

With these words the stranger vanished, leaving Edric to ponder on the wonderful things he had seen and heard.

On the morrow, when Bishop Mellitus, accompanied by his priests and singing-boys, arrived to dedicate with all such honour as he could the Minster of Thorney, he was met by Edric, who held in his hand a salmon, and gave the message which had been delivered to him. Furthermore, he pointed out to him the marks of the twelve crosses of consecration, in memory of the twelve Apostles, on the church within and without. And the Bishop believed his words, for he saw everywhere the signs; so he went from the church saying: "The dedication had been performed sufficiently, better and in a more saintly fashion than he could have done." So he held a service of thanksgiving for this token of heavenly favour, and then made his way back to London, to enjoy with a good conscience the fish which Edric had presented to him.

Quaint and picturesque as is the legend, it is clearly nothing but a legend, told by the monks of St. Peter's for various reasons, the most probable being that they were anxious to prove their superiority over the monks of St. Paul's. It is not even a certainty that King Sebert played any part at all in the history of Thorney Island, for in several of the oldest chronicles we are told about "a dweller or citizen of London by name Sebert who was excyted to make a church in the worship of St. Peter in the West End of London, which that time was foregrowen with bushes and bryeres exceedynglye." But, on the whole, I think we may allow the monks to keep King Sebert as their founder, and accept the story that he and his queen were buried in leaden coffins in this early church, that their bodies were removed to the restored church more than four hundred years later, and once again, in the reign of Henry III., were taken from their resting-place to be laid with great ceremony in the tomb which now you can see just inside the south ambulatory of the Abbey.

A century later we find something tangible concerning the Church and Monastery of St. Peter; for Offa, the wise and strong king of Mercia, made certain gifts to it, and in the charter of 785 A.D. confirming these, he spoke of Thorney Island as a "locus terribilis," by which he probably meant "a sacred spot." But after this again there is silence. Once more Britain lay at the mercy of the invaders, this time the fierce Danes, who, as the Saxons had done, swept ruthlessly over the land, devastating and destroying as they went. The church at Thorney was in far too conspicuous a position to escape their notice; they fell upon it in all their fury, and only a few of the monks managed to reach London alive. So were the buildings "reduced to a very mean and low condition."

In time, however, the hand of the Dane was stayed. For a hundred years indeed had they held their sway of terror, till at last they were decisively beaten by Alfred of Wessex, that ideal warrior-king, who first freed his people from their oppressors, and afterwards, laying aside all personal ambition, devoted himself to the task of ruling them wisely and well.

The Peace of Wedmore was signed in 875, and probably the church and monastery of St. Peter were rebuilt soon after, but we know nothing till we come to the days when Dunstan was made Bishop of London, and "prevailed easily with King Edgar (as indeed he did, and ordered all in Church matters during the reign of that Prince), to have the monastery, then in ruins, restored, and that too at the king's expense; that is, the walls and what else remained of the ruins repaired and the place made habitable. And he brought hither from Glastonbury twelve monks to make it a small monastery of the Benedictine Order." Dunstan had grown up from childhood under the shadow of that famous monastery at Glastonbury, where he had been the pupil of the well-learned and deeply religious men who had come over there from Ireland, and when at last, after many years of varied fortunes, he found himself all-powerful, he made it his first object to introduce the strict Benedictine rule wherever it was possible in religious houses. For during the time when the Danes held the upper hand the people had fallen back into many heathen ways, and the priests no longer held the torch of Christ's religion on high, or sought to lead men from darkness to light. Dunstan was full of zeal, and under his strong influence King Edgar made many grants of lands and provisions to the Abbey of St. Peter, in which place Wulsinus, also a monk from Glastonbury, reigned as Abbot.

But once again the monks of Thorney Island were driven forth from their cells and their cloisters, this time also at the hands of the Danes, who, led by Sweyn, "marched through the land, lighting war beacons" as they went on their way, avenging the treacherous massacre of their fellow-countrymen in Wessex.

King Ethelred, the Unready, offered no resistance to the Danes, but let every city save London fall into their hands, and then fled from his kingdom, leaving Sweyn on the throne. However, in Canute, the son of Sweyn, there arose a friend to what remained of the religious house on Thorney, for he, "of a usurper being none of the worst," as an old writer cautiously admits, conceived a great affection for a good monk, Wulnoth, who had been brought up in the monastery there. When he became king, Canute raised Wulnoth to the position of Abbot, granted many favours to him and his house, and there is little doubt that he built for himself a dwelling-place at Thorney so as to be near Wulnoth, whose conversation pleased him, the Abbot being a man of singular sincerity. It was a rest to him to turn from the cares and responsibilities of his kingdom to the peaceful simple life of the Benedictine house. God had called him to the camp and the court, and he had vowed never to spare himself in what was good or needful for his people. But in his latter days it was the calm of the cloister that he loved. Nothing remains of the palace he built there, save the record that it was burned down in a later reign, but it is probable that the well-known incident of the courtiers and the tide took place on Thorney Isle.

Canute was but forty when he died, and with him died the peace which had been such a blessing to his people while he reigned. For he left three sons, and between two of these, Harold and Hardicanute, there was sharp strife as to who should become king of England. First they divided the land, then Harold became sole king. But three years later he died, and was buried in the Church of St. Peter, under the shadow of the walls his father had loved so well. From thence, however, his fierce brother Hardicanute dragged forth his body and had it thrown into the Thames hard by.

Such a deed as this stamps the man, and shows him as he was, cruel, revengeful, and fierce. His people suffered many things at his hands, and when he died of hard drinking at the end of two years, there was a great longing throughout the land to shake off the last trace of a Danish yoke and to have for king one of their own race. Their hearts turned towards Edward, the younger son of Ethelred the Unready, whose life hitherto had been chiefly spent in Normandy, whither he with his mother, Emma of Normandy, afterwards the wife of Canute, had taken refuge when Sweyn had conquered England. Little did they know of him, save that he was of their blood, and had been exiled from his land and his birthright by a foreign foe. But his face was gentle, like that of a woman, with white skin, pink cheeks, blue eyes and golden hair; his voice was low, his manner serious and kind, his ways were simple and he had a reputation for great holiness.

Earl Godwine, the all-powerful noble who had served under Canute and had vainly endeavoured to restrain his sons, was at one with the people of England in this matter, and so it came to pass that "before King Hardicanute buried were, all folk chose Edward to king at London." For awhile Edward hesitated. A throne had no attractions for him, and he was almost a stranger to English manners and English life. But Godwine, who had gone out to Normandy as the bearer of the message from the people, over-persuaded him and brought him back. The Witan met at Gillingham in Dorset to confirm the choice of the citizens of London, and Edward was crowned in Winchester Cathedral on Easter Day with great ceremony, many foreign princes and ambassadors being present to do him honour.

Almost the first work of the new king was to build himself a palace, and the site he chose was one close to the little Benedictine monastery at Thorney Isle, which now was always called Westminster, a place no longer covered with brambles, but well cultivated by the monks, who were skilled tillers of the soil, and rendered green and fertile by the river which flowed hard by. Of the palace as he built it no traces are left to us, it having been all destroyed by fire, but we know it was made very strong, guarded by outer and inner walls fashioned after the manner of a Norman castle, probably nearly resembling the Council Chamber and Banqueting Hall which still remain in the Tower of London, little altered since the day when the early Norman builders completed their work. The Abbot of Westminster at this time was Eadwine, a very prudent man, and he soon attracted the notice of the king, who was by nature far more fit to rule a monastery than a kingdom. Edward was troubled somewhat in his mind, for when an exile in Normandy, he had taken a vow that should it ever please God to restore him to his rightful inheritance, he would go on a pilgrimage to Rome to do honour to St. Peter there; but now that he was safely established on the throne, his council made strong objections to his leaving the country, lest some evil should befall him or the Danes should take advantage of his absence to invade the land, while "the common people, publicly and with tears, showed their concern, entreating him to desist from so dangerous a voyage." Thus the king knew not how to act, desiring ardently to carry out his vow, and yet being unwilling to disregard the wishes of his people. Possibly it was Eadwine, living as he did so near to the king's new palace as to be often consulted by him, who proposed as a way out of the difficulty that a Bishop, with a fitting retinue, should be sent as an ambassador to Pope Leo, to explain to him how Edward was restrained from journeying thither himself, and to ask for a dispensation. This proposal was quickly carried into action.

Pope Leo readily absolved the king from his vow, desiring that instead he should build or restore some monastery to the honour of St. Peter, and make over to the relief of the poor such a sum of money as his journey would have cost him.

Edward was wonderfully pleased at the Pope's message, and resolved to begin at once a building worthy of the great Apostle. What more natural than that he should choose the little monastery at Westminster, which was very poor? It lay near to the city of London, and to that great river up and down which there was so much coming and going of ships. It lay near also to his own palace, and if the present humble buildings gave place to such an edifice as he intended to raise, where could a more suitable burying-place for himself be found when the time came for God to call him hence? Then, too, Abbot Eadwine found great favour in his eyes; and the monks there, under the strict rule of St. Benedict, had won for themselves a good report concerning the simplicity and holiness of their lives. So it seemed fitting that Westminster should be raised from its lowly state and be refashioned in a manner worthy of the saint whose name it bore.

Just at this time, too, Wulsinus, an aged and saintly monk at Worcester, had a wondrous story to tell of a sacred vision vouchsafed to him, in which St. Peter had appeared bidding him to deliver this message to the king. "There is," declared the Apostle, "a place of mine in the west of London, which I chose and love, the name of it being Thorney: which having for the sins of the people been given to the power of the barbarians, from rich is become poor, from stately low, and from honourable is made despicable. This let the king by my command restore and make a dwelling of monks, stately built and well endowed, for it shall be no less than the House of God and the Gate of Heaven."

The vision was made known to Edward, and shortly afterwards he commanded that a tenth of his entire substance, gold, silver, cattle, and all other possessions, should be set aside for the purpose of pulling down the old church and raising a new one from the very foundation.

So from this time the story of the Abbey passes from misty legend into proven history, and it is with Edward, named afterwards "the Confessor," that the glory must rest of having called into being that great religious house, destined in the future to be most closely linked with all that concerned alike the crown and the country.

CHAPTER II
THE HALLOWING OF THE ABBEY

King Edward had no sooner resolved on the site for his new Abbey Church, than he commenced the task of building it, pressing on the work with zealous eagerness, making it indeed the object of his life. In his character he lacked all those qualities which go to the making of a great king. His prayers and his visions so absorbed him, that in heart and mind he lived in the company of saints and angels, and the duties of government were altogether irksome to him. By birth partly Norman, by education and tastes entirely so, he knew but little of the people over whom he was called to rule, and wherever it was possible he willingly handed over all duties of government to others. Fortunately for himself and for England, there were two men ever at his side, who served both him and his people loyally and well, these being Earl Godwine and his second son, Harold, Earl of the East Saxons. Both were related to him, for Godwine was the father and Harold the brother of Lady Eadgytha, the beautiful and accomplished wife of the king, and both showed themselves to be rulers wise, just, and merciful.

Of the two, Harold was the more beloved by king and country alike; indeed, one chronicler of that time boldly says that Edward's greatest claim to glory lies in the fact that he called Harold to the government of his realm. Tall of stature, beautiful in form and face, he excelled in all things, whether in the battle-field or at the council, and to his many gifts was added a noble and upright character, strong when the need for strength arose, but ever inclined to show mercy and compassion. This was the man on whose shoulders Edward virtually laid all the responsibilities of his realm, while he spent most of his time in his palace at Westminster, so that he might be on the spot to superintend the progress of the building, which went on apace, and to consult with Abbot Edwy as to the form it should take. It was on the church itself, rather than on the buildings of the monastery, that the king lavished his especial care. He meant it to be in the "new style," which he had learnt to love during his exile in Normandy, that land which came forth those master-builders, many of them priests and scholars, whose handiwork is still to be found alike in Norman and in English minsters, beautiful as ever in its strength, its simplicity, and its dignity. Many were the Norman customs and ideas which Edward brought over with his Norman friends, and some of them were vigorously opposed by Harold, who was passionately English.

But as we go through the country and find one after another of those majestic buildings in grey stone, made so perfect as to defy the centuries, we must gratefully remember that it was King Edward who first of all set up this "new style" as a model in our midst.

One characteristic was, that every great church should be built in the form of a cross; in the centre the nave, at the east end the High Altar, and where the nave merged into the choir cross arms on the right and on the left, and so it was that Westminster was the first cruciform church in England.

This is a description of Edward's building, given to us in a French Life of the king, written very shortly after his death:—

"Now he laid the foundations of the church

With large square blocks of grey stone.

Its foundations are deep,

The front, towards the east he makes round,

The stones are very strong and hard.

In the centre rises a tower

And two at the western front,

And fine and large bells he hangs there.

The pillars and mouldings

Are rich without and within.

At the basis and the capitals

The work rises grand and royal.

Sculptured are the stones

And storied the windows.

All are made with the skill

Of good and loyal workmanship.

And when he finished the work,

He covers the church with lead.

He makes then a Cloister, and Chapter-House in front,

Towards the east, vaulted and round,

Where his ordained ministers

May hold their secret Chapter,

Prater and dorter,

And the officers round about."

Considering the size of Edward's building, for it was very little if any smaller than the Abbey as we know it to-day, it is unlikely that all the parts described by the French chronicler were finished during the lifetime of the king. Indeed, the royal builder seems to have known that his eyes would never rest on his work, perfected as he dreamt of it. His longing therefore was that church and choir might be completed and dedicated, and for the rest he made such munificent gifts in land and money, plate and jewels to the Abbot, that he had no fear but that the building of the monastery with its cloisters and dormitories, infirmary and refectory, would be easily accomplished, even if he did not live to see it.

Signs were not wanting to warn him that the hour of his death was near at hand. He had ever firmly believed in dreams and visions, and of late these had been full of solemn meaning to him. He had seen the Seven Sleepers of Ephesus turning from their right sides to their left, and this he judged to be an omen which told of a great upheaval, of wars, pestilence, and famine, which should last for seventy years. Then, too, the Christ Child had appeared to him as he stood near the High Altar in the newly finished choir, and had told him how soon he was to be called hence. And, most wonderful of all, two pilgrims, just returned from the Holy Land, came to the king with a strange story.

Some time before, Edward was on his way to the dedication of a church he had built to St. John the Evangelist, when he passed a beggar who pleaded with him for his charity in the name of the Apostle of Love. The king carried no money with him, and his much-loved Chamberlain, Hugolin, was not at hand. Yet so tender-hearted was Edward that he could not pass the beggar by, and he took from his hand a ring, "large, royal, and beautiful." The beggar took it and vanished. But these two pilgrims told how while they were in Syria and in great straits, having wandered from their path, an old man with a long, white beard, carrying two lighted tapers, stood in their pathway and questioned them. When they spoke of their country and their king, he became very joyous, and declared how great a love he bore to Edward. Furthermore he led them to a hostel hard by, told them that lie was none other than St. John the Evangelist, and gave them the ring, bidding them to take it back to the king with the assurance that in half a year he should stand at his side in Paradise.

Edward accepted the story with childlike simplicity. He fasted more rigorously, he prayed more earnestly, and he decided to hasten on the hallowing of his church.

The Feast of Christmas was at hand, and the king summoned the Witan for the first time to Westminster, that they might take part in the great ceremony. Little did he dream how through the centuries to come Abbey and Parliament would be welded together.

On Christmas Day, though ill, he, wearing his crown, took part in the services, and was present at the Christmas banquet in the palace. He conversed with the bishops and the nobles, and appointed the feast of the Holy Innocents as the day on which the great event for which he had so longed should take place.

But his strength began to rapidly ebb away, and all who saw him knew him to be a dying man. Too weak to do more than set his signature to the charter of the foundation, he still insisted that the hallowing should take place. Death held no terrors for him; it was but the gate through which he must pass ere he could join that white-robed host of saints and martyrs whose presence he had felt so near to him through life. Only, like Simeon of old, there was one thing he desired before he could say, "Lord, now lettest Thou Thy servant depart in peace." Not till his church was consecrated would the desire of his heart be satisfied.

By his bedside stood his wife, the Lady Eadgytha, herself the founder of a convent church at Wilton. In life he had never loved her overmuch; like his kingdom, she occupied a very secondary place in his thoughts. But womanlike she forgot all that in this moment, and thought only how best she could help and comfort him. Calmly she carried out his every wish, and, acting as his representative, went, accompanied by her two brothers Harold and Garth, to the consecration of the Abbey Church by Stigand, Archbishop of Canterbury.

"Magnificently finished was the church," says an old writer, and it is not difficult for us to picture what took place there on this joyous festival. The walls, massive and stately in their simplicity, gleamed in their freshness, and formed a vivid contrast to the colours to be found in the vestments of the bishops and the priests, the robes of the acolytes and singing boys, the distinctive dress of the monks, and the varied costumes of nobles, both Norman and Saxon, who were assembled there. The lights shone on the High Altar, clouds of incense floated around it, and for the first time those walls resounded with chant and hymn and solemn antiphon.

"The work stands finished," murmured the king as the echoes of the music floated across to him.

When the queen returned to his bedside, he lay unconscious, and she, kneeling on the ground, tried to restore to him warmth and life. But for many days he made no sign. Then suddenly, on the last day of the old year, came the final flicker. In a voice clear and strong, he spoke of two holy monks, and all that they had prophesied to him concerning the disaster which would shortly overthrow the land. So earnest were his words that they struck terror into the hearts of all present; only Stigand, the Archbishop, dared declare that the king babbled in delirium. Yet other things did Edward bequeath in those last days. To his friend the Abbot Eadwine he gave his body with the command that it should be laid in the Abbey Church, and to Harold, his brother-in-law, he commended the Lady Eadgytha, who had never failed in her duty towards him, and to whom he desired all honour should be accorded. Neither did he forget his Norman favourites, who had, he declared, left their native land for love of him.

Still there was one all-important bequest to be made, and in that moment Edward seemed to have understood, as he had never understood before, the hopes and longings of his people.

"To thee, Harold, my brother, I commit my kingdom," he said solemnly.

Then once more he became silent till near the end, when he turned to the weeping queen.

"Mourn not, my daughter," he said. "I shall not die, but live. For passing from the country of the dead, I verily hope to behold the good things of the Lord in the land of the living."

So he fell asleep; and to him St. Peter opened the gate of Paradise, and St. John, his own dear one, led him before the Divine Majesty.

The grief of the people was intense, and to it was added a wild terror as to what might now befall the land. Hurriedly, as if in a panic, the royal funeral took place on the Feast of the Epiphany, but one day after the king had breathed his last, and the Abbey became the scene of the deepest mourning. Dirges and penitential psalms filled its walls instead of joyful hymns of praise and thanksgiving.

Edward, wrapped around in beautiful robes embroidered by Eadgytha and her maidens, and wearing the pilgrim's ring, was laid in royal state on a bier, and carried by eight men to the Abbey, there to be placed before the high altar.

"Bishops, and a multitude of abbots, priests, and ecclesiastics, with dukes and earls assembled together. A crowd of monks went thither, and innumerable bodies of people. Here psalms resound, the sighs and tears burst out, and in that temple of chastity, that dwelling of virtue, the king is honourably interred in the place appointed by himself."

THE CONFESSOR'S FUNERAL. FROM THE BAYEUX TAPESTRY.

So, in a halo of sanctity, ended the life and reign of Edward; and remembering all his piety, his humility, the nights of contrition he spent on the cold stones in spite of his wearing sickness, his deep reverence for all things holy, and the noble gifts he made to the Church, men spoke of him rather as a saint than as a king. And indeed as a ruler he left but little mark on his times. Yet the Abbey Church of Westminster is no small memorial for this last king of the Saxons to have bequeathed to the English nation, and for that alone we owe him a debt of gratitude which lends an unfading glory to his name.

Now, you will be wondering how much of the Abbey Church as Edward built it, stands to-day. And alas! there is but little of it left. For when Henry III., who had a special love for the Confessor, resolved to set up some worthy memorial of this "glorious king," he pulled down the greater part of the simple, stately building Edward had so loved, and set up in its place a much more ornate and magnificent piece of work. Edward built to the honour of St. Peter; Henry, to the memory of St. Edward. But generous as was his motive in pulling down that solid Norman building, which otherwise would have been standing firm as ever to-day, we cannot help regretting those vanished Norman arches and massive pillars.

When you stand by the altar rails, you can remember that the bases of the pillars on either side of the altar are those belonging to Edward's church; or if you go from the cloisters, where the south and the east walks join, into the little cloisters, you will pass under an old archway over the entrance, always known as the Confessor's door. Underneath, too, what used to be the ancient dormitory, but is now the great schoolroom of Westminster School, some very massive and solid buildings remain which evidently date from Edward, and there is also again the Chapel of the Pyx, or Chapel of the Chest, where treasures belonging to the sovereign and the monastery were kept. Neither of these latter places are shown to the general public, but when you go to see the Chapter-House, the entrance to which is in the east cloister, you will see to the right of it the doorway of the Pyx Chapel, which is wonderfully strong, and is said to be lined with the skins of Danes. The interior of this, with its stone altar and its solid stone arches, can have undergone very little alteration since Edward's day. You will get, too, what is probably a correct general idea of the whole building as it looked from the outside in those early days if, when you are in the Chapter-House, you look carefully at the pictures which are copied from the Bayeux tapestries. This wonderful piece of work, which was prepared for the rebuilt Cathedral at Bayeux in Normandy, was certainly embroidered during the lifetime of William the Conqueror, and may even have been the work of his wife, Queen Matilda. Most probably it was made in England, and is in itself a valuable addition to the very fragmentary history of those times. All its details seem to be very accurate, copied from what the workers actually saw and knew about, so there is no reason why the picture of the Abbey in that part of the tapestry which shows the funeral of the Confessor should not as accurately represent the building exactly as it stood.

You must notice the part towards the east made round, and the stones which are "very strong and hard," with the main tower and the two smaller towers at the side. And notice too the figure of a man, who is standing on the roof of the Palace, and holding with one hand the weathercock on the east end of the Abbey.

May be the worker only sought to show the buildings of the Abbey and the Palace standing side by side, but all unconsciously that unknown hand prophesied what should be throughout the centuries to come, and told how Church and State should stand firmly linked together.

The members of the Witan had not departed to their homes on the conclusion of the festivities connected with Christmastide and the consecration of the Abbey. They knew the king was dying fast, and that before many days a great duty would rest on them. Rumours may have reached their ears that William of Normandy, cousin to Edward, meant to lay claim to the throne on his death, declaring that the king had promised to make him his heir, and that Harold himself had vowed to support him. But the sturdy Englishmen who formed that council were resolved that never with their consent should a Norman rule over them, and Edward knew full well the man of their choice when he pointed to Harold as their future king. There was an heir to the throne by right of birth, Edgar the Atheling. Still he lived far away unknown to them all, and the days had not yet come when men succeeded to the throne by right of birth alone. On the spot was Harold, the man they loved and trusted, "the shield of the kingdom, the shelter of the oppressed, the judge of the fatherless and the widow."

Edward had done his part. "Death snatched him from the earth, angels bore his white soul to heaven, and in his death he had been glorious, for he had made fast his realm to the noble earl."

The Witan did not hesitate so soon as the throne was theirs to fill, but of their number sent two, who sought out Harold where he stayed, comforting his widowed sister, and offered to him the throne as the man of their choice. Here again the copy of the Bayeux tapestry in the Chapter-House will help you to picture the scene. You will see the two nobles, one bearing the axe of office, the other holding a crown and pointing to the room in which lay Edward, from whence the crown had been borne. And you will see Harold—to quote the vivid words of Mr. Freeman, "at once wistfully and anxiously half drawing back the hand which was stretched forth to grasp the glittering gift. A path of danger lay open before him, and duty, no less than ambition, bade him enter upon the thorny road. And yet the risk had to be run. If he declined the crown, to whom should England offer it? Under him alone could there be the faintest hope that England would offer a united front to either of the invaders who were sure to attack her. The call of patriotism distinctly bade him not to shirk at the last moment from the post to which he had so long looked forward, and which had at last become his own. The first man in England, first in every gift of war and peace, first in the love of his countrymen, first in renown in other lands, was bound to be first alike in honour and in danger."

So Harold was virtually king of England, appointed by Edward, chosen by the Witan. Yet "full king" he was not until before the altar he and his people had given each other their solemn pledges, until "the blessing of the Church and the unction of her highest ministers had made the chosen of the people also the anointed of the Lord."

There was no time to lose. Already the members of the Witan had lingered for a much longer period than was their wont, and they were anxious to return to their homes. But to delay the coronation until their next meeting was too dangerous to be dreamed of. England could not be left without a king. The burial of Edward and the coronation of Harold must take place at once.

So it came to pass that amid unusual sorrow Edward was buried, as I have already described to you, in the dim light of the Epiphany morning, and a few hours later all was in readiness for the solemn coronation rite.

There can be but little doubt that it was in Westminster Abbey that the ceremony took place. Harold, led by two bishops, walked to the high altar followed by a long procession, the singers chanting the prayer that justice and judgment might be the foundations of his throne, that mercy and truth might go before his face. Then the king elect fell on his knees, and the grand strain of the *Te Deum* rose to the skies.

And now Eldred, Archbishop of Northumberland, turned to the crowd and demanded of the prelates, the Theyns, and the people of England whether it was their will that Harold should be crowned king?

Their answer was a mighty shout of assent, which came from their very hearts. Then Harold, on his oath, swore to protect the Church of God and all Christian people, to forbid wrong and robbery to men of every rank, to strive after justice and mercy in all his judgments; and first the Bishop and afterwards Eldred prayed that the God who had wrought such mighty works, would pour down His best gifts on him chosen to be king of the Angles and Saxons, that he might be faithful as Abraham, gentle as Moses, brave as Joshua, humble as David, wise as Solomon, so that he might protect both the Church and his nation from all visible and invisible foes.

So the oath was taken and the prayers were ended. But there was yet to follow that sacred rite of mystic meaning, which was enacted as Eldred poured the holy oil on the head of the king, beseeching God, that as of old, kings, priests, and prophets were anointed, so now the oil poured on the head of His servant might be a true sign of the sanctifying of his heart, a means of grace for His glory and the welcome of His people. The crown was placed on his head; the sword was handed to him; sceptre and rod were given one after the other into his hands; while with each act the solemn voice of the Archbishop rose in prayer that a yet brighter crown in the heavenly country might be his, that he might ever with the sword defend the Church and the people against all adversaries, that his sceptre might be a sceptre of righteousness, and that he who had been anointed with the holy oil might stand fast in the strength of God.

Thus was Harold set upon the royal throne; on his head was the crown, in his hand the sceptre, his sword was borne by two chiefs, "while all the people saw him with wonder and delight."

Directly the coronation ceremony was over, the Mass was celebrated. Then all adjourned to the Palace hard by, and a great banquet was held on this

Twelfth Night, the last day of the Christmas festival, into which so many and varied scenes had been crowded.

Little had those members of the Witan dreamt when they set out from their homes, of all that would have have happened ere they returned—Christmas festivities and meetings of the Council; the consecration of the new church; the death of King Edward; the choosing of King Harold; the burying of the old king and the crowning of the new, all had followed one after the other in those short wintry days.

And the Abbey itself had been the centre round which all these events had taken place.

It could never sink back into being a mere Benedictine monastery of seventy monks, attached to the Church King Edward had built. A greater future lay before it, and I doubt not that the Abbot Eadwine, shrewd man that he was, conscious of the charter which gave him and his successors a peculiar independence, rested well satisfied on that old Christmas night.

CHAPTER III
SAXONS AND NORMANS AT WESTMINSTER

"Cynge Harold lytel stilnesse gehed."

King Harold, like King Edward, spent much more time in London, and consequently at Westminster, than any of his predecessors had done, though not for the same reason. Edward was reluctant to leave the building in which he took so deep an interest; Harold, knowing full well the unsettled state of the kingdom he had to defend, held that London, "guarded alike by strong walls and the strong hearts of its citizens," was the best starting-point for any expedition he might be called on to undertake. So instead of spending the Easter Feast at Winchester, as had been a long-established custom, he came to Westminster and there assembled the Witan Gemot. He had faithfully carried out every request made to him by the dying King Edward. In every way his position was stronger than it had been three months before, and this Easter festival saw him at the zenith of his power. Suddenly a sign appeared from Heaven, which brought terror and desolation to the hearts of men. The Easter hymns were still being sung in the Abbey, when "the sky became ablaze with a mighty mass of flame, which some called a comet." This appearance brought about a state of panic in those days of superstition. First one interpreter and then another stood up to declare what it might portend, and to prophesy of terrible events about to be accomplished. One and all said the same, the sword of the Lord was drawn by this token, and who should tell where it was destined to fall?

Over the seas in Normandy, William had heard in simple but sufficient language of all that had taken place at Westminster in those first days of the year 1066. A messenger, who had come on an English ship, brought the news, "King Edward has ended his days, and Earl Harold is raised to the kindom."

William's wrath was intense. "Oft times he laced, and as oft unlaced his mantle; he spake to no man, and no man dared speak to him." The crown of England he declared was his and his alone, promised to him by Edward years before, when he went on a visit to the English court, and Harold, shipwrecked on the coast of Normandy, had sworn to support his claim. At once he sent a message, or probably several messengers to Harold, demanding from him the crown. The Englishman's answer was given with no uncertain sound. Had William really been chosen king by Edward and the Witan, he would have supported him, but things were all changed now, and he, Harold, could not give up a crown set on his head by the will of the nation, except at the nation's will. William then decided on an appeal to force. His people, bold and adventurous, rallied to his side, and set about preparing a fleet in which to cross the seas, and his chief counsellor, the Abbot Lanfranc, obtained for him from Rome the sanction and blessing of the Church on his undertaking, representing that it would be for the spiritual welfare of England. For even in those early days England had shown an independence and a restiveness under Roman control which could not be allowed to continue unrebuked.

William was indeed a formidable foe, and he was not the worst or only foe, for Harold was suddenly called on to face his own brother, Tostig, who had turned against him, demanding half the kingdom, and who to enforce this claim had enlisted on his side Harald Hardrada, the warrior king of Norway, whose fame as a fighter was known from Iceland to Africa. With an army, these two landed in the North and moved on to York, fighting their way victoriously. But from London Harold was marching at the head of his house-carls, drawing into his train ready volunteers. As they came along the Roman road with a speed almost incredible, their hearts beating high at the thought of an encounter with traitors and a foreign foe, they told one another how King Edward had appeared to Harold on the night before their start, bidding him be strong and very courageous, for the victory would be surely his. On the 25th of September the armies faced each other, and there came a messenger from the enemy's camp offering terms. Harold's answer was characteristic. To his brother he promised peace and forgiveness, "for he is an Englishman. But to Harald Hardrada, who is a foreigner and an enemy, I will give him six feet of English ground; or, as I hear he is taller than most men, I will give him seven feet. But this is all the English ground he will get from me."

The battle was a fierce one and bravely fought, but the Norsemen were utterly vanquished, and Harald Hardrada was left sleeping on that seven feet of ground which the king had offered him. As was his wont, Harold of England showed nothing but generosity to those of the conquered Norsemen who remained, and sent them back in four-and-twenty ships to their own shores. Then with the remnants of his own army he set out by the way he had come to London, having first summoned a hasty Witan Gemot where he was, to tell them that the Normans had landed in the South. He told them of the work which lay before them, and they answered him with a shout, "The heart of Harold failed not, and the hearts of the Englishmen beat with their king."

October the 5th found him in London at his palace of Westminster, and here to his standard flocked brave and trusty men from the shires of the east, the south, and the west, impelled by a passionate patriotism. Even from the cloisters there came willing soldiers, for many of the monks refused to stay and pray in safety when they could strike a blow for England on the battle-field.

S. EDMUND'S CHAPEL. SHEWING TOMB OF JOHN OF ELTHAM, YOUNGER SON OF EDWARD II.

There was much coming and going of armed men round Westminster during those days of preparation, and it was to Westminster Palace that Huon Margot, a monk, came, bearing a message to the king from Duke William. The message was a demand for submission, a challenge, and Harold proudly sent back the answer, "Tell the Duke I will seek him out and do battle with him." Then Gurth, the brother of Harold, found him in the Palace, and thus besought him—

"Fair brother, remain here, but give me your troops; I will take the adventure upon me and will fight William. And while I fight the Normans, do you scour the country, burn the houses, destroy the villages, and carry away all the swine, goats, and cattle, that they may not find food or anything wherewith to subsist."

All the men who stood round in the chamber said—

"This is good counsel. Let the king follow it."

But Harold sturdily refused to hold back from danger which he was called upon to face, neither would he allow the country to be harried.

"Never," he declared, "will I burn an English village or an English house; never will I harm the lands or goods of any Englishman. How could I injure the people I should govern? How could I harass those I would fain see thrive under my rule?"

And a few hours later, the king at the head of his army marched through Kent and Sussex to the high ground of Senlac, where he pitched his camp, within seven miles of the Norman invaders.

I am trying to tell you of scenes in history which are linked with the Abbey or Palace of Westminster, so I must not dwell on the days that followed. Harold, the fearless soldier, lay dead beneath the standard he had so gallantly defended, and around him lay the flower of his race, faithful to the end. The men who remained were leaderless and hopeless; they could no more offer resistance to the ruthless Norman soldiers, and at last they gave way.

William did not immediately march on London. Tidings came that the citizens of London were eager to fight again. So he first subdued the country around, and forced Dover, Winchester, and Canterbury into submission. Then harrying and burning wherever he was opposed, he made his way through Surrey, Hampshire, and Berkshire, purposing to lay waste the north and east of London, as he had done the south and west. He did his work all too well; even the stout hearts of the Londoners quailed, and at Berkhamstead a deputation came to him owning him as conqueror, laying the crown at his feet. It was a bitter moment for the men who undertook this shameful errand, but no other way was open to them in that dark hour, and immediately arrangements were made for the coronation ceremony. William, who consistently professed the deepest respect for the memory of King Edward, his "predecessor," declared that he would only be crowned in Westminster, "which peculiar respect," says Dart, "seems not only to arise from the pretence of his title from him, but the better to ingratiate himself with the people, with whom he stood but indifferent, by expressing extraordinary reverence for their buried favourite."

On Christmas Day, in the year 1066, the Abbey once again saw a great gathering. A guard of Norman soldiers waited without; inside mingled together wise men of two races, Saxon and Norman. Before the high altar, on the gravestone of the Confessor, stood the Conqueror, on one side a Norman Bishop, on the other, Eldred, Archbishop of York. Once again the monks chanted the *Te Deum*, and then followed an innovation. For half that multitude assembled there knew not the English language, and the question as to whether they would have this man to be their king had to be twice asked, once in English, once in Norman.

"Yea, yea, King William," was the answer, given with a shout which so startled the Norman soldiers outside, that at once they imagined some disturbance was being made, or some insult was intended to their king. In their wild anger, they began to set fire to the buildings near at hand, and as the flames dashed upwards, the astonished people rushed out of the Abbey to see what all this might portend. So the body of the great church was empty, and in dramatic solitude the Archbishop went on with the service, surrounded only by the monks. William was greatly overcome as he stood thus alone before the altar; there was something terrible in the loneliness and the stillness of the deserted church. He trembled exceedingly, and could scarce command his voice. It seems as if he had shrunk from wearing the crown of Edward, or still older crown of Alfred, "made of gould wyer works, sett with slight stones and two little bells," for he had caused to be brought a new crown, very heavy with gems, and this was the diadem set on his head by Eldred, after he had made the usual vows, with one specially added, in which he solemnly undertook to rule his people as well as the best of the kings who had gone before him.

Still from without came the sounds of tumult and excitement, still within the gleaming choir the solemn service was continued to the end, and thus was William the Norman crowned and anointed, made king indeed of England, but never king of the English people.

Westminster did not fare ill under the new king. Abbot Eadwine was discreet and wise, with much of the courtier in him, and he managed to preserve himself and his house in the good graces of the Conqueror. The building went steadily on, for money was not wanting, it was no part of William's policy to hinder any of the work undertaken by the Confessor. On the contrary, he confirmed all the charters, and when Abbot Eadwine gracefully yielded to him the lands of Windsor, which the king desired to enjoy, it being very convenient; for his retirement to hunting, he gave in exchange many other lands, besides making rich offerings. Moreover William set a rich pall over Edward's grave, presented a cloth of great splendour with two caskets of gold for the altar, and attended Mass in the Abbey Church most diligently.

Eadwine, the last Saxon Abbot, died in 1071, and was buried in the cloisters; he lay near to the very centre of all the life in the monastery which had so developed under his wise rule. Here in the cloisters the monks walked and talked, studied and transcribed; here the novices and the boy scholars sought their recreation; here was the great refectory, and close by the infirmary and St. Catherine's Chapel; overhead was the long bare dormitory. Surely it was fitting that the Abbots of Westminster should be laid in the cloisters, and so they continued to be till the year 1222. You will find the names of many of them recut on the stone benches in the south cloister, if you look for them, only unfortunately this was very carelessly done, and in many cases the names are put over the wrong graves. It seems, too, that Eadwine's body was moved from the south cloister and laid in the passage leading to the Chapter-House, close to the faithful Hugolin, who was the Chamberlain and close friend of the Confessor.

William appointed in Eadwine's place Geoffrey, a Norman, but so evil were his ways that at the end of four years, "having been first admonished by the king and Archbishop Lanfranc, but not amending upon the admonition," he was deprived and sent back to Normandy in disgrace, where he died. He was followed by Vitelus, Abbot of Bernay, held by William to be wise and a man of business, as indeed it was necessary the ruler of a large monastery should be, and among other things "being a stirring man, he let the monk Sulcardus, the best pen they had belonging to the Abbey, draw up the history of the place to give it a figure in the world."

During the rule of Geoffrey, the Lady Eadgytha, widow of Harold, died at Winchester, and was buried with great honour in the tomb of her husband, a tomb which each year became more and more of a holy place to the people of England. Under the hard rule of William, who, in the words of that honest chronicler Master Richard Wuce, "was eke so stark a man and wroth that no man durst do anything against his will, beyond all metes stark to those who withstood his will," the hearts of the people turned to that tomb of an English king, as the source from which they might hope for deliverance, as the spot of comfort from whence came signs from heaven that the saintly king still watched over his sorely tried people.

On one day, a council of Norman clergy was assembled in St. Catherine's Chapel at Westminster, their object being to deprive the holy Wulstan, Bishop of Worcester, of his see, on the ground that "he was a very idiot, being unacquainted with the French language." Lanfranc ordered him to deliver up his staff and ring. But Wulstan was before all else an Englishman.

"Truly, my Lord Bishop," said he, "you claim from me the pastoral staff which it was not you who crave me. In deference to your judgment I resign it, though not to you, but to Saint Edward, by whose authority I received it."

Then he walked to the tomb of the glorious king.

"Thou knowest," he said in Saxon, "how reluctantly I undertook this burden. Only to thee can I resign the charge of those thou didst entrust to my care. Receive thou my staff; give it to whomsoever thou mayest choose."

Thus speaking, he struck his staff into the stone tomb, and behold it sank in and stood erect, so that they who stood by could not move it neither to the right nor the left. Word was sent to Lanfranc, who had remained with the council in St. Catherine's Chapel, and he indignantly sent Gundulph, Bishop of Rochester, to put an end to this foolish story and carry the staff away. But Gundulph was powerless to move it, and on his evidence Lanfranc himself came with the king. Still every effort was in vain, and at last Lanfranc commanded Wulstan to take back the staff.

"My Lord and king," entreated the Bishop, "I pray thee give now thy decision." And the staff yielded itself into his hands.

So the king and the Archbishop, frightened at what they had seen, ran up to Wulstan, begging his forgiveness, and he, having learned from the Lord to be meek and humble of heart, threw himself in his turn upon his knees.

I need not tell you that this is but a legend, and between legend and history there is a great gulf fixed. But it is through legends that we often learn the beliefs and ideas held by the mass of the people, and this story is one of many which explains how the tomb of Edward became a holy shrine.

William of Normandy was not buried in the Abbey; he did not even die in the country it had been his great ambition to conquer and possess. For in making war against the king of France, he set fire to the town of Nantes, and his horse, treading on a red ember, plunged violently, throwing him to the ground, with such injury to himself that he never recovered, but breathed his last in a monastery at Rouen.

A hard ruler, indeed, he had been, yet Master Wace, whom "himself looked on him and somewhile dwelt in his herd," bids us remember that he was "mild to good men that loved God, and made such good peace in the land that a man might travel over the kingdom with his bosom full of gold unhurt, and no man durst stay another man."

"Wa, la wa! May God Almighty have mild-heartedness on his soul, and give him forgiveness of his sins. And may men after their goodness choose the good in him withal fleeing from the evil, as they go on their way that leadeth to God's kingdom."

Such are the kindly words in which Master Wace ends his "Chronicle of the Conquest."

CHAPTER IV
THROUGH SEVEN REIGNS

I am going to take you along very quickly through the reigns of the Norman kings—William Rufus, Henry I, Stephen, Henry II., Richard Coeur de Lion, and John, and not make a long pause till we come to the year 1216, when Henry III., the royal builder of the Abbey as we know it, came to the throne. The Church of Westminster, from the days of the Norman Conquest onwards, became, as if by right, the coronation church, "the head, crown, and diadem of the kingdom;" and Oxford, Winchester, and St. Paul's, which had witnessed so many coronations in the time of the Saxon kings, were no more thought of for this purpose. But rather curiously none of the Norman kings were buried here. Of a foreign race they were, and some among them rested in foreign tombs—the Conqueror at Caen, Henry II. and Coeur de Lion at Fontrevault, while Rufus, killed in the New Forest, was carried to Winchester, Henry I. to Reading, Stephen to Faversham, and John to Worcester, this last-named king having left instructions that he should be dressed like a monk and laid next good Bishop Wulstan, hoping by this subterfuge to take in the devil!

The fact, however, of the Abbey being the recognised place of coronation gave the Abbot a somewhat unique position, for he it was who had to prepare the king for the great ceremonial, though the actual crowning became the right of the Archbishop of Canterbury. All the regalia, too, such as the crown of Alfred, the sceptre, the ring of Edward the Confessor, were kept at Westminster till the seventeenth century, when all that remained of them after the destructive days of the Commonwealth found a safer resting-place in the Tower of London. Yet still are they carried to the Abbey the night before a coronation and placed for the night in the Jerusalem Chamber, while the Dean and Canons of Westminster still have the proud privilege of standing within the altar rails by the Archbishop.

William Rufus had all the worst qualities of his father without his sense of justice, and he was a cruel, selfish king, but he left his mark on Westminster, though not on the Abbey. The Palace was not large enough for his requirements, and he intended to rebuild it on a great scale. However he accomplished little beyond the Great Hall, which to-day is known as Westminster Hall, and leads to the Houses of Parliament.

PICTURE AND TAPESTRY IN THE SANCTUARY.

PICTURE AND TAPESTRY IN THE SANCTUARY.

This hall, repaired and strengthened by Richard II. and George IV., is in its way as full of interest as the Abbey, for here always took place the banquet, a part of the coronation ceremony, here were councils held, and here was the scene of many a great state trial. Thanks to the affection felt by Rufus for Gilbert the Abbot, the monastery was not taxed in the heavy way which had once seemed likely during a reign under which the whole nation groaned, and indeed the king granted some new charters to it, for the belief steadily grew that the burying-place of King Edward was the burial-place of a saint, and this general feeling of veneration could not be without its influence on Rufus. A new dignity, if that were needed, became attached to the royal tomb at this time, for on its being opened by Lanfranc, Archbishop of Canterbury, in company with many other bishops, the king was found to be sleeping there as peacefully as if he had been buried but a few hours, with no sign of change on his fair white face.

On the news that Rufus had been found dead in the new royal forest he had himself appropriated, his younger brother Henry arrived in hot haste at Westminster, to urge that he should be chosen and crowned king before his eldest brother, Robert, could get over from Normandy. He was better known, and therefore better liked, than Robert, so it came about as he wished; but as delay was thought to be dangerous, the ceremony was quite simple, "good swords being more thought of than costly robes." The fact, however, that Henry came to the council, asking for their support, gave them a power over him which they were ready to seize, and before the deed was finally done they obtained several important pledges from him as they met him in Westminster Hall. This partly explains, too, the reason why Henry sought to win the goodwill of the English nobles and the English people, for if Robert had come over from Normandy to fight for the crown, the Norman nobles could not all have been counted on. And so, to please the English, he determined to marry a princess of their race, the Princess Matilda, daughter of Malcolm of Scotland, and great-grand-daughter of King Edmund Ironside. Only one obstacle stood in the way, Matilda was a nun in the Abbey of Ramsey, but a nun against her will, forced to take the veil by her aunt Christina. "In her presence I wore the veil with grief and indignation," she said, "but as soon as I could get out of her sight I did snatch it from my head, fling it on the ground, and trample it under foot. That was the way, and none other, in which I was veiled."

Anselm, the large-hearted Archbishop of Canterbury, declared that a vow so taken was not binding, and to the great joy of the nation it was decided that she should be married and crowned on the same day in the Abbey. It was an English crowd which gathered to Westminster on that great Sunday of November 11, and the shouts of Englishmen resounded the heartfelt "Yea, yea," when Anselm from the pulpit asked them if they would that this marriage should take place.

Matilda, who was "a very mirror of piety and humility," and who was, moreover, shy at the sight of the "prodigious multitude" assembled to gaze on her, blushed a rosy red, the colour of her crimson robes, and was greatly overcome. She took up her residence at Westminster Palace, and the fame of her good deeds cemented still more closely the affection felt for her by her subjects. Henry loyally redeemed the promise he had made before his coronation, and this was put down entirely to the influence of his queen.

"Many are the good laws that were made in England through Matilda, the good queen, as I understand," wrote the monk Robert of Gloucester.

To the Abbey adjoining her palace she was a generous benefactress. Each day in Lent she went thither barefoot clothed in hair-cloth, and herself waited on the poorest beggars who sought the charity of the monks, even washing their feet.

"Madam, for Godde's love, is this well ado?" asked a courtier.

"Sir," answered the Queen, "our Lord Himself example gave for so to do."

Both Henry and his eldest son William were away in Normandy when this good queen died at Westminster in the year 1115, after eighteen years of happy married life "withouten strife," and she was buried close to her great-uncle, Edward the Confessor, all people mourning her with sad tears.

Henry died in the year 1135, leaving no son, as Prince William had been drowned in making an heroic effort to save his sister Mary, and England was still so much under foreign influence, that instead of his being succeeded by his daughter Matilda or Maud, his nephew, Stephen of Blois, was chosen king and crowned on St. Stephen's Day. In spite of this, a constant struggle went on against the supporters of Maud, who were many, and the whole reign was one of misery and misrule for England.

"King Henry had given peace to the realm and had been as a father to his people, but now was the whole kingdom thrown into trouble and confusion."

Westminster suffered many things at the king's hands, for he forced on the monastery an Abbot, Gervase de Blois, who "managed very ill, disposing of many Abbey lands, and being so lavish with the goods of the monastery, that the monks were afraid he would have made away even with the regalia," while many Abbey lands were ravished and laid bare as the result of the civil warfare between the Empress Maud and Stephen.

At last a compact was made that Stephen should reign for his lifetime, and that Maud's son, Henry of Anjou, should succeed him; and one year after this had been agreed upon, Stephen died, lamented by no one. Henry was a strong character, a great lover of justice and order; indeed, he may be called the father of English law, and to him we owe the system of trial by jury. He found two great powers in the land, the Church and the Barons, and he determined to hold in check the influence of both.

Westminster was fortunate in having for Abbot, Lawrence, a man of much learning, and what was even more important, of much tact, for he managed to keep on excellent terms with the king, whom he persuaded to repair and cover with lead the roofs of the building. It was he who gained for the Abbey the great honour for which the whole nation had been longing, and as the result of a sermon he preached before the king, the nobles, and a great assembly of people, an embassy was sent to Rome, praying that Edward the Confessor might be raised to the honour of a saint. More than once had this appeal been made and refused, but now the Pope, who feared Henry and had a great regard for Lawrence, decreed that "this glorious light was to be no more hid from the world."

Perhaps, too, the large sum of money, willingly offered by pious Englishmen, carried some little weight.

At midnight on October 13, 1163, Abbot Lawrence with the Archbishop Thomas à Beckett opened the grave of Edward, and the "body of the glorious king, who was henceforth to be honoured on earth as he was glorified in heaven," was removed into a "precious coffin," made ready by the order of Henry II. The celebrated "pilgrim ring" Lawrence drew from his finger to keep in the monastery as a precious relic, and the anniversary of this day was solemnly kept for many a long year.

The king was so anxious to make safe the succession of his eldest son, Prince Henry, that he insisted on his being crowned during his lifetime. But Prince Henry did not live to succeed to the throne, and it was Richard Coeur de Lion who was crowned as the next English king. A very vivid account has come down to us through the Chronicle of De Hoveden describing the doings on this day, telling how from the Palace to the Abbey the ground was covered with woollen cloth over which walked the long procession as it wended its way to the ringing of bells, the swinging of censers, lighted tapers shining everywhere. Then before the altar Duke Richard swore that he would all the days of his life observe peace, honour, and reverence towards God and the Holy Church, that he would put an end to any bad laws or customs that were in his kingdom, and confirm all good laws, in token of which Baldwin of Canterbury anointed him with oil on his head, his breast, and his limbs to signify glory, valour, and knowledge, afterwards placing the crown on his head.

But the people who were gathered together for the ceremony were filled with great forebodings of evil at the sight of a bat who fluttered round the king, though it was the bright part of the day, and at the sound of a peal of bells which rang mysteriously. And when some among them caught sight of a party of Jews, whose curiosity had overcome their prudence, Jews and witches having been commanded by a royal proclamation not to come near the Abbey or Palace lest they should work evil to the king, they fell upon them and beat them to death, thus laying the train for a series of horrible Jewish massacres throughout the country.

Richard, as you know, devoted himself to fighting the battles of the Cross in Palestine, and England was left to the mercy and the conflicts of the Barons.

When he fell in battle, his brother John succeeded in getting himself elected king, though by this time a right of inheritance had been established, and there was living Arthur, the son of John's elder brother, and therefore the lawful heir. Never perhaps has a king been crowned in Westminster who was so false to God, to man, and to his people. Even on his coronation day he jeered and mocked during the celebration of the Mass, and through the years which followed no gleam of light breaks through his deeds of treachery, cruelty, and crime. "Hell itself is defiled by his presence," wrote the uncompromising chronicler of his reign.

Although the desperate Barons had forced him to sign the Great Charter, they had no belief that he would abide by it, and certain of them therefore entered into treaty with Louis, the Dauphin of France, who came over to England prepared to accept the crown. Just at this moment, however, John died, and the French Prince was too hasty in assuming that the throne was his, for he began to divide up the kingdom and give lands to his French followers in a manner which roused the indignation of the stalwart Barons. John had left a little son of ten. Why not make him king, they reasoned? The Council could rule the land, and for adviser to the little Prince, who would be more likely to carry out the spirit of the Great Charter than that wise and trusted noble, William, Earl of Pembroke? So after a short struggle, Louis, who had taken possession of the Abbey and many other places in London, went back to France, and the boy king, who had been hurriedly crowned at Gloucester to make him secure, was crowned again in Westminster with great rejoicings on the Whit-Sunday of 1220. Once more the people of London felt that peace and prosperity would now be theirs, and never before had a coronation day been kept with such spontaneous joy.

The Abbot of Westminster was a certain Humez, a Norman, "the last of that country," Widmore tells us with glee, and he was anxious that the Abbey should not be behind the other great churches of the day through not having a special chapel dedicated to the Virgin Mary. For everywhere cathedrals and abbeys were being enlarged, and the Lady Chapel, stretching behind the high altar, held the place of honour.

Humez had obtained the necessary money from certain pious persons, and with much wisdom begged that the boy king should lay the foundation-stone of this new chapel on his coronation day. Henry, who from his childhood was deeply religious, readily agreed; perhaps it was on that day that the dream came to him of leaving behind him some such memorial as this of King Edward. Certainly it was from watching the building of this Lady Chapel, with its light pointed arches and its graceful form, representing as it did the "new style," that his dream took shape, so that twenty-five years later he commenced the work of completely rebuilding Edward's massive Abbey on the beautiful Early English lines. His reverence for the memory of Edward almost amounted to worship, and like his ancestor—for he proudly claimed to be of Edward's stock through Queen Matilda—his religion was more to him than anything else, for he spent the greater part of his days praying or in attending masses. But he was also a great lover of all that was costly and beautiful, and having married a French Princess, he had become familiar with many of the magnificent buildings of

France. So he felt that the Abbey with its stately simplicity was not splendid enough to hold the shrine of the sainted king, and he determined to raise a building which was to be "the most lovable thing in Christendom."

It is for giving us this most lovable thing that we owe to Henry III. a deep measure of gratitude, and yet heavy was the price paid for it at the time by those who, being weak and defenceless, were powerless to resist the heavy taxes laid on them. The new Abbey was paid for by the people: sometimes money was cruelly extorted from them; sometimes a great fair was arranged in the fields near Westminster, and all the shops in the neighbourhood were commanded to be closed for many days, so that the crowds would be forced to flock round the Abbey and spend their money there; sometimes large sums were extorted from the Jews; sometimes the king was driven as a last resource to pawning the Abbey jewels and treasures. At all costs money had to be found, and money in abundance, for Henry's ideas were all on the most lavish scale, and could not be carried out with less than £500,000 of our money.

So, in every sense of the word, the Abbey is the church of the nation, built with the gold of the people. And there is another striking fact to remember. Gradually the clear-headed and patriotic among the Barons were beginning to realise that though they had made the king swear to observe the Great Charter, they had no power of putting into laws which had to be observed the different provisions of that Charter; and though Henry was neither cruel nor tyrannical by nature, as his father had been, he was weak, impulsive, changeable, and extravagant. His idea of power lay in the carrying out of his magnificent ideas at Westminster, regardless of the cost, till, says Matthew of Paris severely, "Oh shame! his folly, by frequent repetition, came to be looked on as a matter of course."

This is not the place to tell you at length how one of the barons, Simon de Montfort by name, fought the good fight by means of which the Charter became a living power in the land; you must read of him in other books, and learn how he came to be called the father of English Parliaments. What I want you to remember now is that it was he who determined to check the unjust taxation which was being imposed by Henry in his efforts to raise the money for the building of the Abbey. "Let the king," he said, "call together the barons and citizens, and let him tell them how much money it is that he wants, and what he wants it for, and then it will be for the barons and people to say how much money they will give, and how it shall be collected. If the king asks what is right and just, then what he asks will be given to him."

There was only one way by which king and people could thus come face to face—Henry must summon to Westminster a Parliament to discuss those matters with him, and it must be a Parliament not made up of bishops and barons only; all England must be represented.

So in the year 1265 the first real Parliament assembled at Westminster—twenty-three barons, a hundred and twenty churchmen, two knights from every county, and two burgesses from every town.

To-day the Houses of Parliament and Westminster Abbey stand side by side, a truly wondrous group of carved grey stone; but as you look at them, I want you to remember how it was through the building of the Abbey that the first Parliament which at all represented the people of England came into being.

Can you not imagine some of the scenes which took place round Westminster during those days? Can you not fancy the interest and anxiety with which those knights and burghers, many of them perhaps in London for the first time, walked around the nearly completed building, struck with amazement that so fair a thing could be fashioned out of stone? How closely they must have watched the workmen, some of them foreigners of great skill, but many of them entirely English, masons, carpenters, builders, carvers, all doing their part, all carrying out the designs of that unknown architect, now held to be an English master of the work, who had been sent by the king of France to learn there the new style. How eagerly they must have chatted with the monks, who during this rebuilding were living in the most uncomfortable manner, but who nevertheless would be ready enough to take the strangers inside, and point out to them one beauty after another. How their eyes must have been dazzled by the wealth of colour and the exquisite carvings in marble, stone, and oak. How they must have marvelled at the fairy lightness of those arches, the delicate tracery of the windows, the glint and glitter of the glass mosaic, the soft colours of the marble.

For in very truth this building of King Henry's exceeded everything they had dreamt of or imagined. In every way the new Abbey was far larger than the old, though a limit was set on its length by the Lady Chapel of Abbot Humez, which is now known to you as the Chapel of Henry VII. The old form of the Cross was kept, but a ring of chapels encircled the east end, while transepts, aisles, and cloisters were all made longer and far loftier. But the central point of magnificence was the shrine of Edward the Confessor, which lay immediately behind the high altar, made to stand even higher than the altar by a mound of earth said to have been brought all the way from the Holy Land.

On the 13th of October 1269, the choir and east end being all complete, the coffin of King Edward, which had been kept during the rebuilding, first in the "quire where the monks do sing," and then in the Palace of Westminster, was solemnly carried back to the Abbey by the king and his brother, his two sons and many nobles, followed by a vast procession of clergy and citizens, and placed with great pomp and ceremony in the newly-made shrine.

The next time you go into Edward the Confessor's Chapel, you must wander back in imagination for more than six hundred years, and picture to yourself that solemn service of the "Translation of St. Edward."

THE CONFESSOR'S CHAPEL.

THE CONFESSOR'S CHAPEL.

The workmen had done their work right well, and we know at least the names of some of them; for Peter, the Roman citizen who wrought the mosaic, has left an inscription telling us that he finished the work in 1269; and among the Fabric Rolls of Westminster we can find accounts sent in by Robert de Beverley, mason; Brother Ralph, the convert; Alexander, the carpenter; and Adam Stretton, clerk of the works, "for the wages of masons serving before the shrine, carpenters, painters, plumbers, glaziers, inferior workmen, and workmen sent to divers places."

The tomb of the Confessor was in the middle of the shrine, set on high "as a light to the church," and was divided into three parts: the base, in the niches of which sick people were to be laid, that the Saint might heal them; the tomb itself, of soft Purbeck marble, rich with mosaic work of coloured gems and stones, and above this a shrine of pure gold set with all manner of costly jewels, sapphires, emeralds, and rubies, whilst images in gold and silver of the Virgin and the Holy Child, John the Evangelist and Peter, stood around as guardian spirits.

Much of the old magnificence has vanished; time has wrought its work, but more deadly than time have been the ravages of covetous men who longed to possess its treasure, or violent men who believed it to be little better than an idol set up in their midst.

Yet it has a mellow beauty of its own, a dignity enhanced rather than lessened by the traces everywhere apparent of its former glory, and we see in it not only an exquisite piece of work, but also that shrine which, like a magnet, drew so many of England's kings and queens to rest beneath its shadow.

TOMBS OF EDWARD I. AND HENRY III.

CHAPTER V
WITH KINGS AND QUEENS IN EDWARD'S SHRINE

As you stand in the Confessor's shrine, you will see all around you the tombs of kings and queens, and in the next chapters I am going to tell you something of those who were thought worthy to lie in a place of such high honour.

Henry III. was not at first buried in this chapel, on which he had lavished so much thought and wealth. He died in the November of 1272, and was carried to Westminster, the Knights Templars, who had given some precious gifts to the Abbey, undertaking to provide the coffin and to pay all the expenses of the funeral, that it might be on a scale befitting one who had been so princely in his dealings with the Church and all matters concerning religion. There is something pathetic in the ending of Henry's life, for though he had reigned nearly sixty years, he had not won the love or trust of his people, and it has been truly said that "in his time England did nothing great except against him." The old king was alone when the end came, for his son Edward was away on a Crusade, and his brother, Richard, had died the year before, broken-hearted at the murder of his son Henry by a son of Simon de Montfort. But the Templars spared nothing that could make the funeral costly, so that, as the solemn procession passed along, men declared that "the king shone more magnificent dead than he had appeared when living."

He was laid before the altar, in the very place from which the coffin of Edward the Confessor had been removed, for it was considered that special virtues still hovered round that spot.

Very different must the new choir have looked, with its immense height, its delicate work, and its mysterious flying buttresses, to the low, simple choir of the Confessor's day. Round the High Altar itself was a blaze of colour, for all the mosaic work on the floor, which you still can see, was freshly brought from Rome by the Abbot Ware, who had gone there to do homage to the Pope, the monks of Westminster having refused to hold themselves subject to the Bishop of London, and it was dazzling in its richness. Quarrels between the monks of Westminster and other dignitaries seem to have occurred very often in those days, as the monks, somewhat elated at the royal favours showered upon their church, were inclined to be overbearing and to resent any authority; while once at least during Henry's reign there had been a serious fracas between the "citizens of London" and the "men of Westminster" on the occasion of some sports. For when the "men of London" seemed to be getting the mastery, the Baylif of Westminster, with some men, harnessed themselves and fell to fighting, so wounding the citizens that they resolved to be revenged. Spurred on by one Constantine Fitz-Henulfe, they issued forth without any order, fought a civil battle round Westminster, and pulled down as many houses as they could belonging to the Abbot and Baylif. Nor when Constantine was captured would he express any sorrow for his misdeeds. On the contrary, he affirmed gladly that "he had done it all, and had done much less than he ought to have done." The fact that King Henry, among other punishments, forced the citizens to pay many thousand marks for this raid, did not tend to soften down the ill-feeling which existed.

Even at Henry's funeral the dignity of the Abbot had to be asserted, for he refused to allow the Archbishop to read the service until he had signed a paper explaining that his so officiating was not to be made a precedent, or to rob the Abbot of any privileges.

So, with quarrels going on around him to the end, King Henry was buried, and the Earl of Gloucester, laying his hand on the coffin, solemnly swore fealty to "Lord Edward," the lawful heir, then far away in Palestine.

Edward I. was in a special sense a child of Westminster, for he had been born in the Palace there, and had been christened Edward after the Confessor. With all his faults, Henry was devoted to his wife and to his children, and the young Edward spent much more of his boyhood with his parents than was usual in those days. He was delicate too, and often his mother had greatly upset the old monks in the monastery at Beaulieu by going to nurse him there when he had fallen ill while on a visit. He was kept during his boyhood under her watchful eye at Westminster. Probably he was taught by one of the Westminster monks, and though we hear that he was "fonder of actions than of books," he learned to speak eloquently in French and English and to understand Latin. As he grew stronger he showed a great liking for all outdoor sports, riding, hawking, hunting, and sword exercises, and with his cousin Henry, the son of Richard of Cornwall, his young French uncles, who had taken up their abode at the Court, and the sons of Simon de Montfort, he played many a game and had many a boyish adventure round Westminster. His affection for the place never failed. Had not he watched it growing in grace and beauty, and was there a single corner of it with which he was not familiar? The deeply religious influence of King Henry, too, could not fail to leave its mark on his son, who, in spite of being his opposite in every other way, had always an intense reverence for sacred things. Henry was the dreamer, Edward the doer, but among the many fine qualities the young Prince possessed, one of the most charming was his loyalty and patience towards his father, which had never wavered, however sorely he had been tried by Henry's utter incapacity to hold the reins of government.

It was nearly two years after the death of Henry before Edward was able to reach England, and yet all had gone on quietly during the interval. The new king had been proclaimed; the assembly of prelates, knights of the shire and citizens had met, had solemnly bound themselves by the same oath as that taken by the Earl of Gloucester at Henry's funeral, and three men, the Archbishop of York, Robert Mortimer, Lord of the Welsh Marches, and Robert Burnell, all trusty friends of Edward, were appointed to carry on the government for the time being.

On August 1, 1272, Edward landed at Dover, and on August 19 he was crowned with his dearly loved wife Eleanor, who had been at his side through all the perilous years which were past. "Nothing ought to part those whom God has joined, and the way to heaven was as near from Palestine as from England," she had declared.

Great were the rejoicings in London that day, for the beautiful Eleanor had a warm place in all hearts, and of Edward all had high hopes. "In face and form he is comely. By a head and shoulders he outstrips most every man," the citizens said as they marked his white determined face, his eyes, which, though soft, could flash like fire, his hair the colour of burnished gold, and his well-knit figure straight as a dart.

And throughout his reign the nation understood Edward. His was a great simple character which appealed to them. His faults were the faults of a strong man who will not be turned aside from his purpose; his ambitions were bound up in England only. To make her a strong united kingdom was the dream of his life, and though in this cause, he fought relentlessly, alike against Llewellyn of Wales and Wallace of Scotland, he strove with equal vigour to give his people good laws, fair taxation, and just representation. "That which touches all should be approved by all," was his creed, and it was he who developed the Parliaments of Simon de Montfort, until, under his guidance, what was called the Model Parliament was assembled at Westminster in 1295. So large was this new assembly, that it was no longer an easy matter for all to sit together in the hall of Westminster Palace, and a division was made, the Barons remaining in the Palace, and the Commons, or representatives of the people, using the wonderful new Chapter-House, which formed part of Henry III.'s work in the cloisters of the Abbey. This Chapter-House was the place in which the monks, with the Abbot and all the other dignitaries of the Abbey, met once a week for conference. Here complaints were listened to, here misdeeds were inquired into, here, tied to the central pillar, those older monks who had offended were publicly flogged. It was designed for a meeting-place, with its rows of stone benches and its stall at the east end for the high officials; and what more natural than that the Abbot should offer it to the king as the place where the Parliament should assemble?

ENTRANCE TO THE CHAPTER HOUSE.

The story goes that the prudent Abbot made one condition with the offer, and stipulated that the Chapter-House, being lent to the king for the use of the Commons, the Crown should keep it in repair. No doubt the story is true, nor can we blame Abbot Wace for making the best terms he could. Can you not see the knights and the burgesses making their way up the cloisters, where the monks were working or walking, through the door, with its wealth of gold and of carving, past the graves of Chamberlain Hugelin, with his wife and daughter, Abbot Eadwyn, and the chronicler Seculdus, into that "incomparable building" which Henry had determined should be unequalled in beauty? Handsome indeed had been their old meeting-place, but this exceeded anything they had ever seen. "In the centre rose a slender pillar of grey marble, or rather a group of shafts held together by moulded bauds, from which seemed to spring the vaulted roof;

the building was eight-sided, in itself a new idea; the walls were richly painted with frescoes setting forth the glories revealed to St. John in his vision of that New Jerusalem, the city not built with hands; the large windows had glass of wondrous colours; saints stood in their niches, and from within and without the Virgin Mother watched over the place."

Edward I., throughout his life, held the Abbey in great reverence, and besides carrying on his father's work and completing the choir stalls, he caused several magnificent tombs to be set up there. Always a devoted son, he resolved that the tomb of Henry III. should lack nothing in beauty; so he sent to Purbeck for the marble, to Rome for the gold and glass mosaics, and to these he added the precious stones of jasper to be brought from France, while to a certain William Torrel he entrusted the work of carving in gilt bronze the fine effigy of the dead king, which, save that it has been robbed of its jewels, is still in perfect preservation, stately in its simplicity. To this tomb the body of Henry was removed; only his heart, as he had himself desired, was carried to the Abbey of Fontrevault in France, there to be placed near to where his mother, his uncle, Richard Coeur de Lion, and others of his race lay buried.

In the same year the greatest blow of his life fell on Edward, for after thirty-five years of the happiest married life, Queen Eleanor, "the good merciful lady beloved of all the English," died of slow fever near Lincoln.

"I loved her with a great love while she lived; I cannot cease to love her while she is no more," said Edward. And his people loved him all the more for his deep grief. He came straight away from his journey to Scotland, to follow that sad funeral procession which slowly made its way to Westminster, and at each place where they paused to rest, he caused a cross to be erected to the memory of the "Chère Reine," one of which, as you know, stood close to Charing Cross station. She was buried in King Edward's Chapel at the feet of Henry III., and once more the skilful hands of William Torrel, "goldsmith and citizen of London," fashioned in gilt copper a wonderfully wrought figure, "the finest in any country" a great authority has declared, which shows us a sweet strong face at peace with God, a sleeping form, queenly and beautiful. Another English workman, Master Thomas of Leghton, made the screen of wrought-iron which protects this monument, round which run the words—

"Ici Gost Alinor, jadis Reine de Engleterre

Femme Al Rey Edward, Fiz le Rey Henri

E Fille Al Rey de Espagne, Contesse de Puntiff

Del Alme de li Dieu pur sa pitié eyt merci.

Amen."

"The king, who loved her well, as she deserved, gave to the monastery seven or eight manors, to the yearly value of two hundred pounds, for religious services, and for an anniversary to be performed for her, and for wax tapers to be kept burning on her tomb both day and night."

THE CORONATION CHAIR.

It being in the chapel of the Confessor that she who was dearer than all else was laid, he brought here, as if to lay it at her feet, his greatest trophy wrested from the Scots, the famous stone of Scone, on which so many kings of Scotland had been crowned. This was put at his command into a chair by a certain Walter of Durham, who was paid one hundred shillings for his work, with an extra sum of about £2, 12s. for carving, painting, and gilding two small leopards, for the wages of carpenters and painters, and for colours and gold employed.

- 47 -

When you look at this chair, remember that on it every sovereign of England has been crowned from the reign of Edward II.

Another trophy had been offered to the shrine of the Confessor a few years before, and that was the golden crown of the conquered Welsh Prince Llewellyn. The offering had been solemnly made by Edward's own little son, Alphonso, a boy of twelve, who, dressed from head to foot in chain-armour, and wearing a long cloak, followed by nobles and knights, had laid it down at the feet of the blessed King Edward, the jewels thereof being applied to adorn the tomb. In the same year the little prince died, and was buried in this chapel of the kings.

More than one great disturbance agitated the Abbey during the later years of Edward's reign. First a fire, which began in the Palace, spread rapidly and caused much damage to parts of the building; then there were several quarrels with some of the Begging Friars, a new Order which was highly disapproved of by the regular monks, for those begging orders got a great reputation among the people, and likewise were in high favour with the Court of Rome. But worst of all, a terrible scandal arose, which ended in forty of the Westminster monks being thrown into prison.

King Edward, when he went to Scotland, left all his jewels and treasures, with a sum of money, amounting all told to the value of £100,000, in the care of the Abbot, who carefully put away most of this charge in the strongly made Chapel of the Pyx, and the rest in the Refectory. In the April of 1303 a great quantity of treasure was stolen, and the king, very wroth, ordered a strict investigation to be made, which ended in the discovery that a certain small merchant or pedlar, named Roger Podlicote, had got into the Abbey during the night on several occasions, and had carried away his booty in bags. That he could have got in unaided was impossible; he must have had accomplices within the Abbey. Besides, the Sacrist was found with a gold cup, which he said he had picked up outside St. Margaret's Church. William the Palmer, keeper of the Palace, declared he had noticed the Sacrist, the sub-Prior, and many of the monks, coming and going unusually often, carrying bags and hampers; while John Abbas, a workman, told how Alexander the monk had caused him to make tools of a special design, threatening to kill him if he spoke aught of this.

PYX CHAPEL.

PYX CHAPEL.

Podlicote, a most adventurous spirit, made a full confession, in which he generously took all the blame upon himself, saying he knew the ways of the Abbey and where the treasury was; and being poor, he had thought how easily he could obtain the goods which were in the Refectory, which he had seen. But considering that this wholesale robbery went on for many months, it is impossible to believe that Master Podlicote's nightly visits to the Abbey through a window in the Chapter-House were quite unknown to the monks, and no one had much pity for them when they were committed to the Tower for two years. Still it was a great disgrace to fall on a monastery which held its head so high; besides, to quote Widmore, "it was a peculiar baseness to wrong a prince who had been so kind to their house, had readily renewed their charters, had improved some of them, and had been very bountiful in giving them lands of great value."

One action taken by the Abbot at this time, however, greatly pleased both the king and the people. For a certain brave knight, John de St. John, governor for Edward in Aquitaine, having been decoyed and taken prisoner by the French, and being too poor to pay the large ransom they demanded, was presented with a generous offering by Abbot Wenlock, "a commendable and charitable thing of public service," comments an old writer, "seeing that monasteries did not always lay out their money so well as for the liberty of a person in high command, a gallant man whom, while fighting valiantly for his prince, the chances of war had made prisoner."

Edward's eventful reign was drawing to a close; already he was the oldest king who had ruled England, and his life had been a hard one. He had never spared himself in mind or body; he had never wavered in his great aims; and his favourite motto, *Pactum serva*, "Keep troth," words he had desired should be carved upon his tomb, was the motto to which he had consistently been faithful. And yet over these closing years a dark cloud hung, for his son, young Edward, showed no signs of rising to his great responsibilities. Tall and handsome to behold, he was weak, changeable, and careless, given to gambling and low society, a tool in the hands of first one and then another of his worthless friends. The old king knew all too well how useless it was to dream that his son would carry on the work to which he had devoted himself, but the knowledge was a veritable cup of bitterness. He had always sought to inspire him with high thoughts, great enthusiasms, and now, as the end loomed on the horizon, he made one more effort, and appealed to the deepest feelings of the young prince. At the festival of Whitsuntide in Westminster Abbey, he admitted his son, with many other young nobles, to the order of knighthood, and throughout one long night the Prince of Wales kept his vigil before the altar at the shrine of the Confessor. Then at the royal banquet which followed, Edward, though so weak he could barely stand, swore solemnly to march at once to Scotland to crush the rebellion which had broken out afresh when all seemed peaceful, and to avenge the death of Comyn, who had been murdered in the church at Dumfries by Robert Bruce. The Scotsmen had not kept troth, and the king was fierce with indignation. But to this vow Edward added another, which was made also by the prince and all the newly dubbed knights in the ball at Westminster; they pledged themselves that so soon as Robert Bruce was conquered, they would no more bear arms against Christendom, but would go to the Holy Land and conquer the infidel, or die in the attempt to do so.

Without delay, king and army set off for Scotland, but the great triumph for which he had longed was not to be his. His spirit was as strong as ever, only his body failed him. He struggled bravely on, then came a day when he could only ride two miles, and at last he had to own that he was face to face with an enemy before whom even his strong will lay powerless. Near Carlisle he died, knight and warrior to the end. He entreated his son to tear himself away from his favourites, and to set before himself the conquest of Scotland and the recovery of the Holy Land, and he asked that his bones might be carried about with the army till Scotland was subdued, that his heart might go with the knights to the Holy Land. Then with a prayer for mercy on his lips he passed away.

Edward II. had not even the grace to carry out one of these dying requests. Four months later Edward was buried in the Confessor's Chapel near to his father, his brother, and his wife, while to his memory was raised only the plainest tomb, in striking contrast to the beautiful monuments around it. The new king scattered his money among his favourites with too free a hand to have anything to spare for the building of a costly tomb.

Yet, after all, as you stand by the grave of this "greatest of the Plantagenets," and look at the simple unornamented monument, I think you will feel with me that in its very simplicity and strength it is unconsciously a truthful memorial of Edward, a striking description of those qualities which in life he loved and strove after. He was a man of action, not of words; a soldier, not a saint; a statesman, not a dreamer. For Edward the Confessor there was a beautiful shrine, the delicate work, the gold, the jewels, the angels, and the martyrs. For Edward the First there was the uncarved block of grey marble, and the blunt inscription—

> "Here lies Edward the First, the Scourge of Scotland.
> Keep troth."

CHAPTER VI
EDWARD III. AND QUEEN PHILIPPA

"The character of the reigning Prince, King Edward II., will not give leave to expect anything of great service to this place," wrote grimly a chronicler of the Abbey. Indeed, beyond the fact that he was crowned here, that a riot nearly took place at the coronation, so angered were the people at Piers Gaveston being given the place of honour and allowed to carry the crown, in defiance of the old king's last request, and that he made an offering of two images to the shrine of the Confessor, there is nothing to tell of Edward's reign in connection with Westminster Abbey.

The country bore with the king for nearly twenty years. Then the Parliament assembled at Westminster asserted itself. The king, all were agreed, had shown himself unfit to rule; he had violated his coronation oath, he had oppressed his people, and had lost Scotland. It was only right, therefore, that he should be deposed, and his son, a boy of great promise, be chosen in his stead. Out of that great assembly only four voices were raised for the king, and a deputation was sent to him telling him what his Parliament had resolved to do. To his honour, the young Prince Edward refused to accept the crown unless with his father's consent, but Edward II., "clad in a plain black gown," submitted without a word to the decree of the assembly, and listened unmoved as they told him how they "rendered and gave back to him, once king of England, their homage and fealty, counting him henceforth as a private person, without any manner of royal dignity."

So Edward III. was crowned on the 29th of January 1327, and the shield with the sword of state, Scottish trophies of his grandfather's which were carried before him, are the identical shield and sword which exist to-day.

Only fourteen years old when he was crowned king, young Edward had already impressed all those who came in contact with him. Men saw in him a worthy successor of Edward I., whose great qualities stood out in shining contrast after the second Edward's disastrous reign. He was strong, he was brave; he, like his grandfather, passionately loved justice and passionately loved England. Nothing could have been more unfortunate than his boyhood or his early education. For neither his father nor his mother could he feel the smallest respect, and the influences about the Court were of the worst. A weaker character would have been swamped by circumstances, and would have sunk to the level of its surroundings; Edward fought his way through, and came out triumphantly on the other side. When he was sixteen he married Philippa of Hainault, and a year later a son was born to them. The delight of the nation was intense; Edward was deeply touched at the signs of affection everywhere shown to him by his subjects, and he resolved all the more earnestly, with the growing strength of his young manhood, to be a king indeed, to rule his people justly, to lead them wisely, to live up to the great things expected of him. England in those days was a young nation, just beginning to feel its power, rejoicing in its strength and its freedom, ready for action, for adventure, for enterprise, and Edward represented in the highest degree all these enthusiasms and aspirations. He was able to lead; he grasped the spirit of his people; king and nation were at one in their aims, so that into the years which followed were crowded great deeds and great victories, victories made all the more honourable by the chivalrous conduct of the conquerors.

I should like to linger over the stories of Edward and his men-at-arms, the knights, the hobblers, and the archers, who won such fame for England on foreign battle-fields, but that would be to wander far away from Westminster, so we must leave Crecy, Calais, and Poitiers, and come back to the Abbey and the Monastery, this little world of itself, where life went on in its own way, regardless of wars in Scotland and France.

As usual, there were several disputes in progress, and one between the Abbot and the king's treasurer ended in a lawsuit which lasted both beyond the Abbot's and treasurer's time. The quarrel was as to who had the right to visit the Hospital of St. James, a hospital founded and endowed by some citizens of London for fourteen leprous maids, on the ground where now St. James's Palace stands. No fewer than six chaplains were attached to this hospital, to perform divine service for the afflicted fourteen lepers, and as the building stood within the parish, the Abbot declared that these chaplains were under his authority. To this the king's treasurer would not agree, and hence the dispute. Apparently at last the verdict was given in favour of the Abbot, but the original Abbot and treasurer being dead, and the new Abbot being indolent, while the new treasurer was grasping, it ended in an actual victory for the latter.

Another quarrel centred round the little chapel of St. Stephen's, which had been founded by Edward I. within the Palace at Westminster, and so liberally endowed by Edward III. that it possessed its own dean and canons.

In this chapel masses were said daily for past and present kings, while altogether nearly forty priests were attached to the foundation, all of whom lived in the Palace. Quite naturally the Abbot of Westminster was not well pleased at this rich foundation within a stone's throw of his Abbey, and insisted that it should be placed under his jurisdiction, a claim which was warmly supported by the Pope. But in this "the people of St. Stephen's," who had the Court on their side, did not acquiesce; and at last the king, who was not greatly interested in these matters, proposed a compromise, which was accepted. The Abbot was to have the right of appointing the dean, and was to be paid a yearly sum of money as a tribute to his authority; while, on the other hand, the dean and canons were to order their own services and control their own affairs.

This chapel of St. Stephen's was very beautiful, more beautiful, we are told, than St. George's Chapel at Windsor. But no traces remain of it or of its cloisters and its chantry except the crypt. In the reign of Henry VIII. Westminster Palace was seriously destroyed by fire, and the chapel was then altered, turned from its original use, and given over to the House of Commons as their Parliament House, another link, you see, between the Palace, the Church, and the People.

In the year 1349 the Black Death, that most terrible plague, swept over England, killing nearly one half of the people; fifty thousand of its victims were buried in London, and the Abbey was not spared, for the Abbot and twenty-six of the monks caught it and died. They were buried in one grave in the south cloister, covered by a large stone, which you will easily find, although it has a wrong name, that of Gervase de Blois, carved upon it; and that vast stone, says Dean Stanley, "is the footmark left in the Abbey by the greatest plague which ever swept over Europe."

Abbot Bircheston, who thus died, had not been very satisfactory. "It is well of this place that he continued no longer," says the chronicler severely; "for he ran the house into a great deal of debt, being himself extravagant and his relations being wasteful people." His successor was that remarkable man Simon Langham, the only Abbot of Westminster who ever became Archbishop of Canterbury, and he did such great things for the monastery that he won for himself the name of the second founder. Not only did he pay off the debts of his predecessors, but he managed with great prudence all the estates and revenues under his care, saved large sums of money by his frugality, and, perhaps most difficult task of all, brought the house once more into excellent discipline. This is what Plete, himself a monk at Westminster, has to say of Abbot Langham: "He rectified many abuses which had crept in, truly a service as it is most useful to any place, so commonly is it the most difficult also; and accordingly it cost him a great deal of study, pains, and resolution to effect it, as having many ill tempers to deal with, some being indolent, others odd and particular, some extravagant, and others perverse."

While he was Archbishop, and afterwards when made a cardinal and living abroad, he never forgot the Abbey where he had been educated and where he had laid the foundation of his great career, but left to it a sum equal to £200,000 to be spent on building, and desired that he should be buried there. So you will find his tomb of marble and alabaster in the little chapel of St. Benedict at the entrance to the south ambulatory, the first monument of any importance set up to the memory of a bishop or abbot.

He was followed by the Prior, Nicholas Litlington, "a stirring person, very useful to the monastery," whose mind was set on improving the buildings. This was an easy task enough, thanks to the legacy of Langham and the good favour in which he stood with king and queen. So at once he set to work, the monastery being the object of his care. He built the south and west cloisters, setting his initials on the roof; the Abbot's Palace, the College Hall, the Jerusalem Chamber, houses for the bailiff, the cellarer, the infirmaries, and the sacrist, a malt-house and a water-mill; and besides this he presented the Abbey with much valuable plate and many rich vestments.

"But," remarks an old writer severely, "as he was enabled to do all this with the money left by his predecessor Langham, he should have put some memorial of the Cardinal upon the buildings. Instead, he has his own arms and the initial letters of his name on the keystone of the cloister arches."

The Abbot's house built by Litlington is the present Deanery; but the College Hall, once the Abbot's refectory, now the dining-hall of the Westminster scholars, and the Jerusalem Chamber, the room into which the Abbot's guests used to pass when they had dined, are open to the public at certain hours, and you must not forget them when you are walking through the cloisters. The Jerusalem Chamber has been restored since the days of Litlington, though the fine roof and the actual building stand now as then. The glass in one of the windows, however, is very old, as is the wonderful stone reredos, which once must have been part of the high altar. In the dining-hall you must notice the gallery at the one end in which the minstrels used to perform, and the fine pointed windows; for as the Norman architecture had given way to the Early English, and the Early English had developed into the beautiful Decorated style, so now another change was taking place, of which Litlington's building is an early example, and the Perpendicular style, which was entirely English, was creeping in.

While Litlington was abbot, another royal funeral took place in the Confessor's Chapel, for in 1369, "that moost gentyll, moost lyberall, and moost courtesse fayre lady, Phillipp of Heynault, died."

This is how a writer living at the time quaintly describes the sad event: "There fell in England a heavy case and a comon, righte pyteouse for the King, his children and all his realme. For the good Queen of England fell sicke, the which sickenesse contynewed on her so longe, that there was no remedye but deathe. And the good lady whenne she this knewe and perceyved, desyred to speke with the Kynge, her husbande. And she sayde, 'Sir, we have in peace, ioye, and great prosperyte, used all our time toguyer. Sir, nowe I pray you at our departyng, that ye will grant me my desyres.... I requyre you, that it may please you to take none other sepulture whensoever it shall please God to call you out of this transytorie lyfe, but besyde me in Westmynster.'

"The Kynge all weepynge sayde, 'Madam, I graunt all your desyre.' Then the good ladye made on her the sign of the Cross, and anone after she yielded up her spiryte, the which I beleeve surely the Holy Angels receyved with great ioy up to Heven, for, in all her lyfe, she dyd neyther in thought nor dede, thynge whereby to lose her soule, so farr as any creature coulde knowe."

Her tomb was ordered to be made of "neat black marble, with her image thereon in polished alabaster, and round the pedestal, sweetly carved niches, with images therein." But what makes this monument specially interesting is that the figure of Queen Philippa is really a likeness and not a beautiful fancy picture, so that as you look at that kind, motherly face you can quite easily picture to yourself the queen who pleaded for the lives of the citizens of Calais, and of whom it was said at her death, "She had done many good deeds in her lyfe; having succoured so many knyghts and comforted ladyes and damosels."

Eight years later, King Edward was laid beside her, all the glory of his life having passed from him with her.

"In his time, England had seemed to shine in her meridian; learning was encouraged; gallantry, and that the most honourable, was practised; the subjects were beloved; the king was honoured at home and feared abroad." But after Philippa's death strength of mind and body alike failed him; his favourite son, the Black Prince, had died; his other sons neglected him, his courtiers robbed him, and when the end came, there was only a poor priest by his bedside, who pressed the crucifix to his lips and caught his last dying word—Jesus.

His funeral, however, was magnificent; he was carried through London with his face uncovered, followed by his children and by the nobles and prelates of England, and afterwards a fine tomb was set up to him with figures of his twelve children kneeling around.

But it was only round the tomb and in the sculptor's fancy that those strong, high-spirited sons of Edward and Philippa knelt in one accord, for from them arose the quarrels and strife which later on brought to England the greatest calamity which can come to any nation—a civil war in its midst.

TOMBS OF RICHARD II. AND EDWARD III.

CHAPTER VII
RICHARD II. AND QUEEN ANNE

Edward the Black Prince, that flower of English chivalry, had left his little son Richard as his legacy to the people who loved him so well.

"I commend to you my son," he said, as he lay dying in Westminster Palace, "for he is but young and small. And I pray that as you have served me, so from your heart you will serve him."

One year afterwards, this boy of eleven was crowned in Westminster, and so "young and small" was he that the long day with all its wearying ceremony was too much for him; he fainted away, and had to be carried from the Abbey to the Palace on a litter.

Never before had there been a coronation on so magnificent a scale: the citizens of London, with their good wives and daughters, were learning to enjoy pageants and holidays, and it was now better than half a century since a king had been crowned. First Richard had spent some days in the Tower, that great fort of the capital, and then had come the wonderful procession through Cheapside, Fleet Street, and the Strand, the boy riding bareheaded, surrounded by a band of young knights in new attire, forerunners of the knightly Order of the Bath, winning all hearts by his beautiful face and his lavish generosity. For the young king was from the first recklessly extravagant, and while he with his nobles feasted in the Palace at the coronation banquet, he caused the fountains outside to pour forth wine in abundance, that all who would might drink to their heart's desire.

John of Gaunt, his uncle, one of those many sons of Edward III., was made Regent, and Richard, with the approbation of all, was placed under the tutorship of that accomplished knight, Guiscard d'Angle, Earl of Huntingdon, to be instructed in the paths of virtue and honour.

But those were not peaceful days in England, and John of Gaunt made the fatal mistake of defying the knights of the shire and burgesses who composed the House of Commons, and who really represented the thoughts and feelings of the people.

"What do these base and ignoble knights attempt?" he asked contemptuously. "Do they think they be kings or princes in the land?"

Nevertheless, in the end he was forced to flee from England, so bitter was the feeling against him. The cause of the universal discontent was the heavy taxation, the result of the long French wars, and the Bishop of Rochester, in his sermon at the coronation, had boldly touched on this with words of solemn warning. For the first time the great peasant population of England, who had hitherto suffered in resentful silence, was in a position to lift up a voice of protest, as the Black Death had so ravaged the country that those labourers who were left were able to make terms for themselves, and to refuse to work without payment. The tax which brought the discontent to a crowning point was the poll-tax, which was a tax of twelve pence (about eighteen shillings) to be paid by every person over fifteen; and when a certain Wat the Tiler killed a tax-collector, who, not content with trying to force him into paying this poll-tax, insulted his little daughter, the men of Kent rallied in their thousands round Wat and marched on London. Richard was now only fifteen, but he was at his best, full of courage, full of strength, worthy grandson of Edward III., true son of Edward the Black Prince. He determined to ride out with a small escort and meet these thousands of rebels face to face. It was a bold stroke, and he knew the risk. But he would not be stayed. There is a story, most probably true, that he consulted the aged Anchorite of the Abbey, for every monastery of importance had its Anchorite, a monk who voluntarily set himself apart for the rest of his life to live in one cell, praying for the house; and more than one of the Anchorites of Westminster had given counsel to the kings who sought them out, the words of these holy men being held as sacred. Certain it is that, on the morning of this eventful day, he, with his escort, heard mass in the Abbey, paid his devotions, and made his offerings at King Edward's shrine, "in which," says an old writer, "the kings of England have great faith." Then he rode out to Smithfield.

"Here is the king," said Wat Tiler to his men. "I will go speak with him. When I give you a sign, step forward and kill every one except the king. Hurt him not, for he is young and we can do what we will with him. We will lead him with us about all England, so shall we be lords of the kingdom without a doubt."

But in a few minutes, as you know, the scene had changed. Wat Tiler lay dead, and the boy king, ordering that not one of his attendants should follow him, rode forward into the midst of the excited crowd, and said calmly, "Sirs, what aileth you? I will be your leader and captain. I am your king."

The men were Englishmen, and this cool courage won their hearts on the spot. They crowded round the king begging for pardon, which he granted to them at once, forbidding his followers to strike a blow. And so the great rebellion ended.

As he rode back to London, Richard stopped to reassure his mother.

"Rejoice and thank God, madam," he said, kissing her, "for I have this day regained my inheritance and the kingdom which I had lost."

If only the king had been true to the promise of his boyhood, he might have ranked among the greatest of our rulers. As it was, he went on his way unchecked, uncontrolled, till one after another his good points sank into the background; cowardice took the place of courage, cruelty of chivalry, and he who had said confidently to his people, "I will be your leader and your captain," proved himself to be utterly incapable and helpless.

A year later Richard married Princess Anne of Bohemia, the sister of that "good King Wencelaus," about whom was written the Christmas Carol you know so well, and on their wedding day there were great feastings at Westminster. All the city guilds and companies, splendidly arrayed, came out to do honour to the rosy-cheeked and smiling girl queen, herself only sixteen; and when at his coronation she entreated the king as a favour to set free all prisoners in the country, the delighted citizens gave her the name of "Our Good Queen Anne."

The young king spent much of his time in his Palace of Westminster, and as you look to-day at Westminster Hall, the only part of the fine building which stands, I want you to try and imagine all the busy life which centred there round the court and the church. Everything connected with Richard was done on a magnificent scale. He had a body-guard of four thousand archers; he had a band of nearly four hundred workmen—carpenters, jewellers, armourers, masons, tilers, furriers—whose duty it was to work everything needed for the king's service, and these, with their wives and children, lived under the shadow of Westminster. Then there were all the servants connected with the royal kitchen, the pantry, spicery, buttery, bakehouse, and brewery, and there must have been a goodly number of these, for a writer who belonged to the court tells us that every day ten thousand folk that "followed the Hous" drew their rations of food from the Palace.

Besides all these we must count the higher court officials, the members of the royal household, the judges who sat in Westminster Hall, the priests of St. Stephen's Chapel, the bishops and abbots and nobles with all their retinues, and then we may have some idea of the bustle and life round Westminster Palace at a time when there was "greate pride, and riche arraye, and all things much more costious and more precious than was before or sith."

Look at Old Palace Yard and New Palace Yard, with the dull old streets leading out of them, and then imagine Richard's Palace, with its towers, its posterns, its great halls and painted chambers, its cloisters, its courts, and its galleries; "gabled houses with carved timber and plastered fronts, cloisters which glowed in the sunshine with their lace like tracery, with the gold and crimson of their painted roofs and walls; everywhere tourelles with rich carvings, windows of tracery most beautiful, archways, gates, battlements; chantry chapels, oratories, courts of justice, and interiors bright with splendid tapestry, the colours of which had not yet faded, with canopies of scarlet and gold, and the sunlight reflected from many a shining helm and breastplate, from many a jewelled hilt and golden scabbard." Would that the Great Fire which destroyed all this had left us one little glimpse of its old splendour.

Inside the monastery, too, there was plenty of life of a different sort, though the monks were by no means cut off from the great world which lay at their door. For the Abbey of St. Peter was the richest of all the great houses, and was now at the height of its glory; and Litlington's new buildings greatly added to its importance, as the Abbot freely entertained in his new palace the highest in the land.

Yet a daily routine was carried out. Eight hours were given to sleep and eight were spent in church; the remainder were devoted to work—that is to say, some monks taught the young, others studied and transcribed, others had duties in the refectory and dormitory, and so on. Most of the monks had come here as young boys; many of them spent here fifty and sixty years of their lives, praying, working, teaching, learning. But I think sometimes the young men must have longed for some share in the life outside of which they heard the echoes daily, and saw all the outward splendours and delights.

Certain it is that Abbot Litlington was something more than a monk. For when, during the reign of Richard, there was a great scare that the French were about to invade England, he, though at that time seventy, armed himself and set off with some of his monks to the coast to defend his country. And we find that "one of these monks, Brother John, supposing his courage equal to his stature, was a very proper person for a soldier, being one of the largest men in the kingdom. His armour, the invasion not taking place, was carried into London to be sold, being so big that no person could be found of a size that it would fit."

One other part of vanished Westminster comes into prominence in this reign, and that is its Sanctuary, which stood where now is Westminster Hospital. It was a massive square keep built of stone, each side nearly eighty feet long, with a heavy oak and iron door, stone stairs, strong dark rooms and thick walls, and besides a belfry tower, in which hung those bells which rang for coronations and tolled for royal funerals; it contained two chapels. This place was the haven of refuge alike to innocent and to guilty; so long as they remained within its walls the Church protected them and kept them. Of course, originally these sanctuaries attached to the religious houses had been intended to protect the weak, the helpless, and the oppressed, but gradually all manner of men, thieves, debtors, and lawbreakers, gathered round it, and at Westminster, where all the Abbey buildings were counted as sacred ground, strange and lawless crowds assembled; but the right of sanctuary was jealously guarded.

Outside the world of Westminster the country was full of discontent, which showed itself in parties and in plots. John of Gaunt had fled, and his place had been filled by his brother, Thomas Woodstock, Duke of Gloucester, who, with Gaunt's son, Henry of Bolingbroke, and other nobles, had forced Richard, still a minor, into accepting several of their demands. But directly he was of age Richard had his revenge; and in the Council Chamber he made it clear that he intended to keep all the authority in his own hands or in the hands of those he himself should choose. Francis, a scribe, and the lame Clerk to the Council, has left us a vivid picture of the scene.

"Then Richard stood in the doorway; upon his head he wore a crown; in his hand he carried his sceptre; on his shoulders hung a mantle of ermine, and through the door I saw a throng of armed men, and heard the clank of steel.

"Since the time of David there had not been a more comely prince in the world to look upon than King Richard.... Yet let no one say that his eyes were soft. This morning they were like the eyes of a falcon.

"'Good, my lord,' began the Duke of Gloucester.

"The King strode across the room and took his seat upon the throne.

"'Fair uncle,' he said, 'tell me how old I am.'

"'Your Highness,' said the Duke, 'is now in his twenty-fourth year.'

"'Say you so? Then, fair uncle, I am old enough to manage mine own affairs.'

"So saying, he took the Great Seal from the Archbishop, and the keys of the Exchequer from the Bishop of Hereford. From the Duke of Gloucester he took his office, he appointed new judges, he created a new council. 'Twas a gallant prince. Alas! that he was not always strong; twice in his life Richard was strong—that day and another. That night there was high revelry in the Palace: the mummers and the minstrels and the music made the Court merry. And the king's fool made the courtiers laugh when he jested about the Duke's amazement and the Archbishop's discomfiture."

Richard now fell entirely under the influence of his own favourites, and the friction between himself and his Parliament increased each year. The one good influence in his life was that of Queen Anne; over and over again her sound sense saved the situation. Once Richard, in a fit of sulkiness, had gone to live at Bristol, very privately, and to him there came the Archbishop of Canterbury, who warned him that unless he returned to London the citizens of London and the greater part of his subjects would be very discontented. Richard at first refused to pay any attention to the Archbishop, but at last the good advice of the queen prevailed; he controlled his anger and said he would cheerfully go to London. On his arrival there, a special Parliament was summoned, which made London and Westminster very crowded; the king heard Mass with the crown on his head in the chapel of the Palace; the Archbishop of Canterbury performed the divine service, and was very attentively heard, for he was an excellent preacher; and then came the barons, prelates, and nobles to Richard, with joined hands, as showing themselves to be vassals, swearing faith and loyalty, and kissing him on the mouth.

"But it was visible," adds Froissart, "that the king kissed some heartily and others not."

Possibly, if Anne had lived, her sensible influence might have saved Richard, in spite of the growing irritation of his people at his reckless extravagance. But after only a few hours' illness the queen died at the Feast of Whitsuntide 1394, in Sheen Palace, "to the infinite distress of King Richard, who was deeply afflicted at her death."

Richard was with her when she died, and so uncontrolled was his grief, that, cursing the place of her death, he ordered the Palace of Sheen to be levelled to the ground. He determined that hers should be the greatest burial ever seen in London, and sent to Flanders for large quantities of wax wherewith to have made the torches and flambeaux, though this delayed the funeral by some months. He summoned all the nobles of the land to be present in these words:—

"Inasmuch as our beloved companion the Queen, whom God has hence commanded, will be buried at Westminster on Monday, the 3rd of August next, we earnestly entreat that you, setting aside all excuses, will repair to our city of London the Wednesday previous to the same day, bringing with you our very dear kinswoman your consort at the same time. We desire that you will, the preceding day, accompany the corpse of our dear consort from our manor of Sheen to Westminster, and for this we trust we may rely on you, as you desire our honour and that of our kingdom."

So a great procession followed the queen from Sheen to Westminster, and all were clothed in black, men and women, with black hoods also. Richard behaved as one mad with grief, and when the Earl of Arundel arrived late, he seized a cane, and struck him on the head with such force that the unfortunate nobleman fell to the ground.

A year later the king ordered the beautiful monument which you see in the Confessor's Chapel, and so great was his devotion that he had his own monument made at the same time, with his hand clasped in that of his dearly loved queen. And the touching inscription, of which this is a translation, was of his own choosing:—

"Under this stone lies Anne, here entombed,

Wedded in this world's life to the second Richard.

To Christ were her meek virtues devoted,

His poor she freely fed from her treasures.

Strife she healed and feuds she appeased.

Beauteous her form, her face surpassing fair.

Only July's seventh day, thirteen hundred, ninety four,

All comfort was bereft, for through irremediable sickness

She passed away into eternal joys."

In spite of his grief, which was very real, Richard married again; but the new queen had no influence with him, and the breach between him and his people widened daily. "Nothing but complaints were heard; the courts of justice were closed; the enmities increased, and the common people said, 'Times are sadly changed; we have a good-for-nothing king, who only attends to his idle pleasures, and so that his inclinations are gratified cares not how public affairs are managed. We must look for a remedy, or our enemies and well-wishers will rejoice.'"

So writes Froissart, who lived in England at the time; and he goes on to say how the people declared to one another, "Our ancestors in former days provided a remedy; our remedy is in Henry of Lancaster. Him we must send for and appoint him regent of the kingdom. For these people are most obstinate, and of all England, the Londoners are the leaders."

HENRY OF LANCASTER CROWNED AT WESTMINSTER.

HENRY OF LANCASTER CROWNED AT WESTMINSTER.

This being the feeling in the country, the time was ripe for John of Gaunt's banished son, Henry Bolingbroke, who had long been waiting for his hour. He landed with but thirty men, while Richard was away on one of his highly unpopular expeditions in Ireland; soon he had an army of fifty thousand with which he marched to London, and Richard when he returned agreed meekly, without a word, to all that was demanded. He signed a deed prepared by Parliament in which he said that "he was incapable of reigning, worthy to be deposed, and willing to renounce the throne."

"If it pleases you, it pleases me also," was his feeble remark.

Then he was put into prison, first in the Tower, afterwards in Pontefract Castle, and from this last place he never came out alive. His death was very sudden; some said he fell sick, some said he was starved, almost certainly he was murdered. He was buried at Langley, though many a long year afterwards his body was moved to Westminster by command of Henry V., and laid in the tomb he had chosen close to his wife, after it had been carried through London followed by 20,000 persons, of whom "some on him had pity and some none."

So husband and wife lie united at last under this fine tomb, which cost £10,000 in our money. But in one detail Richard's wish is ungratified to-day, for his hand and hers, which on the monument were clasped together, have been ruthlessly broken off.

Another memorial of Richard in the Abbey is his portrait, which you will find in the choir near the altar, and which is "an ancient painting of the unhappy, beautiful prince, sitting in a chair of gold dressed in a vest of green, flowered with flowers of gold and the initial letters of his name, having on shoes of gold powdered with pearls, the whole robed in crimson lined with ermine, and the shoes spread with the same fastened under a collar of gold." It is valuable because it is the first portrait we have of an English king.

Richard rebuilt Westminster Hall, and built a fine porch called Solomon's Porch, where now stands the great north entrance; but of this porch not a trace remains.

CHAPTER VIII
HENRY V. AND HIS CHANTRY

On the last day of September 1399, Westminster was well astir, for Parliament had met to decide an all-important question.

Richard had renounced the crown, and his cousin, Henry of Lancaster, claimed it.

"Risyng from his place, mekeley makyne the signe of the Crosse, he saide unto the people, 'In the name of the Father, Son, and Holy Ghost, I, Henry of Lancaster, claim the realme of Englande and the crowne, as that I am dyscended by righte lyne of bloode from that good Lord King Henry III." Moreover, he proceeded to make clear, Richard had resigned the crown into his hands, and he had also won it by right of conquest.

Then the Archbishop asked the assembly if they would have Henry for king, to which with one voice they answered "Ye, ye, ye," and after that the Archbishop led Henry to the king's throne and set him thereon with great reverence, making to him a long "oryson" from the words, "When I was a child, I spake as a child; but at the time when I came unto the state of a man, I put away childish things."

"A chylde," he said, "will lyghtly promise and as lyghtly brake his promise, doing all thinges that his fancye giveth him unto, and forgettinge lyghtly what he hath done. By which reason it followyth that great inconvenyence must fall to that people a chylde is ruler and governour of. But now we ought all to rejoyse that a man and not a chylde shall have lordeshype over us, a man that shall govern the people by skylful doyngs, settyne apart wylfulnesse and all pleasure of himself."

And the people answered "Amen" with great gladness; they clapped their hands for joy and did homage to the new king, while the coronation was fixed for the 13th of October, the Feast of St. Edward.

Froissart has left us a vivid account of that great day, which you shall have in his words.

"On the Saturday before the coronation, the new king went from Westminster to the Tower attended by great numbers, and those squires who were to be knighted watched their arms that night. They amounted to forty-six, and each squire had his chamber and his bath in which he bathed. The ensuing day, the Duke of Lancaster, after mass, created them knights, and presented them with long green coats with straight sleeves. After dinner on this Sunday, the Duke left the Tower on his return to Westminster; he was bareheaded, and there were of nobility from eight to nine hundred horse in the procession. The Duke was dressed in a jacket of cloth of gold, mounted on a white courser, with a blue garter on his left leg. The same night the king bathed himself, and on the morrow confessed himself and heard three masses. The prelates and clergy who had assembled, then came in a large procession from Westminster Abbey to conduct the king thither, and returned in the same manner, the king and nobles following. The dukes, earls, and barons wore long scarlet robes, with mantles trimmed with ermine and large hoods of the same. The dukes and earls had three bars of ermine on the left arm, the barons but two. On each side of the king were carried the sword of mercy and the sword of justice, and the Marshal of England carried the sceptre.

"The procession entered the church about nine o'clock, in the middle of which was erected a scaffold covered with crimson cloth, and in the centre a royal throne of cloth of gold. When the Duke entered the church, he seated himself upon the throne, and was thus in royal state, except having the crown on his head.

"The Archbishop of Canterbury proclaimed how God had given them a man for their lord and sovereign, and then asked the people if they were consenting to his being consecrated and crowned king. They unanimously shouted out Ay.

"After this the Duke descended from the throne, and advanced to the altar to be consecrated. He was anointed in six places, and while this was doing the clergy chanted a litany that is performed at the hallowing of a font.

"The king was now dressed in churchman's clothes, and they put on him crimson shoes. Then they added spurs; the sword of justice was drawn, blest, and delivered to the king, who put it into the scabbard. The crown of St. Edward, which is arched over like a cross, was then brought and blessed, and put on the king's head by the Archbishop.

"When mass was over, the king left the Abbey and returned to the Palace, and went first to his apartment, then returned to the Hall to dinner.

"At the first table sat the king; at the second, five great peers of England; at the third, the principal citizens of London; at the fourth, the new created knights; at the fifth, all knights and squires of honour. And the king was served by the Prince of Wales, who carried the sword of mercy.

"When dinner was half over, a knight of the name of Dymock entered the Hall completely armed, mounted on a handsome steed. The knight was armed for wager of battle, and was preceded by another knight bearing his lance; he himself had his drawn sword in one hand and a naked dagger at his side. The knight presented the king with a written paper, the contents of which were, that if any knight or gentleman would dare maintain that King Henry was not the lawful sovereign, he was ready to offer him combat in the presence of the king, when and where he would.

"After King Henry had dined and partaken of wines and spices, he retired to his private apartments, and all the company went. Thus passed the Coronation Day of King Henry, who remained that and the ensuing day at the Palace of Westminster."

But though Henry was thus firmly set on the throne by the will of Parliament, he knew full well that he was not the lawful heir while the Earl of March, the descendant of John of Gaunt's elder brother, was alive, and this fact put him very much at the mercy of his Parliament throughout his reign. He was there by the will of Parliament, and therefore, according to their will he must act. His was a troubled, anxious rule; for rebellions broke out in many different parts of the country, and Henry never felt really secure.

With Westminster he had little to do, save at the beginning and end of his reign, and he has left no memorial of himself in the building. Yet he is the one king who died within the Abbey walls.

To ease his conscience, he had resolved to make a pilgrimage to the sepulchre of the Lord at Jerusalem, and this in spite of the fact that he was suffering from a grave disease.

"Galleys of warre" were made ready for the expedition, and the king came to Westminster, both to meet his Parliament and to pray in the shrine of Edward for the blessing and protection of that saint, though he firmly believed an old prophecy that he should die in Jerusalem would be now fulfilled.

While kneeling in the shrine, he became so ill that those about him thought he would die in that place. But with difficulty they moved him to the fine chamber in the Abbot's house, carrying him on a litter through the cloisters, and "there they laid him before the fire on a pallet, he being in great agony for a certain time."

At last, when he came to himself, he asked where he was, and when this had been told him, he inquired if the chamber had any special name.

He was told its name was Jerusalem.

"Then sayd the Kynge: Laud be to the Father of Heaven, for nowe I knowe I shall dye in this chamber, accordynge to ye propheseye of me aforesayde, that I should dye in Jerusalem."

So, in that dark tapestried room, the king, lying there in his royal robes, just as he had come from doing honour to St. Edward, made himself ready to die. His son, Prince Harry, was with him, though between the two there had been many a misunderstanding and quarrel during the last few years; and Shakespeare, taking his facts from the French chronicler, tells how Henry lay there unconscious, his crown on a pillow at his side, and at last seemed to breathe no more. Whereupon the attendants, believing him to be dead, covered over his face, and Prince Harry first held the crown in his hands, then set it on his own head.

This very act seemed to call the dying king back to life, for he groaned, came to himself, and missed the crown.

"What right have you to it, my son?" he asked reproachfully.

The Prince made answer: "My lord, as you have held it by the right of your sword, it is my intent to hold and defend the same during my life."

To which replied the king: "I leave all things to God, and pray that He will have mercy upon me."

And thus saying he died.

But the English chroniclers give another picture of the Prince, and describe him sobered and awestruck in the presence of Death, kneeling at his father's side as the priest administered the Holy Sacrament, tenderly recalling his wandering mind and saying—

"My lord, he has just consecrated the Body of the Lord Christ: I entreat you to worship Him, by whom kings reign and princes rule."

Then the king raised himself up to receive the cup, blessed his son, kissed him, and died.

Prince Harry wept distractedly, full of remorse as he thought of all the follies and mistakes of his past life, which had so added to the sorrows of the dead king. But all that was good and great in him came to the front now. Alone, in a little chapel inside the Abbey, he passed the rest of that day, kneeling in utter humility before the King of kings, praying for pardon, for peace, and for strength. "Then, when the shades of night had fallen upon the face of the earth, the tearful Prince in the darkness went to the Anchorite of Westminster (whose stone cell lay on the south side of the infirmary cloister), and unfolding to this perfect man the secrets of his life, being washed in penitence, he received absolution, and putting off the cloak of iniquity, he returned garbed in the mantle of virtue." Nor was this sudden change the impulse of a moment, for "Henry, after he was admitted to the rule of the land, showed himself a new man, and tourned all his wyldness into sobernesse, wyse sadnesse and constant virtue."

The king, at his own wish, was buried at Canterbury by the side of the Black Prince; some chroniclers say, because he trembled at the thought of lying near Richard's tomb in the Confessor's Chapel; and nothing disturbed the peace of the Abbey till the following spring, when on Passion Sunday, "a daye of exceedinge rayne and snow," Henry V. was crowned.

His first act as king was to give King Richard an honourable burial in the tomb he had chosen, to order that tapers should burn around his grave "as long as the world endureth," and that dirges and masses should be said for his soul. Then he concerned himself with the building which had stood still throughout his father's reign, and he made as his chief architect the wealthy and generous Whittington, now Lord Mayor of London—possibly the hero of the old story—with a monk of Westminster named Haweden. To those two was entrusted the work of completing the nave and all the western part of the Abbey.

Henry was brave and adventurous, the nobles were longing for war, and France, at that moment divided against itself, almost invited attack. The old pretext did well enough; Henry laid claim to the throne of France and invaded the land, scorning all idea of compromise. Disease attacked his army, so that when he came face to face with his foe he had but 15,000 men to their 50,000. But his courage rose to the crisis, and when one of his knights sighed for the thousands of brave warriors in England, he said warmly—

"I would not have a single man more. If God give us the victory, it will be plain we owe it to His grace."

And the battle there fought and won was the great battle of Agincourt, the victory once again of the English archers. Henry had always been loved by the nation, now he became their hero and their darling.

"Oh, when shall Englishmen

With such acts fill a pen,

Or England breed again

Such a King Harry?"

The news of the triumph was quickly sent to London by a special messenger, and the Mayor, with the commonalty and an immense number of citizens, set out on foot to make their pilgrimage to St. Edward's shrine, there to offer devout thanksgiving for the joyful news.

And to this procession there joined themselves very many lords and peers of the realm, with the substantial men, both spiritual and temporal, for all knew that thanksgiving was due unto God, and to Edward, the glorious Confessor. Therefore went they like pilgrims on foot to Westminster, as aforesaid, passing through the newly built nave.

Later on, when Henry made his triumphant entry into London as the victor of Agincourt, "the gates and streets of the cities were garnished and apparelled with precious cloths of arras, containing the victories and triumphs of the king of England, which was done to the intent that the king might understand what remembrance his people would leave to their posterity of these, his great victories and triumphs."

But the king would not have any ditties to be sung of his victory, for he said the glory belonged to God, and the hymn of praise he commanded was a joyful *Te Deum*, which rang through the vaulted arches of the Abbey, led by the monks, swelled by countless voices of brave Englishmen. Nor would Henry allow his battered helmet of gold and his other armour, "that in cruel battaille was so sore broken with the great strokes he hadde received," to be carried before him or shown to his people. With a fine modesty, he sought in no way to glorify himself. The memory of his early manhood, with its dark side, was ever before his eyes; the conflict with the enemy within was ever waging, and the knowledge of his own weakness swept over him even in the hour of his greatest triumph, so that he could not but be humble as a little child.

Peace was at last made with France, the terms being that Henry should marry the French king's daughter, Katherine, who possessed "a white oval face, dark flashing eyes, and most engaging manners," and that he should succeed to the throne of France on the death of his father-in-law. In the February of 1421 he brought his pretty bride to England, where the people received her "as if she had been an angel of God," and on the 24th of that month she was crowned by the Archbishop.

In the words of Robert Fabyan, an alderman of London, but devoted to the pleasures of learning, "I will proceed to show you some part of the great honour that was exercised and used upon that day."

After the service in the church was ended, Queen Katherine was led into the great hall of Westminster, and there sat at dinner at Henry's side, while close to her sat the captive Prince James of Scotland, the Archbishop of Canterbury, and many great nobles. The Countess of Kent sat under the table at the right side of the queen, and the Countess Marshal on the left side, holding her napkin, while the Earl of Worcester rode about the hall on a great courser to keep room and order. Being Lent, no meat was allowed, excepting brawn served with mustard, but of fish there was a great choice;

"pyke in herbage lamprey powderyd, codlyng, crabbys, solys, fresshe samon, dryed smelt, halybut, rochet, porpies rostyd, prawys, clys roast, and a white fisshe florysshed with hawthorne leaves and redde lawrys." Wonderful ornaments called "subtelties" were on the table, being images intended to symbolise the happy event, and fastened on to these were labels with such verses as—

"To this sign the king

Great joy will bring,

And all his people

The queen will content."

Or—

"It is written

And can be seen,

In marriage pure

No strifes endure."

Katherine's pity was roused by the clever and charming young Scottish prince who had been so long a prisoner, and who was now deeply in love with Lady Joanna Beaufort, a lady he had seen in the gardens of Windsor Castle, and at this banquet she pleaded for him with her husband, with the result that he was eventually set free, and allowed to marry the lady of his love.

In spite of the peace which had been made, the French people were not inclined to submit to their conquerors, and within a few months of Katherine's coronation war broke out again, which sent Henry off in haste to France. He was still victorious, and when besieging Meaux the news was brought that Katherine had given him a son. At the same time came a loving letter from the queen herself, begging that she might join him in France so soon as her health would permit. The permission was readily granted, and she came, but not too soon; for Henry, who had bravely fought illness as he fought all other enemies, was conquered at last, and died at Vincennes, he, "mighty victor, mighty lord, being carried there helpless on a litter."

In the third year of his reign Henry had made his will, in which he had set down careful instructions as to his own burying, which was to be at Westminster, among the kings; and as by now there was but little room left in the Confessor's Chapel, he directed that at its eastern end, where the relics were kept, a high place should be made, ascended on each side by steps, and that there should be raised an altar, while underneath it his body should be laid. To this altar he bequeathed plate, vestments, and a sum of money for the Abbey, in token of which three monks of the Abbey were daily to say three masses there for his soul.

He had been a great benefactor to the Abbey, for besides having completed the nave, he had paid to it a thousand marks yearly, restored to it a ring valued at a thousand marks, and given such valuable presents as a Psalter and other fine books; so the monks were anxious to do him all honour, while the people of London were determined to worthily show their sorrow and their love.

The great funeral procession set out from France, and by slow stages reached London. The coffin had been set on an open chariot, and behind it was carved an image of the king made of leather and painted to look lifelike, clothed in purple with ermine, holding a sceptre, crowned and sandalled. The queen and King James of Scotland followed as chief mourners; a thousand men in white bore torches; throughout the day chants, hymns, and sacred offices were sung by the priests, and wherever his body rested for awhile in a church, masses were said.

From Paris to Calais, Calais to Dover, Dover to Canterbury, and Canterbury to London, this solemn journey of many weeks was made, while once on English soil the procession was greatly lengthened. The streets of London were draped in black; each householder stood at his door with a lighted torch; before the royal coffin rode the king's favourite knight and standard-bearer, Sir Louis Robsart, and many lords bore the banners of saints. Men at arms, in deep black and on black horses, formed the guard of honour; behind came his three chargers, then followed the royal mourners, and once more came a touch of relief from the rich vestments of the bishops and abbots, and the white robes of the priests and singers.

"So with great solemnity and honour was that excellent prince brought unto the monastery of Westminster, and there at the feet of St. Edward reverently interred, on whose soul, sweet Jesus, be merciful."

The little king of England was not yet a year old, but directly after the funeral Parliament met, and Queen Katherine rode through the city of London in a chariot drawn by white horses, surrounded by the nobles of the land. She held her baby in her arms, and in the words of one who watched, "Those pretty hands which could not yet feed himself, were made capable of wielding a sceptre, and he who beholden to his nurses for food, did distribute law and justice to the nation." By his Chancellor the infant king saluted, and to his people spoke his mind, by means of another tongue. Alice Boteler and Joan Ashley were appointed by this year-old child to be his governess and nurse, "from time to time reasonably to chastise us as the case may require, to teach us courtesy and good manners, and many things convenient for our royal persons to learn."

The building of the chantry over the grave of Henry V. was not long delayed, and all his instructions were carefully carried out. You will see it is a little chapel of itself at the east end of the Confessor's Chapel, standing so high, that at first the people from the farther end of the Abbey could see the priests celebrating mass at its altar.

HENRY V.'s TOMB

But before long the stone screen put up about this time, to the further honour of St. Edward, cut it off from view. How exquisite must that screen have been, with its lacework tracery, its niches full of saints, its brilliancy of gold, of crimson, and of blue! You must look carefully at the carvings, which tell the story of Edward's life, fact and legend blended together. Here

I will tell you shortly what each scene is meant to represent, beginning from your left as you face the screen.

The first two describe the birth of Edward; the third, his coronation; the fourth, his dream of the devil dancing for joy over the piles of money collected by the much-hated tax called Danegeld, a dream which so alarmed the king that he did away with the tax. The fifth shows how Edward had mercy on a thief who tried to steal his gold, for the king said, "Let him keep it; he hath more need of it than us." The sixth tells how Christ appeared to the king at the Holy Sacrament; the seventh and eighth describe the crowning of the king of Denmark and a quarrel between Harold and Tostig. The ninth and tenth go back to legend, the vision of the Seven Sleepers and the appearance of St. John as a pilgrim; while the twelfth and thirteenth describe St. John giving back the ring to the pilgrim, and the pilgrim's bearing it to King Edward. The eleventh shows the king washing his hands on the right, and on the left are three blind men, waiting for their sight to be restored to them when they wash their eyes in the water Edward had used; and the two last tell of the king's death and the dedication of the Abbey.

The chantry of King Henry was less ornate than this screen, but it was nevertheless very beautiful. You must look at the pattern of the open work on the iron grating which is round the tomb gates, and pick out the fleur-de-lis, the emblem of France, claimed by Henry as his inheritance. The figure of the king was the special gift of his widow, and was carved of the best English oak, with a head of silver, and its value made it too great a temptation to some "covetous pilferers about the latter end of Henry VIII., who broke it off and conveyed it clean awaie."

Over the chantry you will see a helmet, shield, and saddle; and though the helmet is certainly not the one which Henry kept hidden from all people at the Agincourt festival, it is certainly as old as the funeral day, and was probably made for that occasion.

In the year 1878, Katherine of Valois, who had first been buried in Henry III.'s chapel, then left for more than two hundred years in a rudely made coffin, open to the public gaze, by her husband's tomb, and afterwards laid in a side chapel, was at last buried under the altar slab in the Chantry Chapel of Henry V., and here within the calm shelter of Edward's shrine were carried the remains of two other queens, Eadgytha, the wife of Harold, and good Queen Maude, the wife of Henry I. Here, too, rest two tiny royal children, Margaret of York, the baby daughter of Edward IV., and her niece, Elizabeth Tudor, the three-year-old child of Henry VII. and Elizabeth. Their little marble tombs are plain and bear now no name. One other royal prince is buried here, Thomas of Woodstock, the uncle and for some time the adviser of Richard II., who certainly suffered heavily for any advice he gave, good or otherwise, for he was smothered to death at Calais with Richard's consent. And one man not of royal birth lies here—John of Waltham, Bishop of Salisbury, for whom this same Richard II. had so great a liking, that, defying every one, he ordered him to be laid among kings, close to the tomb of the Confessor.

I wonder if by now you know thoroughly that chapel which holds our earliest and some of our greatest kings and queens? Does that stately tomb in the centre call to your mind Edward, the dreamer and the builder, the dramatic ending of his life, the splendid ceremony of his burial within these walls, when he was honoured not alone as king of England or founder of the Abbey, but as a saint of the Church? Does the tomb of Henry III., with its remains of soft coloured marble and gilt mosaics, tell you of Westminster's second great builder, a lover of beauty and religious observances, but withal weak and extravagant, and incapable of rising to his great responsibilities? Does the rugged, undecorated monument of Edward I. show you the man, strong, stern, and steadfast, or the tomb of his beloved Eleanor speak to you of his wonderful love for her and of her sweet goodness? And when you look at the resting-place of Edward III. and Philippa, does it not call up to your mind the days of chivalry and the feats of English soldiers, the victories of Poitiers and Crecy, the siege of Calais and the compassionate pleading of the kindly queen? You stand by the tomb of Richard and Anne, united at last, and do not you think, "Oh, the pity of it," when you remember how Richard might have been strong and brave, had only he kept true to his best self? And then, do you not turn with a thrill of pride to the lofty chantry which encircles the grave of Henry V., the best loved king England ever had, the king who set a glow of patriotism alight in his realm, who rose above his failings and his faults, and gave to his people the fine example of a man who was victor over himself as well as victor over his foreign foes? Worthily I think does Henry's chantry crown the Confessor's shrine.

If some of these thoughts have come to you, this chapel will have taught you more history than any number of books or any number of dates. Because history only grows real to all of us, when the men and women about whom we read and learn cease to be mere figures and become our familiar acquaintances, till we fit them in as it were to their proper places in the story of England—places which are not always bounded by the years of a reign, which often cannot be bounded even by centuries.

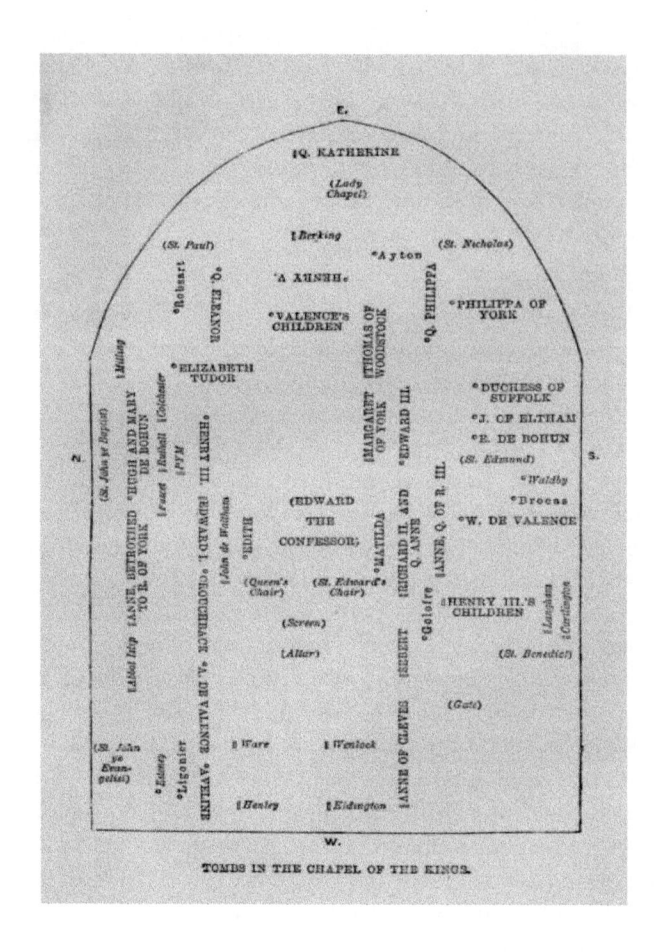

TOMBS IN THE CHAPEL OF THE KINGS.

CHAPTER IX
THE WARS OF THE ROSES AND THE THIRD ROYAL BUILDER

Little Henry VI. was not crowned till he was nine years old, and one old writer says that "so small was he, he could not wear the crown, and a bracelet of his mother's was placed on his head." He was a dreamy, gentle boy, and, far from being excited or happy on his coronation day, we hear how "very sadly and gravely he beheld all the people round about him, at the sight of which he showed great humility." His mother, Katherine, had married a Welshman named Owen Tudor, much to the anger of those about the court and the nobles, who considered that by so doing she had demeaned herself, and after this she was allowed to see very little of her son, who was therefore left entirely to his uncles, the Duke of Bedford and the Duke of Gloucester. Like Edward the Confessor, Henry was fit for a cloister but not for a crown, and he was called to reign in troublous times, when strength of will and purpose were more needed in a king than saintliness or simplicity of life. His uncles, who realised his weakness, arranged that he should marry Margaret of Anjou, a woman who was brave, ambitious, and masterful; but the fact that she soon got Henry completely under her control only brought about in the end his destruction and hers. In France the English lose all that they had won, for a deliverer of France had arisen in the girl Joan of Arc, who gave fresh courage and hope to her fellow-countrymen and led them on to victory as though she had been a saint sent by God. Then back to England came those many thousands of soldiers who had been fighting abroad all these years, and they were not inclined to settle down to a peaceful life; they wanted adventure, excitement, and plunder, and they were ready to flock round any leader who could promise them the chance of a fight. You will remember how, when you looked at Edward III.'s tomb, with the figures of his sons kneeling round, I told you that the descendants of those sons brought civil war upon England; and it was in the reign of Henry VI. that this terrible war broke out. Henry, as you know, was descended from John of Gaunt, Duke of Lancaster, and his grandfather, Henry IV., had gained the throne by will of Parliament and by right of conquest, but not by right of inheritance. Now there was living Richard, Duke of York, who was descended from the Duke of Clarence, the elder brother of John of Gaunt, and when, owing to Henry's weakness and the jealousies of the great nobles, two parties gradually began to form themselves, these parties naturally became divided into those who supported the king, that is to say, the House of Lancaster, and those who supported the House of York. At first there was no thought of civil war; these two parties merely opposed each other and schemed one against the other; but before long feeling ran so high that open warfare became inevitable, and each side took as its badge a rose.

So began the Wars of the Roses, and there followed those terrible battles of Northampton, Wakefield, St. Albans, Towton, Barnet, and Tewkesbury, in which thousands of Englishmen were slain (20,000 at Towton alone), the victory resting first on one side and then on the other, though finally with the Yorkists. The Duke of York had been killed early in the campaign, but his place had been filled by his young son, Edward, and at last, after the battle of Tewkesbury, King Henry and Queen Margaret were taken prisoners, their son Edward having been killed in battle or murdered afterwards. Both were taken to the Tower, and one night, between eleven and twelve, King Henry was put to death, the Duke of Gloucester and divers of his men being in the Tower that night. So Edward of York ascended the throne, the fourth king of that name, and the first stage of the War of the Roses was ended.

Henry was not buried at Westminster; in the darkness of the night his body was carried from the Tower, put on to a lighted barge, and, "without singing or saying," conveyed up the dark waters of the Thames to his silent interment at Chertsey Abbey. And yet this gentle, humble king had loved the Abbey well, and had greatly longed to lie near to St. Edward, by his father and his ancestors, having chosen the spot where the relics had been kept, as a "good place."

Edward IV. reigned for twelve years, but he did not reign in peace; and once his wife Elizabeth was in such distress and danger that, with her three little girls, Elizabeth, Mary, and Cicely, and one faithful attendant, Lady Scrope, she fled to Westminster for sanctuary, and threw herself on the mercy of Abbot Mylling. In this gloomy place of refuge her son was born, she being tended by a certain Mother Cobb, who also lived in sanctuary, while the Abbot sent her some few things for her comfort, and a kind butcher named Gould provided "half a beef and two muttons every week."

It was a strange birthplace for an English prince; but his christening, which took place in the Abbey, was not without honour, though the ceremony was carried out as though he were a poor man's son. He was given the honoured name of Edward, the Abbot was his godfather, and the Duchess of Bedford with Lady Scrope stood as his godmothers. When peace was restored, Edward IV. at once came to Westminster to comfort his queen, and he did not forget to reward those who had helped Elizabeth in the hour of her distress. To Nurse Cobb he gave £12 a year; from the butcher he ordered a royal shipful of hides and tallow; while the Abbot, for "his great civility," was made a Privy Councillor, and afterwards Bishop of Hereford.

But though Elizabeth left the Sanctuary, she was once more to return to its kindly shelter. She had always a mistrust of her husband's favourite brother, the Duke of Gloucester, and when King Edward died in 1473, she at once went back to Westminster with her daughters and her second son, the Duke of York. Her eldest boy, Edward, was already in his uncle's power and in the Tower, although the Duke of Gloucester had made him enter London in state, he riding bare-headed before him, and saying to the people loudly, "Behold your prince and sovereign." But the queen was not to be deceived by this. "Woe worth him," she said bitterly; "he goeth about to destroy me and my blood."

This time Elizabeth and her children were given room in the Abbot's palace, probably in the dining-hall, and there the Archbishop of York came to her to deliver up, for the use of her son, the Great Seal, entrusted to him by Edward IV. He found her sitting on the floor, "alone on the rushes, desolate and dismayed, and about her was much rumble, haste, and business with conveyance of her household stuff into sanctuary. Every man was busy to carry, bear, and convey these stuffs, chests, and fardels, and no man was unoccupied." In the distance could be heard the noise of the workmen already beginning the preparations for the coronation of King Edward, which the Duke of Gloucester was apparently pushing forward with all haste. But as the Archbishop looked out of his window on to the Thames, he saw the river covered with boats full of the Duke of Gloucester's servants, keeping a watch over the queen's hiding-place.

Richard of Gloucester's next move was to get possession of the little Duke of York, and as he was now appointed Protector, having altogether deceived the Council as to his real intent, this was no very difficult matter. And the poor queen had only a mother's love and a mother's fears to set against these mighty men and the fair sounding argument "that the little king was melancholy and desired his brother for a playmate."

"I deliver him into your keeping, my lord," she said to the Archbishop of Canterbury, her face white, her voice trembling, "of whom I shall ask him again before God and the world. And I pray you, for the trust which his father reposed in you, that as you think I fear too much, so you be cautious that you fear not too little."

Then she threw her arms round the boy and covered him with kisses.

"Farewell, mine own sweet son," she sobbed; "God send you good keeping. And God knoweth when we shall kiss together again."

Her worst fears were realised. She never saw her boys again, never knew how they were murdered in the Tower, or even where they were buried. And from her dwelling-place within the Sanctuary precincts she could see and hear all the preparations that were being made for the coronation of Richard III., while she "sobbed and wept and pulled her fair hair, as she called by name her two sweet babes, and cried to God to comfort her."

For nearly a year she remained where she was, then Richard, having taken an oath before the Lord Mayor and the Council to protect her and her daughters, she moved out of Sanctuary into some humble lodgings near Westminster, where her one friend seems to have been a doctor named Lewis, who was also a priest, and apparently something of a politician too, for he began to plan with the queen for the marriage of her eldest daughter, Elizabeth, with Harry of Richmond, who, through his mother, Margaret Beaufort, was the hope of the Lancastrian party.

Richard III. was already hated in England, and as the story of the way in which he had caused his little nephews to be murdered became generally known, the hatred increased tenfold. So the Lancastrian party thought the moment had come for them to make another effort. Harry Richmond landed at Milford Haven from France with 3000 men, and soon an eager, willing army flocked to his standard. At Bosworth field he met Richard in battle.

"Let courage supply the want of our numbers," he cried. "And as for me, I propose to live with honour hereafter, or die with honour here."

Evening found him the victor of the day; Richard lay dead on the field, and his crown, which he had worn into battle, was found hanging on a bush. There on the scene of his triumph the crown was set on Henry's head, while the soldiers shouted joyfully, "God save King Henry VII.," and then burst into a solemn *Te Deum*.

In October Henry was formally crowned in the Abbey, and in the Abbey, too, a few months later, he married the Princess Elizabeth, once the helpless, homeless Sanctuary child. So were the Houses of York and Lancaster made one; so were the red roses and white roses grafted together, and the people of London celebrated the happy event with bonfires, dancing, songs, and banquet. Cardinal Bourchier, himself of Plantagenet stock, performed the marriage ceremony, and so, as an old writer prettily puts it, "his hand held the sweet posie wherein the white and red roses were first tied together."

Not till a year later was Elizabeth crowned, and by then a little son had been born to her, named Arthur at his father's wish, in memory of the stainless King Arthur, whom Henry VII. claimed as an ancestor through his Welsh grandfather, Owen Tudor.

It was about this time that a great change came over the people of England in regard to their opinion of Henry VI. They had begun by pitying him for his misfortunes; then they had called to mind his patience and humility, his kind deeds, his love of learning, and his pure life, till at last in their eyes he became nothing short of a saint. Richard III. had caused his body to be removed from Chertsey to Windsor, much to the anger of the priests at Chertsey, who had spread abroad stories of wonderful miracles performed at his tomb, which stories, being readily believed, had drawn many pilgrims to the place. And pilgrims never came empty-handed.

Henry VII. came under the influence of this feeling, and he resolved that honour should now be done to this king, whom men had liked and pitied, but had never honoured in life. He had already decided to build a new chapel to the Virgin Mary in the Abbey, or rather to entirely rebuild the Lady Chapel of Henry III., and here he intended Henry VI. should be reburied under a costly tomb. He went so far as to petition the Pope to add King Henry's name to the list of saints; but the Pope would only agree to do so for an extravagant sum of money, and Henry Tudor thought the money could be more profitably spent in other ways. So the matter was allowed to drop, and although the council which had been summoned to decide where Henry should finally be buried—in Windsor, Chertsey, or Westminster—gave their judgment in favour of Westminster, it is very doubtful if his body was ever moved to the Abbey at all. Certainly no monument was raised to his memory. However, the building of the Lady Chapel went on apace, only its purpose was changed. It was no longer to be the chantry of Henry VI., but the chapel of Henry VII., the burying-place of the Tudor kings and queens of his race.

Henry was a curious mixture of a desire to hoard up money, and a desire to build what he undertook on a very lavish scale. He saved more money than any other English king, and he certainly spent less, for he was simple in all his tastes, a silent, gloomy man. But he has left behind him in Westminster Abbey a piece of work as beautiful as wealth and art could make it, a building "stately and surprising, which brought this church to her highest pitch of glory," and though his original ideas as to its purpose were frustrated, his longings that here "three chantry monks should say prayers for his soul so long as the world endured," being ruthlessly disregarded by his own son, Henry VIII., his chapel still stands, so that with Edward the Confessor and Henry III. he ranks among the three great royal builders of the Abbey.

Before you go into this chapel stand for a minute in King Edward's shrine, with its stately simplicity; then pass under the chantry of Henry V., simple too, but telling of strength, of life, and vigour; walk up the steps of Henry's Chapel into the dark entrance, and then stay still in the doorway to drink in the matchless beauty before your eyes. Here, simplicity is a word unknown; everywhere, inside and out, is a wealth of carving; no spot or corner was deemed too hidden away to be ornamented; roof and walls alike are covered with delicate lacework and rich embroidery made out of stone.

"They dreamed not of a perishable house who thus could build."

The foundation-stone was laid one afternoon in the January of 1502 by Islip, "that wise and holy man who was Abbot of the Westminster monks," and the building was solemnly dedicated to the Blessed Virgin Mary by order of Henry VII., king of England and France and Lord of Ireland. The work went on quickly, for money was not lacking. Abbot Islip was a man of action, and Henry was feverishly anxious that the building should be completed in his lifetime. Here it was that he meant to be buried, for just because his claim to the throne was not a very good one, he was doubly anxious to link himself on by many different ways to the kings of the past. Everywhere in his chapel, round his tomb, on the roof, and on the doorways, you will find his different badges set up, as if to say, "Each one of these badges gave me the right to be king of England." You will see over and over again the York and Lancaster roses; the portcullis and the greyhound, both of them Beaufort badges, which had come to him through his mother, Margaret Beaufort, the direct descendant of John of Gaunt, Duke of Lancaster; the red dragon of Cadwallader of Wales, the last British king, whom Henry alone of all the English kings proudly claimed as his ancestor, through Owen Tudor, his father; and the lion, which always figured in the royal arms of England. These badges, everywhere carved, were Henry's challenge to any one who might dispute his claim.

"We will," said Henry, "that this chapel be wholly and perfectlie fynished with all spede; and the windows glazed with stories, imagies, badgies, and cognoisants; that the walles, doors, archies, windows, vaults, and imagies, within and without be painted, garnished, and adorned in as goodly and rich manner as such a work requireth and as to a king's work appertaigneth."

But in spite of all the speed the king died before the work was finished, and never saw his chapel in all its costly beauty. Only a few days before his death he gave the Abbot £5000 more, "in redy money by the hande," for the carrying on of the work, and his will showed how deep his interest lay, for he solemnly charged his executors to advance whatever money was needful, and to choose for the high altar "the greatest Image of our Lady we have in our Juel house; a Crosse of plate of gold upon tymber, chalices, altar suits, vestments, candlesticks, and ornaments," all of them to bear the royal badges. "And for the price and value of them," he concluded, "our mynde is, that thei bei of suche as appertaigneth to the gifte of a prynce; and therefore we wol that our executours in that partie have a special regarde to the lawe of God, the weal of our soule and our honour royal."

Queen Elizabeth had died some years before her husband, and had been impressively laid in some side chapel of the Abbey. Now, on Henry's death, both were buried together in the tomb which the king had ordered should be in the middle of the Chapel by the high altar, and about which he had left minute instructions as to the images of himself and the queen, the inscription, the tabernacles round the tomb with the images of saints and angels, and the grating of copper and gilt for its protection.

Certainly the tomb was made worthy of the exquisite chapel which enshrined it, and Henry's wishes were faithfully carried out in this respect. An Italian, Torregiano, made the images of the king and queen in gilt bronze, and Torregiano was something of a genius, for all his images have a wonderful life of their own. Yet he must have been anything but a pleasant visitor to the monastery precincts, for he was a bold man, with a loud voice, frowning eyebrows, and fierce gestures, who daily boasted of his feats among the beasts of Englishmen, and told how he had broken the nose of his rival Michael Angelo; or how he had shattered to pieces an image of the Virgin, because there was some dispute about the price to be paid him. However, we must forgive him his violent temper out of gratitude for his beautiful work.

The grating round the tomb was made by English workmen, and here again you will see everywhere the king's badges. And I want you to notice, too, the little angels who stand round the king and queen, for they look as if they had just flown there for a moment, so lightly are they poised. Then you must look at the carvings round the tomb, those Saints whom the king had chosen to be his guardians: the Virgin Mary with Christ in her arms and St. Michael at her side; St. John the Baptist pointing to a picture of the Lamb of God; St. John the Evangelist holding his Gospel in his hand, an eagle standing at his feet; St. George of England standing on the vanquished Dragon, and with him St. Anthony dressed as a monk; Mary Magdalene with her box of precious ointment; St. Barbara holding a three-windowed tower; St. Christopher bearing on his shoulder the Christ Child, and St. Edward the Confessor crowned in glory.

Just outside the screen must have stood a beautiful altar, also the work of Torrigiano, an altar of white marble, gilded with fine gold, enriched by inlay and carving, the central figure being "an image, erth coloured of Christ dead;" but this was wrecked by a fanatic named Marlow in the time of the Commonwealth, whose "ignorant zeal was such that he brake it into shivers, though it was a raritie not to be matched in any part of the world."

As you stand in the chapel I want you to gaze up at the vaulted roof, which seems as though it hung in mid air, so wonderful is the design with its fairy grace and lightness; for here you see a beautiful example of that fan-tracery vaulting which was peculiarly English in its style, and which in this case was probably the work of two English masons, John Hyharn and William Vertue. Then you must look around at the army of Saints and Martyrs who guard the walls; king, apostle, saint confessor, all are here, and the niches in which they stand are delicately carved and decorated. And you must try to imagine the glory of the windows in those early days when, filled with "goode, clene, sure, and perfyte glasse of oryent colours, and the imagery of the story of the olde lawe and the new lawe," they reflected their rich hues around. Now only one little part of those many painted windows remains, but that is a figure of Henry VII., who looks down over the chapel which he raised.

The carved oaken stalls intended for the monks were not all finished at this time, and as is so often the case with such stalls, there is nothing sacred about the character of the ornaments carved on them. On the contrary, they aim at being amusing; and you will find quaint figures of monkeys winnowing corn; of foxes in armour riding on the backs of cocks; of fiends seizing a miser; of turkeys chasing a boy; a bear playing on bagpipes, and so on. In the year 1725 George I. reconstructed the old order of Knights of the Bath, and as from the days of Richard II. it had been the custom only to create such knights at a coronation and when a Prince of Wales was created, the Order had many associations with Westminster. So this Chapel of Henry VII. was set apart as the Chapel of the Order, just as the Chapel of St. George's, Windsor, was set apart for the Order of the Garter; and here for nearly a hundred years every knight was installed; here was hung his banner; and here was fastened up over his stall the plate on which was emblazoned his coat of arms. But gradually the Order became so large that the many ceremonies connected with it had to cease, and now only the banners which hang here tell us of bygone days.

GATES OF HENRY VII.'s CHAPEL.

GATES OF HENRY VII.'s CHAPEL.

As you come out, take a last look at the massive gates of oak and metal serried with badges, and then stand once more in the middle of the sixteenth century, when that mass of carving was made yet more rich and beautiful by the colours which blazed everywhere, from the crimson, blue, and purple of the windows; the gold and silver vessels on the altar; the gleaming brass of the images; the gorgeous vestments of the priests; the dazzling whiteness of the marble; the glitter of the tapers round the tomb. Think of how Abbot Islip must have gloried in this new gem of dazzling beauty now added to the Abbey, already so rich in treasure; for Islip was of "a wakeful conscience" and held himself the steward of the house of God, so that he too did some building to this place, and evidently won the confidence of the king, who made him paymaster of the workmen.

As for Henry himself, the chapel has become a far greater memorial of him than he can ever have deemed possible. It matters little to us now what was his real motive in raising it, even if it were possible to point to any one unmixed motive which inspired him. For us it is enough that the chapel stands, and though we need not, with Fabyan the chronicler, wax enthusiastic over "the excellent wysdome, sugared eloquence, wonderfull dyscression, the exceedynge treasure and rychesse innumerabyll" of this silent, almost gloomy king, let us with the same chronicler "remember his beautyfull buildyngs and his liberell endowments at Westminster, and pray that he may attain that celestyall mansion whych he and all trew Christen soules are inheritors unto, the whyche God hym graunt."

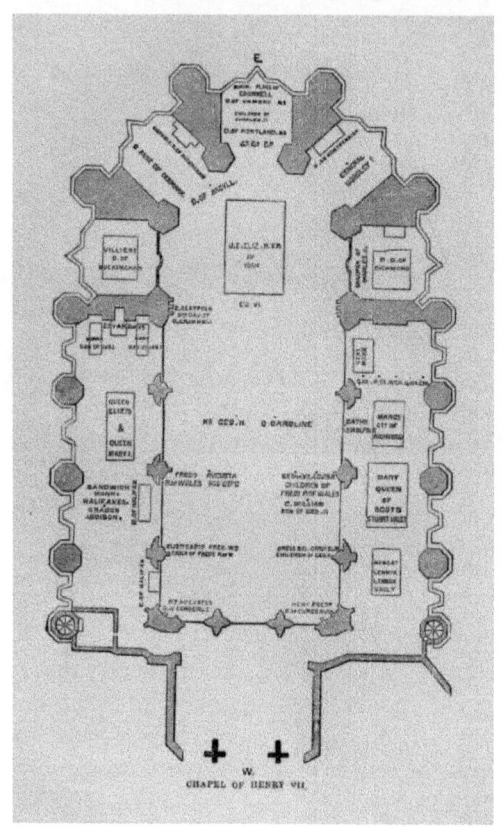

CHAPEL OF HENRY VII.

CHAPTER X
THE ABBEY AND THE REFORMATION

A few months after the death and burial of Henry VII., another royal funeral took place in this beautiful chapel of the Tudors, the funeral of his mother, Margaret, the "venerable lady," whose influence was far-reaching, and whose holiness had won for her such universal love and reverence.

"It would fill a volume to recount her good deeds," says her biographer, and he goes on to tell how she lived a life of prayer and simplicity, being a member of no leas than five religious houses; how she herself waited on the poor, the sick, the dying, and how she freely gave of her wealth for the encouragement of learning. "Her ears were spent in hearing the word of God, her tongue was occupied in prayer, her feet in visiting holy places, her hands in giving alms." She provided an almshouse for poor women near Westminster Abbey, and another at Hatfield, and besides founding schools and colleges, she maintained many poor scholars at her own expense. She also translated many works in the English tongue. It was in Westminster that she desired to be buried, and she made many gifts to the place which her son was so richly beautifying, stipulating in return that prayers should always be said here for herself and all her family. She was destined to outlive son, daughter-in-law, and grandson, and it was not till 1509 that her useful life of close on three-score years and ten came to an end, and she passed peacefully away, "the almoner of God, the friend of the poor, the supporter of true religion, the patroness of learning, the comforter of the sorrowing, the beloved of all." As you stand by her monument in the south aisle of Henry VII.'s Chapel, look at her strong, noble face, beautiful in its calm old age, her hands clasped in prayer as was their wont; and while you are lost in wonder at the skill of the sculptor, probably Torrigiano, I think you will realise something of the goodness and purity of Margaret Richmond, which this sleeping figure makes so vivid, and will understand how "every one that knew her loved her, for everything she said or did became her." It was well for her that she did not live long enough to see her clever imperious grandson seeking to destroy so many of the things which she had loved and guarded.

Henry VIII. came to the throne with splendid opportunities. He was gifted far above the average: his manners were genial and taking; he could talk many languages; he was devoted to sport, a good musician, an admirable wrestler; fond of amusement, but fond also of more serious things; and the people were prepared to love their King Hal, for he was in every way a contrast to his father, who had never won their affections. Henry was a strong man, who resolved to be no puppet in the hands of any party or minister. Yet it was his will which ruined his character, for it was a will entirely bent on gaining its own ends, unchecked by any sense of duty, untouched by any appeal to high or noble motives. What he desired he must have, and all that stood in his way must be swept aside: he would spare no one who thwarted him; nothing weighed in the balance against the gratification of his own whims and fancies.

You will remember that he was not the eldest son of Henry VII. His brother Arthur, Prince of Wales, had died in 1501, a few months after he had married Katherine, the Infanta of Spain, and chiefly because the idea was at first strongly opposed, Henry made up his mind to marry his widowed sister-in-law. When he came to the throne, he at once carried out his will in this matter, and brushed aside all the objections that were raised on account of the close relationship existing between the two. The marriage took place at Greenwich, and the double coronation followed at Westminster on Midsummer Day in the year 1509, "amid all the rejoicings in the world." Katherine made a beautiful queen, dressed in white with cloth of gold, her long hair hanging down to her feet, and little dreamt any of those who cheered her on her way of all that was to spring out of that marriage, for Henry seemed to be the most devoted of husbands. In 1511 their son was born, and had such an elaborate christening that he took a cold from which he never recovered. "His soul returned to among the Holy Innocents of God," says a Westminster manuscript, and we are told how "the queen made much lamentation, but by the king's persuasion she was at last comforted." The baby prince was certainly buried in the Abbey, though exactly where is unknown. But his death, unimportant as it must have seemed at the moment to those who took part in the funeral, had in reality a deep significance. Henry was incapable of loving any one for long, and as he began to grow weary of Katherine, he made it a grievance that her other child was a daughter and not a son. Furthermore, he argued to himself that he had done wrong in marrying his brother's widow, so that the death of his son was the sign of God's wrath, and then he began to devise how he could dissolve his marriage with her, to wed instead her fascinating maid of honour, Anne Boleyn. Only the Pope could grant him the divorce that he desired, and accordingly Henry sent his all-powerful favourite, Wolsey, to Rome to get this consent. But the Pope, much as he feared Henry, feared the Emperor Charles V., the nephew of Queen Katherine, much more, and Wolsey, on his side, was anxious not to offend the Pope, as his ambition was to succeed him, so it all ended in his going back to Henry without having the desired permission. Henry was furious, and Wolsey, disgraced, died broken-hearted. The king's next step was to defy the Pope, and to send round to all the ministers in Europe, asking them whether in their opinion his marriage with Katherine had been a legal one. But their answer in almost every case was the opposite answer to what Henry had determined on, and their opposition only increased his determination, till at last, urged thereto by Thomas Cromwell, Wolsey's successor in his favour, he took the bold step of declaring that he himself was the head of the Church in England, the defender of the faith, and that therefore the Pope had no power to forbid the divorce. He was clever enough to know that for many a long day the independent spirit of the English nation had rebelled against the power of the Pope in the land; that the revival of learning had set men thinking for themselves; that the teaching of Luther and the other reformers had prepared the way for a great change in England, and that he could count on his Parliament to support him in declaring himself supreme head of the Church in this land. Thus whilst pretending to cleanse and purify the Church, and reform the many errors which had crept in, Henry really was true to his general policy of sweeping out of the way any obstacle to his wishes. The Pope had opposed him, so from henceforward he would deprive the Pope of all authority in England. He divorced Katherine, and married Anne Boleyn, while those few men who refused to go against their conscience by declaring the king to be in the right on this question of his marriage, when they felt him to be in the wrong, did so at the cost of their lives.

But the king had not yet finished with the Pope; urged thereto by Cromwell, who earned for himself the name "The Hammer of the Monks," he proceeded to attack all the monasteries and religious houses in England, and there were many hundreds of them, which were under the immediate jurisdiction of Rome. To these religious houses England owed no small debt of gratitude: the monks had been teachers, scholars, chroniclers, architects, carvers, painters, translators, and illuminators; they had nursed the sick, they had relieved the needy; they had been the great employers of labour, the tillers of the soil, and, untouched by the ebb and flow of the tide outside, they had gone quietly on with their daily round of work and prayer, keeping their lights ever burning before the altar to signify that their house was "always watchynge to God." But, as they became rich and powerful, they fell away from their high ideals; the threefold vow of poverty, obedience, and purity ceased to sanctify their lives; luxury took the place of plain, frugal living; the monks no longer laboured with their own hands, but kept great retinues of servants, and the money that should have been spent for the glory of God and the church was squandered in extravagant living. The abbots were under no control save that of Rome, and Rome was far away, so that there was no power from outside to correct, to reform, and to purify. Gradually, too, the monasteries had lost their hold over the people; resting on their past, they made no effort to keep pace with the present; they bitterly opposed any education save that which they held in their own hands; they resented progress and enlightenment; they were no longer centres of light and learning; their fire had burnt out, quenched by covetousness, by wrong-doing and by luxurious living.

Cromwell saw in them an opportunity which Henry was all too ready to grasp. A Commission was formed to visit and report on the universities and all religious houses; and when the visitors had finished their work, which they had done carefully and thoroughly, they laid their verdict before the House of Commons in the famous Black Book, which was destroyed some years later by order of Queen Mary. Much of what it contained is therefore lost to us, but as the Commons, who sat, remember, in the Chapter-Room at Westminster, heard clause after clause read out, which told, with a few honourable exceptions, a terrible story against the monasteries, they could not restrain themselves, and over and over again shouts of "Down with the monks" rang through the vaulted building. Generally speaking, the largest of the monasteries had come well out of the inquiry, and Parliament therefore began by only dissolving the smaller houses, at the same time ordering that the lands and incomes of these latter should be handed over to the king, as head of the Church, to be spent in the "high and true interests of religion." Certainly the Commons had none but high motives in passing this Act, and never dreamt of a general dissolution, or the appropriation of all that immense wealth for anything but religious or educational purposes. They had not realised Henry's greed, "which no religion could moderate, or the force of his will, against which nothing, however sacred, seemed able to stand."

The monks at Westminster naturally heard very quickly all the particulars of the deliberations which had taken place inside the Chapter-Room. How they must have lingered about the cloisters that day; how eagerly and excitedly must they have talked during those hours when talking was allowed, wondering in what way all these things would end; how they must have speculated as to their own future, and that of the few other large monasteries in which the Commissioners had declared that "thanks be to God, religion had been right well kept and observed." They had not long to wait.

A general order issued shortly afterwards, ordering the removal of all shrines, images, and relics, made it clear that Henry and his ministers had other ideas beyond the reformation of religious houses; and the monks, who gauged the character of the king, hastily moved the body of St. Edward to some sacred spot, that, at least, this holy possession of the Abbey might not be lost to it. They managed, too, to hide some of the treasures which beautified Edward's shrine, but much of the gold and many of the jewels became the property of the king. Altogether nearly 800 monasteries fell into the hands of Henry, and without any compunction he appropriated their lands and their wealth, giving away to his favourites of the moment what he did not desire to keep for himself. Inside the religious houses the greatest excitement prevailed, and much diversity of opinion; for some there were among the abbots and monks who were prepared to lose their lives rather than willingly surrender themselves to the king's will, while others, more the children of this world than the children of light, deemed that by submission could they best hope to save something in this overwhelming deluge.

At Westminster, under Abbot Benson, the monks chose a prudent course, the abbot being one, as an old writer severely remarks, "whose conscience was not likely to stand in his way on any occasion," and in the January of 1540 the Abbey with all its wealth was voluntarily handed over to the king.

Partly perhaps on account of this absolute submission, but much more because even Henry had still reverence for a place which was peculiarly royal in all its associations, Westminster was in some degree saved. The old order indeed was destined to pass away; its wealth was to be a thing of the past, save for the wealth of beauty in sculptured stone which could not easily be taken from it, and which still remained unrivalled even when all the gold and jewels and plate excepting a silver pot, two gilt cups, three hearse clothes, twelve cushions and some other clothes, had been carried away to satisfy greedy courtiers, "leaving the place very bare."

But Henry converted the building into a cathedral, giving it a bishop, a dean, prebendaries, minor canons, all these offices with the exception of the Bishopric being filled by the monks belonging to the establishment. The Bishop, Thirleby, was ordered to make the abbot's house his palace; Abbot Benson, now Dean, took up his residence in humble quarters, and all the old glory of the monastery departed for ever, while Henry was quite £60,000 a year richer in our money. Those of the monks for whom no place could be found under the new system were pensioned off, and many of the buildings, such as the refectory and the smaller dormitory, no longer needed for the cowled figures who for so many generations had used them, were pulled down or put to fresh uses.

Nor was the monastery the only part of Westminster which fell from its greatness. Earlier in the reign of Henry a fire had destroyed much of the old Palace, and the king, who cared but little for it, set his heart on York House close by, at Whitehall, once the London house of the Bishops of York, afterwards the residence of Wolsey.

The Cardinal lived in state; indeed Westminster was but a humble dwelling compared to this magnificent palace, and on his disgrace, Henry took possession of it. For more than a hundred and fifty years it was the royal palace, with fine courts, halls and chambers, its own chapel and offices, its bowling-green, tent yard, cock-pit, and tennis courts, and meanwhile the gabled, sculptured Westminster Palace, the home of Saxon, Norman, and Plantagenet kings, fell to pieces. For us, both are now but phantom palaces, with hardly a trace of either remaining to recall the glories of the past.

But in the story of the Abbey, this change from Westminster to Whitehall had more than a passing effect; from henceforth the old intimate association between the Palace and Abbey ceased to exist, and Henry thus broke one more link with the traditions of his ancestors. Not even the chapel of his father, now no longer called the Lady Chapel, but instead St. Saviour's Chapel, had any attractions for one in whose nature reverent affection for old associations was entirely absent, and at his own desire, Henry was buried at Windsor, by his "true and loving wife, Jane Seymour," who had kept in his good graces by giving him a son, and then dying before he had time to grow weary of her. Of all his wives, only the plain and placid Anne of Cleves was buried in the Abbey, on the south side of the Altar, and "she had but half a monument," says Fuller, though her funeral was an elaborate one, by order of Mary, who was then queen.

King Edward VI., just ten years old, succeeded his father; and the members of his council, especially his uncle, the Duke of Somerset, strongly in favour of the Reformed Church, were determined that the Pope should not win back any of his old authority. In this, all the thinking people were of their opinion, but some of the poor people, who had formerly received much in charity from the monks, were very bitter, and there was more than one rebellion in favour of the monasteries. However, these were put down, and the reformers went on with their work. Edward was crowned as Head of the Church in England, and, for the first time, a Bible, translated into the English tongue, was set in his hands at the coronation service. For only within the last ten years had the Bible been read to the people in a language they could understand, and you will remember how first Wycliffe, and then Tyndale, had failed in their attempts to place this book in the hands of all, that all might read and learn of God's teachings, by the light of the understanding which God had given them. Two years after the coronation a Prayer-Book was published, also in English, not exactly the same Prayer-Book as we use now, for as time went on the spirit of the people changed in favour of a still simpler service than that which found favour with the early reformers in England, and in the reign of Charles II. a revised Prayer-Book was issued, as in the reign of James I. our present translation of the Bible was authorised. But it was in Edward's reign that an English Bible and Prayer-Book first found their way into the Abbey.

The plan of having a Bishop at Westminster does not seem to have succeeded. Thirleby was removed to Norwich, and Richard Cox became the Dean. But he remained in the simple quarters, near the Little Cloister, which had been assigned to Dean Boston, and the Abbot's house passed into the possession of a layman for the time being. Protector Somerset had certainly no feeling of veneration for the grand old pile of buildings. Not only did he put the Abbey under the Bishop of London, and insist on cartloads of stone, which once had formed part of the solid monastery buildings, being used for his own palace, Somerset House, but of the few lands which still remained to the Abbey, he took some and made them over to St. Paul's, from time immemorial the rival of Westminster. You have often heard the saying "robbing Peter to pay Paul;" now you know its origin. And as if to cut off every possible association with the past, the House of Commons moved from the Chapter House to St. Stephen's Chapel, part of the old Westminster Palace, and there met until the great fire in 1834, after which the present Houses of Parliament were built.

But with the death of Edward, who had reigned seven years, and the defeat of the Protestant party, who had tried to set Lady Jane Grey on the throne, there came a flicker of prosperity to the Abbey, a dim reflection, as it were, of its bygone greatness. For Queen Mary was a devout Roman Catholic, and so soon as it lay in her power, she dissolved the chapter or cathedral body, restored the monastery, and gave the post of Abbot to Fakenham, who was "a person of learning, good-natured, and very charitable to the poor."

Edward was buried at Westminster, close to his grandfather, Henry VII., and underneath the altar of Torrigiano, of which I have already told you, so that the last Roman Catholic and the first really Protestant king of England lay side by side, under the same exquisite roof, a striking commentary on the fact that the Reformation was not a complete wrench with the past, but a transition from old to new according to the unchangeable law of progress.

Mary was crowned on October 10, and on the coronation morning she journeyed in the royal barge from Whitehall to the private waterstairs of old Westminster Palace, and from thence went into the Parliament chamber, where she robed. Blue cloth covered the ground all the way from Westminster Hall to the choir in the Abbey, but here the altar blazed with cloth of gold, and rich covers hung all around, while the floor was strewn with fresh rushes, a quaint contrast to everything else. The Archbishops of Canterbury and York and the Bishop of London were already in the Tower as prisoners, so it was Gardiner, Bishop of Winchester, who met the queen and performed the service, at which there was much dismay among the people, for they said it had ever boded ill for England when the Archbishop did not crown the sovereign. The old coronation service with its full ceremonial was used, and the queen was very devout, kneeling long in silent prayer.

Four days later, the queen again rode to the Abbey, this time to open her Parliament. But the occasion did not pass by without some disturbances, for some who refused to kneel while the Mass was being celebrated were turned out by force.

The restoration of her religion was the object dearer than all others to Mary's heart, and her unfaltering belief that in so doing she was working the will of God, added to her passionate enthusiasm for her faith, are the only excuses we can plead for her, when we shudder at the cruel persecutions which made England a land of terror during the next few years. Here it is only necessary to say that, as always, persecution purified and strengthened the very cause it was destined to destroy, and Mary, during her five years' reign, made her people hate her so bitterly, that nothing but her death prevented a general rebellion.

She died a wretched, lonely woman, conscious of her utter failure.

"My oppressed heart is pierced by many wounds," she said bitterly at the last.

Her funeral took place with much state, but the only real mourners were the priests and monks, who feared for their own fate. Mary had entreated that she might not be buried in royal array. Her crown had brought her no happiness, she said, and she did not wish to be encumbered by it now. Behind her coffin rode her ladies, with black trains so long that they swept the ground. Mass was said before the High Altar for the last time, while Fakenham, the last Abbot of Westminster, as he himself well knew, preached a great sermon on the dead queen, and, in a voice trembling with deep feeling, told how she was too good for earth, a veritable angel, who had found the realm poisoned with heresy, and had purged it.

But his words found no echo in the heart of those around, and the funeral ended in a scene of disorder, for the people had no respect for the dead, and plucked down all the hangings and draperies, while the Archbishop of York, "in the midst of the hurly-burly, pronounced that a collation was prepared," whereupon the lords, ladies, and knights, with the bishops and Abbot Fakenham, hurried to another part of the building for dinner.

And no monument was erected to the memory of her who was the last queen of the old faith to be buried in the Abbey.

CHAPTER XI
IN THE CHAPEL OF HENRY VII.

On November 17, 1558, Mary died, and that very day Parliament met in old Westminster Palace "to proclaim without further halt of time the Lady Elizabeth as queen of this realm." Shouts of "God save Queen Elizabeth" resounded through the walls, and outside the cry "Long live our Queen Elizabeth" was taken up with heartfelt intensity by the people, who believed, and not in vain, that with her their deliverance had come. She had suffered, they had suffered, both in the same great cause, and now together they were standing in the dawn of a day which promised to be fair and radiant. The Spanish influence, which they hated passionately, as Englishmen have ever been wont to hate foreign interference, had received its death-blow, for here was a queen, "born mere English, here among us, and therefore most natural to us," who understood them, and whom they could freely trust. No wonder that there were no signs of mourning for the dead queen, only irrepressible joy and relief at the accession of the new sovereign they were prepared to love so loyally. But no wonder either that the echoes of the cheers which reached the Abbey fell on some hearts which could not respond to them. To Fakenham, with his handful of monks, those shouts of joy were as a death-knell, though the Abbot himself may have had some hopes that Elizabeth would remember how he had pleaded with Mary for her freedom.

The coronation festivities, which began January 15, put London in a delirium of rejoicings, and though the royal exchequer was so low that there was no money available for costly preparations, the people more than compensated for this by the pageants and decorations they organised out of the fulness of their hearts. "The queen," says an officer who followed the procession, "as she entered the city was received with prayers, welcomings, cries and tender words, with all those signs which argue the earnest love of subjects towards their sovereign. She, by holding up her hands and glad countenance to such as stood afar off, and most tender language to those that stood near, showed herself no less thankful to receive the people's goodwill than they to offer it, and to such as bade 'God save her Grace,' she said in return, 'God save you all,' so that the people were wonderfully transported at the loving answers and gestures of the queen."

Only one bishop could be found to read the coronation service, as those few Protestants who had escaped with their lives across the seas had not yet returned from their exile, and the Roman Catholics refused to assist, though no alterations were introduced into the service, excepting that the

Litany, the Gospel, and the Epistle were ordered to be read in English. This bishop, with the singers, met the queen at Westminster Hall on the following day, a Sunday, and to the fine old hymn, "Hail, Festal Day," the procession wended its way into the Abbey, and the solemn ceremony took place.

Nor did Elizabeth at first make any changes in the Abbey services. It was her desire, she declared at the opening of her Parliament ten days later, "to unite the people of the realm in one uniform order," and though she was determined that the English Church should be utterly severed from Roman control, and that the Bible should be an open book, she understood the bulk of her people well enough to know that, as Bishop Creighton has so clearly put it, "what they wished for was a national church, independent of Rome, with simple services, not too unlike those to which they had been accustomed." So, at the state service in the Abbey on this occasion, the Mass was celebrated with the usual ritual, though the sermon was preached by a certain Doctor Cox, who was a vigorous Protestant.

Elizabeth's first Parliament gave over to her all the religious houses revived by her sister, and she decided to once more make Westminster a Cathedral church, though without a bishopric. Possibly if Fakenham had been a more time-serving man, he might have managed to stay on under the new regime as Dean, but he was uncompromisingly true to his principles; he refused to acknowledge any one but the Pope as head of the Church, and in the House of Lords he made a strong speech against the English Prayer-Book. His reign at Westminster had been a short one, but he had not failed in his duty towards the precious trust committed to his care. The Confessor's Chapel, shrine of the English saint, was still the greatest treasure of the Abbey, and to this he had caused the body of the king, hidden, you will remember, by the monks at the first threat of dissolution, to be carried back "with the most goodly singing and chanting ever heard," after he had repaired the shrine itself to the best of his ability, assisted by Queen Mary, who had sent him some jewels. Moreover, in Parliament he successfully defended the right of sanctuary, so that this remained for some time longer at least an Abbey privilege, and altogether it is pleasant to remember this last Abbot as one who was true to the light as he saw it, a kindly, moderate, honest man, a firm friend, a fair enemy, a fine solitary figure standing out among his fellows. It is said that when in 1560 the bill was passed in Parliament which decided the fate of Westminster and the other remaining monasteries, a messenger who came to bring the news to Abbot Fakenham found him busy planting young elms in the Dean's yard.

"Cease thy labours, my lord Abbot," he said. "This planting of trees will avail thee nothing now."

But the old Abbot was not so mean-spirited.

"I verily believe," he made answer, "that so long as this church endureth, it shall be kept for a seat of learning."

And he went on contentedly with his work.

He lived for twenty-five years after he left the Abbey, under a certain amount of restraints, and great efforts were made to induce him to change his faith. But he never wavered, and so far as possible withdrew from all controversy, spending his time and his substance among the poor. "Like an axil tree, he stood firm and fixed in his own judgments," says Fuller, "while the times, like the wheels, turned backwards and forwards round him."

Westminster stood aloof from the keen religious controversies which raged around, and quietly stepped into its new position. It was now neither a monastery nor a cathedral, but a "collegiate church," as it is to-day, with its Dean and Chapter and its school. Very little, if anything, happened to disturb the peace of the Abbey under the rule of its three excellent Deans appointed by Elizabeth—Bill, Goodman, and Andrewes; the only sign of the times which deserves noticing being that more and more it became the custom to bury distinguished people not of royal blood within these honoured walls. Otherwise we may well quote the words of Widmore, who in summing up this epoch in Westminster history, concludes—"It may here be remarked that though misfortunes and disturbances in a place give opportunity to an historian to make observations and show his eloquence, while they also entertain the reader, yet peace and quietness are good proofs both of the happiness of the times and the discretion of those who govern."

On the 24th of March 1603, Elizabeth died after a reign of forty-four years, during which she had never lost her hold over the hearts and minds of her people. As a woman she had her failings and weaknesses, but as a queen she had done right well for England, and "round her, with all her faults, the England we know grew into the consciousness of its destiny.... She saw what England might become, and nursed it into the knowledge of its power."

The outburst of grief at her death was her people's acknowledgment of the debt they owed her. They had trusted her, and not in vain; she had understood them, had served them, and had loved them. On the day of her burying at Westminster "the city was surcharged with multitudes of all sorts, in the streets, houses, windows, leads, and gutters, and when they beheld her statue lying on the coffin, set forth in royal robes, having a crown upon the head thereof, a ball and sceptre in either hand, there was such a general sighing, weeping, and groaning as the like hath not been seen or known in the memory of man, neither doth any history mention any people, time, or state to make the like lamentation for the death of their sovereign."

Nor did her memory fade away with her life, for her tomb, which you will find in the north aisle of Henry VII.'s Chapel, became familiar to her people throughout the length and breadth of the land, "a lovely draught of it being pictured in the London and country churches."

The monument raised to her memory by James I. is a fine one of its kind, and the sculptor has given us an impression of her strength and power as she lies sleeping there in royal state, guarded by lions, though I think we cannot help missing the exquisite little figures of saints and angels banished in deference to the increasingly severe views of the English Churchmen. Here is the translation of the Latin inscription round the monument, which certainly described, and in no way exaggerated, the feelings of the nation towards her:—

"To the eternal memory of Elizabeth, Queen of England, France, and Ireland, Daughter of Henry VIII., Grand-daughter of Henry VII., Great-Grand-Daughter of Edward IV. Mother of her Country. A Nursing Mother of religion and all liberal Sciences, skilled in many languages, adorned with excellent adornments both of body and mind, and excellent for princely virtues beyond her sex. Religion to its primitive purity restored; peace settled; Money restored to its just value; Domestic Rebellions quelled; France relieved when involved with internal divisions; The Netherlands supported, the Spanish Armada vanquished; Ireland, almost lost by rebels, eased by routing the Spaniards; the Revenues of both Universities much enlarged; and lastly, all England enriched. Elizabeth, during forty-five years, a very prudent Governor, a victorious and triumphant Queen, most pious and most happy, at her calm death in her seventieth year, left her remains to be placed in this Church which she preserved, until the hour of her Resurrection in Christ."

In arranging for this lengthy epitaph, James could not fail to be reminded that Queen Mary, who lay in the same tomb as Elizabeth, was passed over in cold silence, so he added a simple sentence pathetic in its restraint, almost an appeal on behalf of the one whose life had been such a failure.

"Here rest we two sisters Elizabeth and Mary, fellows both in throne and grave, in the hope of one resurrection."

TOMB OF QUEEN ELIZABETH.

In life everything had tended to separate them, but in death they lay together at peace.

James erected another monument in this chapel, on the southern side, and this was to the memory of his mother, the ill-fated Mary Queen of Scots. She had been buried at Peterborough, but her son, when he came into the inheritance which was his, through her, very rightly caused her to be buried among the kings and queens of England. Here again death reconciled two implacable foes, so that Mary Queen of Scots lies opposite to Elizabeth in this chapel of the Tudors. The marble figure, with its sweet, finely-cut face and its graceful draperies and its delicate lacework, is full of charm, and makes familiar to us one whose fascinating beauty was her own undoing.

And now we come to a new phase in the history of the Abbey; for though after the days of Queen Elizabeth several kings and queens of England were buried within its walls, to none of them was a monument raised, not so much even as an inscription was cut on the stones over their graves. With the Stuarts began a new race of kings, and under their rule there grew up a new set of relations between king and subjects. They preached the doctrine of the divine right of kings, declaring themselves to be above any laws which their people might desire to make through Parliament, so the battle had to be fought out between king and Parliament, a battle so fierce that it brought once more civil war to England, cost Charles the First his life, and caused James II. to flee to foreign lands. But from that struggle with its many errors there at last developed

"That sober freedom out of which there springs

Our loyal passion for our temperate kings,"

which holds together to-day the throne and the nation as never before in our island story.

So you will see how, as the people became more and more the ruling force in England, it was the representatives of the people—statesmen, soldiers, sailors, writers, musicians, travellers, thinkers, discoverers, and benefactors—who stepped into the foremost places, and who were thought worthy of a resting-place among the great kings of old in the Abbey, while, with a few exceptions, the sovereigns of England were buried at Windsor, now the most important of all the royal palaces.

It is in Henry VII.'s Chapel that James I. himself was buried in the founder's tomb, and his wife Anne of Denmark lay close to him. Near at hand you will see a beautiful little monument of a baby in a cradle, which marks the grave of Princess Sophia, a baby daughter of James I. The king gave orders at her death that she should be buried "as cheaply as possible, without any solemnity," but in spite of this, and although she was only two days old, a great number of lords, ladies, and officers of state attended, followed the little coffin, which was brought up on a black draped barge from Greenwich, and which was met at the Abbey by the heralds, the dean and prebends, with the choir, while an antiphon was sung to the organ. The royal sculptor, Nicholas Pourtian, was allowed the sum of one hundred and forty pounds for her monument, and he must have been a great lover of children or he could not have thought out anything so charming as this yellow-tinted, lace-covered cradle with its tiny baby occupant.

Nor is the inscription less pretty in idea than the monument, for it tells us how Sophia, "Royal Rosebud, snatched away from her parents, James, King of Great Britain, Ireland and France, and Queen Anne, that she might flourish again in the Rosary of Christ, was placed here."

Next to her is her sister Mary who lived to be two, and then died of fever, saying many times over in her wanderings these same words, "I go, I go, away I go." Hers too is a very natural little figure, in spite of the stiff straight clothes and the quaint cap; and the carver has put a great deal of life into the weeping cherubs, to whom surely not the most rigid Puritan could have objected. In this same corner were laid, some years later, the bones found by some workmen under the stairs at the Tower of London, supposed to be those of the little princes who had been murdered there, so that at last King Edward the Fifth and his brother were honourably buried near their more fortunate sister Elizabeth of York.

The tomb of Mary Queen of Scots is really a Stuart vault, and it might almost be called the vault of Royal Children, for more than thirty are buried under it. Here, without any monument, but an inscription on the floor, lies Henry, Prince of Wales, the eldest son of James, who gave such high promise both of character and ability, that he had won the hearts of the people, and more especially of the Puritans, in a remarkable degree. James, though holding very unsatisfactory views as to the rights and duties of a king, had nevertheless brought up his son wisely and had educated him most carefully. Before he was six he had been instructed "how to behave towards God, how to behave when he should come to be king, and how to behave in all those matters which were right or wrong according as they were used;" and when he was only nine he wrote in Latin to his father giving an account of the books he had been reading, which included Cicero's Epistles.

According to the law of Scotland, the heir to the throne was not allowed to be brought up by his parents, but was sent to Stirling Castle, to be under the care of the Earl of Mar, who held the right to be the hereditary guardian, and this accounts for the many letters which passed between the little prince and the king and queen. When Elizabeth died and James became king of Great Britain, he had to go hastily to London, but about a year later he sent for the queen to come "with the bairns to Windsor, where he prayed God they should all have a blyth meeting." As they arrived there during the festival of St. George, Prince Henry was at once made a Knight of the Garter, and his "princely carriage and his learned behaviour" on that occasion greatly impressed every one who saw him. The coronation of James was fixed for St. James's Day, but because of the plague raging in London, all the fair pageants and the public rejoicings were hastily countermanded, so that the ceremony was almost a private one, even the usual procession through the city being left out. Great was the disappointment of the Londoners, though they were promised that so soon as the plague had disappeared the king, with the queen and their children, would visit the city with all the state of a coronation procession.

One part of this coronation service was of special interest; and to many people it meant the fulfilment of an old prophecy. For more than eight hundred years before these words had been roughly carved on the sacred stone of Scone—

If Fates go right, where'er this stone is found
The Scots shall monarchs of that realm be crowned.

And now, seated on the Coronation Chair which held that stone, James VI. of Scotland was crowned as James I. of England.

Prince Henry was still brought up away from home, first in company with his sister, the merry and witty little Princess Elizabeth, who afterwards married the Elector Palatine. Brother and sister were devoted to each other: both were full of the highest spirits, ready for any adventure; both loved riding and games, and would "mount horses of prodigious mettle;" and it was a great grief to them when they were parted, though, woman-like, Elizabeth fretted the longer. Prince Henry was more of a philosopher.

"That you are displeased to be left in solitude I can well believe," he wrote to her; "you women and damsels are sociable creatures. But you know those who love each other best cannot always be glued together."

Meanwhile Henry took up his residence at Hampton Court. The Gunpowder Plot left a deep impression on him, for had it succeeded he would have lost his life, and he became still more serious and thoughtful, making friends only with those who could teach him something about the many things in which he took an interest, ships, guns, fortifications, books, foreign lands, politics and so on. For Sir Walter Raleigh, that adventurous sailor and treasure-hunter, now a prisoner in the Tower, he had the greatest affection, and spent many hours walking up and down the terrace with him talking of ships and the sea, to the great delight of the old man, who found him an enthusiastic and intelligent companion and at one with him in his opinion that a strong navy meant peace for England. In vain Henry pleaded with his father to set free this prisoner who had committed no crime save that of offending Spain. But James and his son were of very different natures, and James was always doggedly obstinate. "No one but the King would shut up such a bird in a cage," said the boy sadly.

INTERIOR LOOKING EAST.

In 1610 he was created Prince of Wales and there were great festivities in the White Chamber of Westminster Palace, as there, in the presence of the Lords and Commons, he knelt before the king, wearing a robe of purple velvet, to receive the crown of Llewellyn. Once again he won all hearts, and the members of Parliament congratulated themselves that so worthy a prince was heir to the throne. He became more and more the idol of the people, and indeed rarely if ever since the days of Edward, the Black Prince, had a king's son been so full of promise. But to the utter grief of the nation he died two years later, after a short illness.

"Are you pleased to submit yourself to the will of God?" asked the Archbishop, when all hope was given up.

"With all my heart," the boy answered simply.

"I had written him a treatise on the 'Art of War by Sea,'" said Raleigh, when the sad news reached him. "But God hath spared me the labour of finishing it. I leave him therefore in the hands of God."

When the long funeral procession passed through the streets "there was a great outcry among all people," and it was to the sounds of weeping and wailing that the boy-prince, who had won so much love and respect, was carried to Westminster Abbey. There, close to him, was laid more than forty years later, his dearest sister, Elizabeth, Queen of Bohemia, who, after a sadly adventurous life, spent her last few years peacefully in London, cared for and watched over by Lord Craven, whose devotion to her had been lifelong, as unchanging as it was chivalrous.

Another brother and sister are buried here, Anne, the little daughter of Charles I., and Prince Henry, his third son. Anne died before all those troubles began, which saddened the childhood of her brothers and sisters, and made them prisoners in the hands of their father's enemies, as she was only four when she fell into a fast consumption.

"I am not able," she said wearily, the night she died, "to say my long prayer, but I will say my short one. 'Lighten mine eyes, O Lord, lest I sleep in death.'"

Little Henry, the Duke of Gloucester, was extraordinarily like his uncle Henry in every way, old for his age, clever, thoughtful, "with a sweet method of talking, and a judgment much beyond his years." He was taken from his father almost before he knew him, and was, with his sister, also a Princess Elizabeth, kept practically a prisoner in London by the Puritan party. But he was not unkindly treated, for so engaging was he both in conversation and in manners, that many of the Puritans thought he would make a good ruler for England if only he were strictly brought up, and kept away from the influence of his mother or the court.

When the sentence of death was passed on King Charles, he asked to see the two of his children who were in London, and after some delay the request was granted. Awe-struck, the little couple came into his presence, and the king seems to have grasped what was likely to happen. He lifted the Duke of Gloucester on to his knee. "Sweetheart," he said, "they will cut off thy father's head, and mark, child, perhaps they will make thee a king. But you must not be a king while your brothers Charles and James be living."

"I will be torn in pieces first," answered the white-faced child, with a determination which made so great an impression on Charles, that even at that sad moment he rejoiced exceedingly; while the little Duke, who up till now had rarely seen his father, could carry away as a last memory the picture of one whose courage was highest when the need for it was greatest, and who, if he had faced life weakly, met death bravely.

With his sister he was taken to Carisbrooke Castle, but here his existence was very sad, for Princess Elizabeth, like her sister Anne, fell into a consumption, and not being properly cared for, she died. So lonely was he now, that those who had the charge of him, still nursing the idea that one day he might become king, sent him abroad to Leyden, with a tutor, and here he won for himself the pleasant reputation of being "a most complete gentleman and rarely accomplished."

With the Restoration Henry gladly returned to England, and at once begged his brother to find him some work to do, as "he could not bear an idle life." So he was made Lord Treasurer. He proved himself to be a good man of business, while in his leisure hours he gathered round him men of letters and learning, and soon became as popular in London as he had been in Leyden. Then a sudden attack of smallpox killed him, and once again a funeral procession wended its way to Westminster amid signs of very real sorrow. For his fair life had won him many friends and never an enemy.

Of Prince Rupert, who was buried in this vault, that gallant soldier in the Royalist cause, more in another chapter, and this one shall end with a few words about the luckless "Lady Arabella Stuart." She was a cousin to James I., as her father's brother was the Earl of Darnley who had married Mary Queen of Scots; but besides this she was of royal birth, and her grandmother, the Countess of Lennox, whose tomb you will find close by, claimed, as you will see inscribed thereon, to have "to her great-grandfather Edward IV., to her grandfather Henry VII., to her uncle Henry VIII., to her grandchild James VI. and I." Arabella's father had committed the unpardonable offence of marrying without Queen Elizabeth's permission Elizabeth Cavendish, the daughter of the celebrated Bess of Hardwick, and for so doing the young couple were promptly sent to the Tower, in company with both the mothers-in-law, one of whom, the Countess of Lennox, had already twice been imprisoned for matters of love—an early attachment of her own to Thomas Howard, and the marriage of her elder son to Mary Queen of Scots. The young Earl of Lennox died very soon after his marriage, and Elizabeth relented so far as to allow yearly £400 a year to his widow and £200 to his little daughter Arabella.

When she was twelve, Arabella was sent for by the queen to London, and being very handsome as well as clever, she soon began to attract attention. The Roman Catholic party, always on the look-out for a weapon to use against the crown, turned their attentions to her, and her position became a dangerous one, though she herself was entirely loyal and very prudent. The great Lord Burleigh, however, was always her good friend, and when James came to the throne, he gave him a wise hint to "deal tenderly with this high-spirited and fascinating young lady." James took his advice, and Arabella lived at his court, nominally as the governess of the Princess Elizabeth, but actually as if she herself had been a daughter. She was a favourite with all, especially with Henry Prince of Wales, for she was highly educated and a most delightful companion. But though she had many lovers, she would look at none of them, declaring "she had no mind for marriage." However, unfortunately for her, she lost her heart to William Seymour, whom she married in spite of the disapproval of James. And then began her troubles, for Seymour was utterly unworthy of her, and had only married her to advance his own position. When he was put into the Tower, and his wife was kept as a prisoner at Lambeth, his only idea was to make good his own escape, leaving Arabella to her fate; whilst she, still believing in him, risked everything to set him free. It was only when she found that he had fled to Ostend without her that the full force of her sorrows overwhelmed her.

She had hardly a friend, for even Prince Henry seems to have sided for once with his father, and greatest of all was the bitterness of realising that her husband cared nothing for her. He did not even write to her, lest in so doing he might endanger his own safety.

She was sent to the Tower, where first her health, then her mind gave way, and she became as a little child, singing nursery songs, prattling of childish things. Death was a merciful release. Secretly, by dead of night, she was taken from the Tower to the Abbey on a barge, and buried without any ceremony in the vault under the tomb of her aunt. She had often described herself as the "most sorrowful creature living," and, indeed, I think that under this tomb in Henry VII.'s chapel lie three royal women of the Stuart race whose lives were all the saddest tragedies, Mary Queen of Scots, Elizabeth of Bohemia, and the Lady Arabella. "God grant them all a good ending," as the old chroniclers were wont to say. At least now, after life's fitful fever, they sleep well in the calm of the old Abbey.

CHAPTER XII
FROM THE STUARTS TO OUR OWN TIMES

When James I. came to the throne, Lancelot Andrewes was Dean of Westminster, and he devoted himself to the care of the school, which, under Elizabeth's endowments, was now prospering greatly. He had this excellent reputation, "that all the places where he had preferment were better for it," and it is certain that either he must have been a remarkable master or the Westminster boys must have been models of their kind, for this is how Hacket, once his pupil, rapturously describes him:—

"Who could come near the shrine of such a saint and not offer up a few pæans of glory on it? Or how durst I omit it? For he it was that first planted me in my tender studies and watered them continually with his bounty.... He did often supply the place of head-master and usher for the space of an whole week together, and gave us not an hour of loitering time from morning till night. He never walked to Chiswick for his recreation without a brace of this young fry, and in that wayfaring leisure had a singular dexterity to fill those narrow vessels with a funnel. And what was the greatest burden of his toil, sometimes twice in the week, sometimes oftener, he sent for the uppermost scholars to his lodgings at night and kept them with him from eight to eleven, unfolding to them the best rudiments of the Greek tongue and the elements of Hebrew grammar. And all this he did to boys without any compulsion or correction; nay, I never heard him to utter so much as a word of austerity."

Altogether Andrewes was a man of great influence and renown both as a scholar and a preacher, so he was promoted to a bishopric after a short time, and was succeeded by Richard Neile, who had himself been a boy of Westminster School, and who, therefore, in his turn carefully fostered its growth. He too became a bishop in three years, and of the two deans who followed him, Montague and Tounson, we know little except that the one was "a person of wit and entertaining conversation," and the other "one of a graceful presence and an excellent preacher, who left a widow and fifteen children unprovided for."

It is Hacket who again gives us an amusing picture of the excitement among all the divines when it became known that Tounson was to be Bishop of Salisbury and that the Deanery of Westminster was vacant.

"It was a fortunate seat," he says, "near the Court. Like the office over the king of Persia's garden at Babylon, stored with the most delicious fruits. He that was trusted with the garden was the Lord of the Palace."

Among those who earnestly desired the post was John Williams, one of the chaplains to James I., and in these words he applied for it through Lord Burleigh:—

"MY MOST NOBLE LORD,—I am an humble suitor, first to be acknowledged your servant, and then that I may with your happy hand be transplanted to Westminster if the Deanery shall still prove vacant. I trouble not your Honour for profit, but for convenience, for being unmarried and inclining so to continue, I do find that Westminster is fitter by much for that disposition. If your Honour be not bent upon an ancient servitor, I beseech you to think on me."

Fortunately for Westminster he obtained his heart's desire, and in 1620 began his useful rule. He took for his exemplars Abbot Islip and Dean Andrewes, imitating the first by carefully restoring the many parts of the Abbey which through neglect were falling in ruins, and the second by encouraging the school. Then, "that God might be praised with a cheerful noise in His sanctuary," he obtained, as Hacket tells us, "the sweetest music both for the organ and for voices of all parts that was ever heard in an English quire;" and in Jerusalem Chamber he gave many entertainments with music, which "the most famous masters of this delightful faculty frequented." To enlarge the boundaries of learning he turned one of the deserted rooms in the cloisters, of old used by the monks, into a library, bought out of his own means a large number of books from a certain Mr. Baker of Highgate, and was so public-spirited that he allowed men of learning from all parts of London to have access to those precious works.

He was in great favour with James, who made him Lord Keeper of the Seal and Bishop of Lincoln, allowing him to hold Westminster at the same time, and though his enemies had much to say on the subject of his holding so many offices, it must be said in justice that he got through an amazing amount of work. Under him it seemed as if some of the splendid hospitalities which had ceased since the days when the Abbots kept open house were to be revived, for Dean Williams entertained in Jerusalem Chamber the French ambassadors who came over to arrange for the marriage between Prince Charles and Princess Henriette.

Before the feast he led them into the Abbey, which was "stuck with flambeaux everywhere that they might cast their eyes upon the stateliness of the church," while "the best finger of the age, Dr. Orlando Gibbons," played the organ for their entertainment.

You will see a memorial of this banquet in the carvings over the mantelpiece in the Jerusalem Chamber for on one side is Charles I. and on the other side his French bride.

But with the death of James I., Lord Keeper, Bishop and Dean Williams fell upon evil days, for he was disliked by the Duke of Buckingham and Laud, who entirely influenced the king, and was not even allowed to officiate on the coronation day.

JERUSALEM CHAMBER.

JERUSALEM CHAMBER.

Under the Commonwealth the Abbey fared badly, for with a fanatical horror of anything that reminded them of royalty or of Rome, the Parliamentarians had not the smallest regard for it, and delighted in showing their contempt for its past. How far the soldiers were allowed to desecrate its walls and its altars it is difficult to clearly ascertain, and we may fairly believe that the story of how they pulled down the organ, pawned the pipes for ale, and played boisterous games up and down the church "to show their Christian liberty," is a great exaggeration, even if any such thing took place at all. Certainly the altar in Henry VII.'s chapel, under which lay buried Edward VI., was destroyed, the copes and vestments were sold, and many windows and monuments supposed to teach lessons of superstition and idolatry were demolished. No dean was appointed. The church being put under a Parliamentary Committee, Presbyterian preachers conducted morning exercises, which took the place of the daily services, and Bradshaw, the President of the court which tried and condemned to death Charles I., settled himself into the deserted deanery. A strange sight indeed it must have been to those who noted it to watch this man going backwards and forwards between Abbot Islip's house and the Hall of Westminster Palace, holding in the hollow of his hand the life of the king of England!

Westminster School, which, under Elizabeth, had been set on its new and enlarged footing, and since then had vigorously expanded under the various head-masters, alone continued to flourish. Its scholars naturally were closely connected with the life that centred round Westminster: they listened to the debates of Parliament, they flocked to hear the trials in Westminster Hall, they attended the services in the Abbey. Their feelings ran high during the Civil War. Pym, Cromwell, and Bradshaw they hated; the execution of Charles roused their deepest indignation, and they listened in awed horror as Bushby, their master, read solemnly the prayer for the king at the very moment when the scaffold was being erected at Whitehall. It was the strong personality of Bushby and his tactful management which saved the school from being seriously interfered with at the hands of the all-powerful Parliament, so that for fifty-five years this model for head-masters "ruled with his rod and his iron will, and successfully piloted this bark through very stormy seas." He was full of enthusiasm and energy and he was more anxious that his pupils should become men of action and character than accomplished scholars. His monument, which is near the Poets' Corner shows him, in the words of the inscription, "such as he appeared to human eyes;" and the words which follow tell how he "sowed a plenteous harvest of ingenious men; discovered, managed, and improved the natural genius in every one; formed and nourished the minds of youths, and gave to the school of Westminster the fame of which it boasts."

But the Abbey was a national institution, too firmly builded on the rocks to be more than shaken by the passing storms. It had weathered the earthquake of the Reformation, it had survived the tempests of the Revolution. With the Restoration came the calm, and quietly the old life was resumed. I have but little more to tell you of the inner story of the Abbey, nor from this time forward do kings and queens play any very important part in its story. It is the tombs and monuments which now begin, more closely even than before, to cement the tie between Westminster and the pages of English history. So I will only tell you in a few words how Dean Sprat busied himself with the restoration of the great buildings, the architect being Sir Christopher Wren, who, as you know, designed St. Paul's Cathedral, and rebuilt so many of the old London churches which the Great Fire had destroyed, and how Dean Atterbury carried on the work, including the rebuilding of the great dormitory, until his devotion to the Stuart cause and his opposition to George I. caused him to be sent first to the Tower, and afterwards as an exile to France. Atterbury loved well his Abbey, and his last request was that he might walk through it once more, especially to see the glass which was his own gift to it, and which still exists in the beautiful rose window over the north door. But the sad thing about these so-called restorations is that so much of the matchless old work was destroyed, and nobody seemed in the least concerned at this. That was an age when the glories of medieval architecture appear to have lost all their charm in men's eyes, when the love of beautiful things was at its lowest ebb. The Westminster boys played their games in the chapels, and were allowed to skip from tomb to tomb in the Confessor's shrine; hideous monuments were erected and crowded together, nothing old was reverenced, and we can only be thankful that more was not destroyed or hopelessly ruined. And yet, in spite of this apparent indifference, here and there were men who found themselves stirred when they came within those walls as they were stirred nowhere else, so that many a writer, including Addison, Steele, and Goldsmith, and earlier still, John Milton, has paid homage, even in those unimaginative days, to that fair place, "so far exceeding human excellence that a man would think it was knit together by the fingers of angels."

One more dean I must tell you of, and that is Dean Stanley, who, with his wife, lies in the south aisle of Henry VII.'s Chapel. For it was when he was appointed to Westminster in 1864 that once again the Abbey became something more than a great memory of former days. First of all he unfolded the storied past, clearing up many a mystery, setting right many an error, and then, impelled by a deep reverence for all its great associations, he consistently carried on its history. In every trace of his work we find this same wise spirit of sympathy and understanding. To him the Abbey was our greatest national treasure; his ideal was, not only so to keep it, but to make it a living influence among all English-speaking people. And thanks in no small degree to him, Westminster Abbey is to-day a very magnet in the heart of the empire, to which high and low rich and poor, learned and ignorant are drawn from far and near, to drink in, as they are able, its memories and its beauties, to do homage to those great souls whom it honours there to read as from a book stories of Englishmen who whether as kings or statesmen, abbots or deans, nobles or commoners, poets or patriots, added at least some stones to that other building, not fashioned by hands alone, which grew up side by side with Edward's church, and thus became the builders of our nation.

But we have gone forward, quickly, and I must take you back for a moment to Henry VII.'s Chapel, where still after the Restoration some royal funerals took place. With the outburst of loyal feeling, it was felt by many that Charles I., who had been buried at Windsor, ought to be brought here, and Christopher Wren was commanded to prepare a costly monument. But nothing further was done in the matter. Charles II. was buried at midnight most unceremoniously, close to the monument of General Monk, and one who was probably present adds, by way of comment, "he was soon forgotten." Ten children of James II. were laid in the spacious vault under Mary Queen of Scots monument, but he himself, having fled from his kingdom, died abroad and was buried in Paris. William and Mary, Queen Anne and her husband, Prince George of Denmark, all lie near Charles II., and the seventeen children of Anne are just behind in what is really the Children's Vault. One of these children, Prince William Henry, another Duke of Gloucester, though he only lived to be eleven, was such a quaint little boy that his tutor wrote a biography of him. He was always very delicate, but though his body was weak his mind was precocious and his spirits were unfailingly high. From the time he was two his craze was for soldiers, and he had a company of ninety boys from Kensington for his bodyguard, whom he drilled and ruled by martial law. These boys he called his horse-guards, and they wore red grenadiers' caps and carried wooden swords and muskets; but, however much they may have pleased the little prince, who lived at Camden House, they were somewhat of a terror to the people of Kensington, as, "presuming on being soldiers, they were very rude and challenged men in the streets, which caused complaints." This tutor of his, Jenkin Lewis, who entered thoroughly into the spirit of the little Duke, gives a delightful account of a visit paid to him by his uncle, the grave William III., who appears to have been very fond of him.

Altogether the Duke must have been a charming little boy, plucky, generous, and remarkably bright. If he fell down and hurt himself, he would say, "A bullet in the war had grazed me," and though, to please the queen, he learnt dancing from an old Frenchman, he confided to his tutor that the only thing he loved in that way was the English march to a drum.

Greatly to his joy the king decided to make him a Knight of the Garter when he was only six years old, and to add to the honour William tied on the Garter himself.

"Now," said the boy proudly, "if I fight any more battles I shall give harder blows than ever."

He was as quick and interested at his lessons as he was at soldiering, and we bear of his making amazing progress under the Bishop of Marlborough in the history of the Bible, geography, constitutional history, and many other subjects, while his tutor had taught him "the terms of fortification and navigation, the different parts of a ship of war, and stories about Cæsar,

Alexander, Pompey, Hannibal, and Scipio. It was his tutor who put into verse, and persuaded Mr. Church, one of the gentlemen of Westminster Abbey, to set to music, the Duke's words of command to his boys, which ran thus:—

"Hark, hark! the hostile drum alarms,

Let ours too beat, and call to arms;

Prepare, my boys, to meet the foe,

Let every breast with valour glow.

Soon conquest shall our arms decide,

And Britain's sons in triumph ride.

In order charge your daring band,

Attentive to your chief's command.

Discharge your volleys, fire away;

They yield, my lads, we gain the day.

March on, pursue to yonder town;

No ambush fear, the day's our own.

Yet from your hearts let mercy flow,

And nobly spare the captive foe!"

When in 1696 a plot formed against William III. was discovered, the Duke determined not to be behind the Houses of Parliament, who offered their loyal addresses to the king, so he drew up a little address of his own in these words, which was signed by himself and all his boys: "We, your Majesty's faithful subjects, will stand by you as long as we have a drop of blood."

On the 24th July 1700 he was eleven and had a birthday party, which of course meant a sham fight among his boys; and when on the next morning he complained of feeling ill, every one naturally thought he was only overtired or excited. But a bad throat and high fever soon showed that there was serious mischief, and within a week he died. "To the inexpressible grief," wrote the Bishop of Salisbury, "of all good men who were well-wishers to the Protestant religion and lovers of their country."

George II. was the last king to be buried in the Abbey, and he was laid in the same stone coffin as his wife, Queen Caroline. You will find the gravestones in the nave of Henry VII.'s Chapel, and near to it are buried his two daughters, his son Frederick, Prince of Wales, and several grandchildren. Horace Walpole, the son of Robert Walpole, who had for twenty-one years been the Prime Minister of the king, thus describes to us the last royal funeral at Westminster:—

"The procession through a line of foot-guards, every seventh man bearing a torch, the horse-guards lining the outside, their officers with drawn swords and crape sashes, the drums muffled, the fifes, the bells tolling, and the minute guns, all this was very solemn. But the charm was the entrance to the Abbey, where we were received by the Dean and Chapter in rich robes, the choir and almsmen bearing torches, the whole Abbey so illuminated that one saw it to greater advantage than by day. When we came to the Chapel of Henry VII., all solemnity and decorum ceased, no order was observed, people sat or stood where they would or could; the Yeomen of the Guard were crying out for help, oppressed by the immense weight of the coffin. The Bishop read sadly and blundered in the prayers, and the anthem, besides being immeasurably tedious, would have served as well for a wedding.... The Duke of Newcastle fell into a fit of crying the moment we came into the chapel and flung himself back in a stall, the Archbishop towering over him with a smelling-bottle; but in two minutes his curiosity got the better of his hypocrisy, and he ran about the chapel with his glass to spy who was or was not there. Then returned his fear of getting cold, and the Duke of Cumberland, who felt himself weighed down, on turning round found it was the Duke of Newcastle standing upon his train to avoid the chill of the marble."

But though Westminster was no longer to be the church of the royal tombs, there was one ceremony she was still to claim undisputed as her own peculiar right. A Coronation meant the Abbey; no other place was ever dreamt of. Charles II. here commenced his reign with great glory. James II. characteristically grudged spending any money excepting £100,000 for the queen's dress and trinkets. William and Mary were crowned together, for Mary refused to be queen unless her husband became king with her, and it is for this joint-coronation that the second chair of state was made, which stands with the old Coronation Chair in the Confessor's Chapel. The members of the House of Commons were present and "hummed applause at the eloquent ending to Bishop Burnet's sermon, in which he prayed God "to bless the royal pair with long life and love, with obedient subjects, wise counsellors, faithful allies, gallant fleets and armies, and finally with crowns more glorious and lasting than those which glittered on the altar of the Abbey."

Queen Anne, fat, gouty, and childless, found the day a weary one. Unlike her sister Mary, she was crowned queen in her own right, and her husband was the first of the nobles to do her homage.

When George I. was crowned many difficulties had to be overcome, for everything had to be explained to the king, who knew no English, by ministers who stumbled badly over their German. But George II. had learnt the language of his people, and liking great ceremonies as much as his father had disliked them, his coronation day was celebrated in great state. Queen Caroline must have been ablaze with jewels, for besides wearing all her own, she had borrowed what pearls she could from the ladies of quality, and had hired all manner of diamonds from the Jews and jewellers. George IV. spent more money when he was crowned king than any other of his race, but the day was not without a very painful scene, as he refused to prepare any place for his wife, Queen Caroline, and she indignantly tried in vain to insist on her rights and to force her way into the Abbey. She failed, and her failure so broke her spirits that she fell ill, and a few weeks later she died.

William IV. was crowned at a critical moment, for the country was in a state of excitement concerning the Reform Bill, which, if passed, would give a vote to a great number of people who did not possess one, but which was being firmly opposed by the Duke of Wellington and a strong party. To avoid any risks of riots or demonstrations the usual procession was left out, even the usual banquet in the old palace, while everything was as simple and private as possible. But seven years later those old grey walls looked down on a Coronation Day which brought untold blessings to England. On June 28, 1838, Princess Victoria, a slender girl in the first freshness of her youth, was publicly recognised undoubted queen of the realm, and took her solemn oath in the sight of the people to perform and keep the promises demanded of her by the Archbishop. Here in the Sanctuary she was anointed; here the spurs and the sword of state were presented to her, and then laid on the altar; here the orb was placed in her hands and the royal robe about her shoulders; here the ring, the sceptre, the rod were delivered to her; here was the crown of pure gold set on her head, and the Bible, the royal law, placed in her hands; here she ascended the throne, while her nobles did her homage; here, taking off her crown, she received the Holy Communion, and then passed on into the Confessor's Chapel in accordance with the time-honoured usage.

Vastly solemn indeed was the ceremony, calling to mind as it did the long procession of kings and queens who, without exception in that place, almost in those identical words, had accepted the great trust to which they had been called. Some had been faithful; some, through weakness or through wilful wrong-doing, had violated the vow. The strongest men had sometimes wavered, the bravest men had faltered before their task. But Queen Victoria never failed her people. Through weal and woe, through storm and sunshine, through good and evil days, she watched over them and guarded their interests. She ruled over their hearts at home and throughout those vaster dominions beyond the seas, she bound them to her with bonds of loyal devotion, so that when, in the dim light of a winter's day in February 1901, the Abbey was filled with a vast crowd of those who were there to pay their last tribute to her memory, their universal sorrow was no mere formality, but was in harmony with the sense of personal loss which was felt by all who had owned her as their Sovereign Lady.

PART II
AMONG THE MONUMENTS

PRINCE RUPERT.

CHAPTER XIII
PURITANS AND CAVALIERS IN THE ABBEY

By a strange irony of fate, the royal chapel of the Tudors was destined to be, at least for awhile, the burying-place of many Parliamentary leaders, and perhaps stranger still it is to realise how Roundhead and Cavalier, disgraced minister and triumphant reformer, came at last to the old Abbey, which opened its arms to receive them, condemning no man, but committing all unto the care of Him who judgeth with righteous judgment. The Duke of Buckingham and Pym, Cromwell and Prince Rupert, Admiral Blake, Clarendon the historian of the great rebellion, Essex and General Monk, all were buried within a few feet of each other, and their names are still engraved on Abbey stones, though some of them sleep there no more.

These men, in their different ways, stood in the forefront of that hard-fought Revolution, and as I want Westminster to be something more to you than a place of names and monuments, I will try to tell you enough of each one for you to be able to fit them into their proper places in the history of those stormy days.

We will begin with Buckingham, who, as young George Villiers, was brought up to be a courtier, and taught only such accomplishments as would fit him for that part. He was an apt pupil, graceful, witty, versatile, full of charm, and from the moment he entered the service of James I. as cupbearer, his upward career began. He leapt from step to step with dazzling rapidity, and the king became a mere puppet in his hands. "I love the Earl of Buckingham more than anything else," he declared. "Whatsoever he desireth must be done." For awhile Buckingham did not seriously interfere with politics; his ambition was satisfied with personal power and court influence, while his own position concerned him much more closely than the affairs of the country. But eventually he was drawn into the vortex, to his own undoing, for his brilliancy was only superficial, his wild schemes collapsed one after the other, while his reckless extravagance, coupled with his disastrous undertakings, staggered the Parliament, which had for a brief moment believed in him. However, Charles, who was now king, implicitly believed in him through all his failures, and supported his exorbitant demands for money to carry on his unpopular and unsuccessful foreign policy. At last the gathering indignation burst.

"The Duke of Buckingham is the cause of all our miseries," was the deliberate statement made in the House of Commons, followed by a long list of charges, and the determination, for the first time, to hold a minister responsible to Parliament for his actions. The king was furious. "None of my servants shall be questioned by you, or it shall be the worse for you," he said scornfully, and he dissolved Parliament. But the trial of Buckingham was taken out of their hands, for shortly afterwards he was stabbed to death by a certain Fenton, a melancholy, malcontented gentleman, who declared that he did so to rid the country of an intolerable tyrant. He was buried quietly in the Abbey, and the king set up to his memory the elaborate but hardly beautiful monument which you see. You must notice, though, the three figures of his children, for one of them, Francis, a very gallant boy, "of rare beauty and comeliness," fell fighting for the king at Kingston, wounded nine times, yet scorning to ask quarter, standing with his back against an oak tree till he dropped.

General Monk, afterwards Duke of Albemarle, fought on the Parliamentary side, and after the defeat of the Royalists in England he was with Cromwell through his victorious campaigns in Scotland and Ireland, remaining behind as commander-in-chief for Scotland. But it was as a sailor rather than as a soldier that he made his greatest reputation, for when the struggle began between England and the Dutch for the command of the seas, the Dutch challenging the English right to it, Monk, and another Parliamentary officer, Blake, were appointed generals at sea, it being thought that their ability to lead, their energy and their good sense, would more than compensate for their lack of technical experience. So it eventually proved, and after some close fighting Monk was able to report that the English held the coast of Holland as if it were besieged. Parliament rewarded Monk with a vote of thanks, a medal and a chain worth £300, and he assured them that he had "no other thought but to defend the nation against all enemies, whether by sea or by land, as might be entrusted to him."

Not altogether approving of the arbitrary way in which Cromwell treated Parliament, he determined to keep clear of politics and to remain a "plain fighting man." But while employed by the Protector he was entirely loyal to him, and at once sent to him a letter he received from Charles II. suggesting negotiations. "An honest, very simple-hearted man," was Cromwell's remark on him.

But with the death of the Protector the whole aspect of things changed. Monk had fully intended to serve Richard Cromwell as he had served his father, only it became palpably evident that the new Protector was not in any way capable of controlling the country or the army, and within a few weeks dissatisfaction and discontent were evident everywhere—the pendulum had swung back, and England cried for a king once more. With Richard Cromwell at the head of affairs, Monk saw that the days of the Commonwealth were numbered. "He forsook himself or I had never faltered in my allegiance," he explained; for Dick Cromwell was as anxious as any one to be rid of his office. Through his brother, Nicholas Monk, a sturdy Royalist, afterwards made Bishop of Hereford, Charles sent a straightforward letter to the general, judging rightly that plain words were more likely to take effect with him. "If you take my interests to heart," wrote the king, "I will leave the way and manner to you and act as you advise."

For awhile Monk hesitated, then he accepted the situation. He met the king at Dover, and served him faithfully in whatever capacity it was desired of him, assisting in the settlement of Scotland, or going to sea with Prince Rupert, or keeping order in London during those years of panic when first the plague, then the Great Fire produced the wildest terror and confusion. He died "like a Roman general and a soldier, his chamber door open as if it had been a tent, his officers around him," and England mourned an honest, duty-loving man, brave on every point excepting where his wife was concerned, and here he frankly admitted to a "terror of her tongue and passions." The king, who had made him Duke of Albemarle, was present at his funeral, and undertook to pay all the expenses, besides erecting a monument to him. But his memory and gratitude were both short-lived, so that it was left to the second Duke to see that his father's name and fame were duly chronicled in the Abbey, that future generations might know him as "an honest man, who served his country."

Admiral Blake, buried in the Cromwell vault, first went to sea to settle Prince Rupert, who with his tiny fleet was a terror to English ships, and so successful was he, that at last Rupert was thankful to reach France in safety with his one remaining vessel. For reward, Parliament gave him a place in the council of state, and he devoted himself to making the navy more efficient, as he felt sure a war at sea with the Dutch was imminent. He desired to make his sailors men of the same stamp as Cromwell's famous Ironsides, but though he was a great disciplinarian he was very popular, and his men fought for him with a will. The war began with a victory for Blake, which, far from disheartening the Dutch, put them on their mettle, and off Dungeness they compelled the English admiral to retreat on Dover, after a fierce struggle. So elated was Van Tromp at this advantage, that as he passed along the Channel he had a broom fastened to the masthead of his ship to show how he meant to sweep the English from the seas. Blake was sorely grieved at his failure, and for a moment gave way to a depression which led him to entreat Parliament that he might be discharged from "an employment much too great for him." Then his old spirit returned, and he asked "for more men to fight again."

At the battle of Portland the fleets met once more, and it was a terrible fight. Though Blake was badly wounded, the victory lay with the English. He followed up the advantages he had gained, and near the North Foreland took eleven Dutch ships and 1350 prisoners, with a small loss. His wound had by now so affected his health, that he was compelled to return to England, leaving Monk to fight the last great fight, in which Van Tromp was killed, 6000 Dutchmen killed, wounded, or made prisoners, and twenty-six of their ships sunk or taken. However, though the Dutch were settled, it was necessary to assert the English power in the Mediterranean, especially where Spain was concerned, and Blake was the name to conjure with. So, in spite of his painful illness, he set out once more, "the one man able to preserve the commonwealth," Cromwell told him. At Santa Cruz he met the Spanish fleet and conquered it. "To God be all the glory," he wrote in his simply worded despatch which told of this great and popular victory.

Then, feeling his increasing weakness, he asked leave to return home, as "the work was done and the chain complete." But he died at sea, in sight of Plymouth Sound. His funeral in Westminster Abbey was a splendid one, worthy of the splendid service he had rendered to England, Cromwell having ordered that "no pomp was to be spared, so as to encourage all officers to venture their lives." A lasting shame it is indeed that at the Restoration his remains, with those of Deane, one of his admirals, and other Parliamentary officers, were taken from their graves, and buried without any mark of respect in one common grave in St. Margaret's Churchyard. Within the Abbey no monument marks his grave, though he had held for England the supremacy of the seas against vigorous attacks, and had made a reputation for himself "very wonderful, which will never be forgotten in Spain."

The very name of Prince Rupert breathes of romance and adventure. His mother was the fascinating and high-spirited Princess Elizabeth, daughter of James I., who had married Frederick, Prince Palatine of the Rhine, and had persuaded him to accept the crown of Bohemia when it was offered to him by the people, who had just wrested their independence from the Emperor of Austria. But his reign at Prague was short, for the Emperor won back his own, and the Queen of Hearts, as Elizabeth was affectionately called, had to escape with her children as best she could, Rupert being but a few weeks old. Her father, afraid of Spain and the Roman Catholic powers, would do nothing to help her, so she would have fared badly had it not been for some faithful English friends, headed by Lord Craven, and the people of Holland, who looked on the king of Bohemia as a sufferer in the Protestant cause, and who therefore gave his family a home besides a generous allowance. Frederick was not only deprived of his new kingdom, but lost also his old possessions, for the Emperor seized his lands on the Rhine and spoiled his palaces. Many a brave attempt he made to win back the Palatinate, always to be baffled, and at last, after the death of his eldest son, he fell into such a low state of health that he died of a fever. Elizabeth was left with three sons and two daughters, Rupert being her idol, for she believed him born to be a hero. And truly he was a boy to be proud of, excelling in everything he undertook, and such a true soldier that, when he was only fourteen, his tutors declared he was worthy to command a regiment. When Charles I. became king, he invited two of his nephews to England, and, with the queen, at once lost his heart to Rupert, who was then about eighteen. He proposed making him a bishop or marrying him to an heiress, but Rupert would hear of neither plan. A soldier's life, with plenty of adventure, was the only life for him.

On the 22nd of August in the year 1642, the Civil War broke out in England; the royal standard was set up at Nottingham, and Prince Rupert was made General of the Royal Horse, he being then but twenty-three. His very presence, brimming over as he was with enthusiasm, vigour, and determination, brought a breath of new life to the men who "could not hold back when the royal standard waved," yet "who did not like the quarrel, and heartily wished the king would yield and consent to what Parliament desired."

But Rupert was quite untouched by the general feeling of depression. The cause or its merits concerned him but little; he knew nothing of the intensity of the struggle, of the many unredressed grievances, of the arbitrary treatment of the nation's representatives in Parliament, of the total disregard for the opinions of the people which had at last made nothing but war possible between two such conflicting parties. He only saw the romantic side, a king called upon to defend himself in his own realm against rebels and traitors, and so heart and soul he espoused his uncle's cause. A cavalier of the cavaliers was Prince Rupert, with his handsome face, long flowing hair, clean-shaved cheeks, beplumed hat, and scarlet cloak, to which he added a very gallant bearing and a lordly manner. Directly he saw the cavalry he was to command, less than a thousand badly mounted untrained men, he dashed away like a whirlwind, to scour the country in search of more. Here, there, and everywhere he came and went like a flash, "in a short time heard of in many places at great distances," to quote a Parliamentary historian, till the very sound of his name had a magic effect. He charmed some, he terrified others, but he did what he would with them all, and in less than a month he rode back to join the court at Shrewsbury, with a picked force of three thousand men, well horsed and equipped. Contrasted with the indecision of Charles, Rupert's high-handed audacity was refreshing, and when the king left him free "to steer his own course," he at once set out for Worcester, which was threatened by Essex and the Parliamentary army.

The Royalist plan was to march on London, a plan which Parliament saw must at all costs be frustrated, so Essex received imperative orders to intercept and check the enemy. At Edgehill, near Banbury, the armies met, and the king, from his position on a hill-top, took view of Essex and his army in the vale.

"I shall give them battle," he said. "God assist the justice of my cause."

Then he called a council of war, at which many points of difference arose between the old soldiers and the young. Of course Rupert was the spokesman for the latter, and this was not the first time he had come into collision with the other generals of the Royalist army. Caution was a word unknown to him, and patience did not exist in his vocabulary. Slow and steady tactics he abhorred; he scorned the enemy, and pleaded vehemently for bold, dashing movements, which were, he said, best suited to the high-spirited soldiers of the king. As usual he prevailed, for he was never one who could be persuaded to change his opinion. His plan of battle was decided on, which meant that the Royal Horse should charge and drive the Roundhead Cavalry from the field, afterwards falling upon the flank of the enemy's infantry, while the Royalist infantry attacked them from the front.

"Then," he added, carried away by the thought of a victory which seemed so obvious, "the day is ours."

When the battle began in earnest Rupert charged with his cavalry, and so magnificently, that it seemed as if all his prophecies were fully justified, for the Roundheads were swept backwards till they broke and fled. But so excited and eager were the horsemen to pursue their flying foes, that they left all the Royalist infantry unprotected, and when Prince Rupert returned with such troops as he could rally from the chase, he found all confusion and uncertainty. Moreover, it was nearly dark, and no one was ready to support Rupert when he entreated that another charge might be made to settle the day. So, after all, it was only half a victory for the king's army, even though he held the road to London, while altogether quite 6000 Englishmen lay dead on the field.

Charles next made a move to Oxford, where he established his Court, for Oxford was almost the only city at that time "wholly devoted to his Majesty," and from here peace negotiations were again entered into, with the usual result that both sides were left still more bitterly opposed to each other. Rupert was charged with attacking two Parliamentary regiments at Brentford during the negotiations when all fighting was suspended. But with all his faults of impatience and impetuosity he was far too honourable a soldier to have willingly taken any unfair advantage of his foe, and it seems clear what he did was at the king's command, or when he was in ignorance of the stage which had been reached in the negotiations. While the king and the main army lay inactive though full of talk at Oxford, Rupert with his cavalry scoured the country round in search of men, horses, food, and forage, and indeed whatever they could lay hands on; for as Parliament held all the money, the king's soldiers had to live off the country as best they could, and wait patiently for pay which rarely came. The Prince, as was his wont, journeyed far and wide, his special object being to extend the king's territory all round Oxford and to take in all the west of England. So we hear of him, sometimes successful and sometimes baffled, at Cirencester, Banbury, Bristol, Gloucester, Birmingham, and Wales, then moving northwards in Leicester and Northamptonshire, till at the peremptory command of Charles he made his way towards York, which was in great danger, and which, "if lost," wrote the king, "would mean little less than the loss of the crown."

He relieved the town with great dash, but was so eager to press on that he would not even wait to speak to the governor, Lord Newcastle, who was very offended at what he considered to be a want of respect. Still more angry was he when he received a message from Rupert commanding him to follow the cavalry without delay. He made no haste to carry out this order, and Rupert, who was in close touch with the enemy, waited for him in vain. The delay cost the Royalists dear, for the battle of Marston Moor which ensued was a complete triumph for the Roundheads. But even then Rupert did not lose heart, as did so many of his party.

"'What will you do?' asked General King of him. 'I will rally my men,' sayes ye Prince. Sayes General King, 'Nowe what will my Lord Newcastle do?' Sayes he, 'I will go to Holland, for all is lost.'"

The defeat of the Northern army was decisive, and Rupert felt the only help lay in Wales and the west of England. But defeat followed defeat. At Naseby the Parliamentary army was again victorious; Bristol surrendered, then Oxford. Nor was this all. Among the king's nearest advisers were many who disliked Prince Rupert, especially Lord Digby, and when the Prince surrendered Bristol, he saw his opportunity for revenge. Very cleverly he worked on Charles to such an extent that he made it appear as if Rupert had weakly capitulated without any justification, and the king, who all too easily forgot the past, signed an order revoking the military authority and position he had bestowed on his nephew. The Prince was sorely hurt and indignant at this want of confidence. "It is Digby that is the cause of all the distraction," he said quietly, and then proceeded to defend his honour and his action, which he did in a manner that commended itself to all fair-minded men.

Having written a full account of the siege, and proved that holding out longer would have only meant a useless sacrifice of valuable lives, he followed this up by going straight to the king at Newark, in spite of having been forbidden to do so by Digby. "I am come, sir," he said, "to render an account of Bristol." At first Charles would not listen, but Rupert insisted on a court-martial, which at last was granted, and which completely cleared him. The king accepted the verdict, but in a half-hearted way, which nettled the Prince, who was already chafing at the unjust accusations made against his honour. A few days later he vigorously fought the battle of another officer who had been dismissed—also the victim of Digby's jealousy.

"No officer," he declared indignantly, "should be deprived of his commission without being able to defend himself against a council of war."

In his anger he applied to Parliament for permission to return to Holland, but when the message came that this would only be given on condition that he did not fight again, he indignantly refused the terms. His loyalty was deeper than his anger when it came to the test.

Ere long, however, the hopeless, weary struggle reached its end. The king threw himself on the mercy of his Scottish army, who for £400,000 gave him up to Parliament, and he was made a prisoner. Rupert found his way to France, and later on he joined the Prince of Wales in getting together a small fleet which it was proposed to send to Ireland. He entered enthusiastically into this new career. "The royal cause," he said, "is now at sea." Far and wide on the ocean he was to be heard of with his ships, round Spain, Portugal, in the Mediterranean and the West Indies, near Azores and Cape Verde, seizing wherever he could find them the treasure-ships belonging to the English Parliament. His name was a terror by sea as it had been by land, and the adventurous life was quite according to his liking. With the Restoration he came back to England, and Charles settled on him an allowance of £4000 a year, besides giving him an important command in the fleet. But no real scope was allowed him for his powers, and Charles, with all his foreign intrigues, found Rupert too inconveniently straightforward and resolute.

So the end of his life was a disappointment, though when action of one sort was denied him, his eager brain turned to science, chemistry, and inventions. Most of his old friends had vanished; his mother had died many years before, protected and comforted to the last by Lord Craven, who had taken for a motto the words "For God and for Her;" and of his sisters, one was an abbess, the other married to the Elector of Hanover.

He lived alone and quietly at his house in Spring Gardens at the top of Whitehall, and when he died, comparatively young, he was "generally lamented for an honest, brave, true-hearted man, whose life had embraced innumerable toils, and a variety of noble actions by land and by sea."

"It is an infinite pity he is not employed according to his genius," a friend of his mother's had written to her long years before. "He is full of spirit and action, and may be compared to steel, which is the commanding metal if it be rightly tempered and disposed. Whatever he wills, he wills vehemently."

And this criticism, which was true of him up to the day he died, contains the essence of his successes and of his failures.

It was in this vaulted chapel of the Tudor kings that Oliver Cromwell was buried with regal magnificence, his effigy robed in purple, surrounded by a sceptre, a sword, and an imperial crown, being also placed in the Abbey. Many of his friends and followers—Pym, the hero of his early days; Ireton, his son-in-law; Bradshaw, the President of the Court which had tried and condemned the King in Westminster Hall close by—were already by his desire buried in the Abbey, as were most of his immediate family; his old mother, who had always said "she cared nothing for her son's grandeur, and was always afraid when she heard a musket lest he should be shot, and his best loved daughter, Betty, Elizabeth Claypole. The latter was such an attractive girl, and "played the part of princess so naturally, and obliging all persons by her civility," that Cromwell feared lest her very charms should be a snare to her, leading her thoughts from God. His letters to her show all the tenderest side of his strong nature. "I watch thy growth as a Seeker after truth," he once wrote to her. "To be a Seeker is to be of the best sect, next to a Finder. And such a one shall every happy Seeker be at the end."

OLIVER CROMWELL.

Oliver Cromwell was ever a son of strife, and two years after his death, on the anniversary of the king's execution, his body was dragged from the grave by order of the Restoration Parliament and publicly hung, a similar revenge being meted out to Bradshaw and Ireton, and the "pure-souled patriot John Pym."

So to-day we do not even know where he is buried, and only a plate in the floor of Henry VII.'s chapel, put there by Dean Stanley, shows us where once the great man lay.

For great he surely was, even though narrow, relentless, arbitrary, and overbearing; great, that is to say, if high aims, honest ambitions, dogged courage, and unswerving obedience to what he held to be the Divine voice, count for ought in the standard we require of our public men.

CHAPTER XIV
CHAUCER

Geoffrey Chaucer was the first English poet or writer to be buried within the Abbey, and just as the Confessor's tomb drew kings and queens to lie around it, so Chaucer's grave, in a way undreamed of at the time, consecrated one part of Westminster as the Poets' Corner. And what more fitting than that he who has been so justly named the "poet of the dawn, the finder of our fair language, the father of English poetry," should rest, when his life's work was ended, near to those others with whose names our early history is studded?

He was born in London about the year 1335, the son of a merchant vintner, and throughout his life London was to him "a city very deare and sweete." He was well educated, though where we know not, in classics, divinity, astronomy, philosophy, and chemistry, and naturally spoke French fluently, as its use was general. From his boyhood he loved reading only less than he loved nature.

"On bokës for to rede, I me delyte,

Save certeynly whan that the moneth of May

Is comen, and that I here the foulës synge,

And that the flourës gynnen for to sprynge,

Farwel my boke and my devocïoun."

And almost equally, too, he loved to see life, to travel in foreign countries, to study, in a kindly sympathetic spirit, human nature in all its forms, neither criticising harshly nor condemning impatiently, but just observing and understanding.

Those early years of his life marked a great epoch in England, for Edward III. made the land ring with the fame of his victories at Crecy and Poitiers; the valour of his knights and soldiers; the fair and famous deeds done in the name of that chivalry which was then at its height; and young Chaucer seems to have caught the reflection of all that enthusiasm and vigour. He was the child of his age, but he heard its sobs as well as its laughter, the rattling chains of its slaves as well as the clanking steel and the trumpet notes of its armed men. The Black Death and the revolt of the downtrodden peasants made a grim setting to the picture of heart-stirring triumphs in the battle-field, and Chaucer saw both the setting and the picture.

When he was about twenty he became attached to the court in a humble capacity, but his pleasant manners and conversation, his cheerfulness and his straightforward simplicity, soon won him promotion, so that he was made first gentleman-in-waiting, then esquire to King Edward, who more than once spoke of him as his "beloved valet," and who trusted him well enough to send him on many important missions to foreign countries as his messenger. But Chaucer's greatest and unchanging ally at court was the king's brother, John of Gaunt. For more than forty years their friendship remained unbroken through many ups and downs of fortune.

In 1369 John of Gaunt's first wife, Blanche, died, young, beautiful, and beloved. Chaucer had already shown his power of writing excellent verse by a translation he had made from a celebrated French poem "Le Roman de la Rose," so it was only natural that John of Gaunt should turn to him when in the sorrow of the moment he desired the goodness and charm of his lady to be commemorated. The result was the "Book of the Duchess," a story told as an allegory, for Chaucer was under the spell of French literature, which revelled in allegory. In this book he tells how one May morning, the sun shining in at his windows, and the sound of the "sweete foule's carolling," drew him forth into the forest, where, led thereto by a faithful dog, he found a knight dressed in black, mourning all in a quiet spot among the mighty trees. His hands drooped, his face was pale, he could not be consoled. But finding the poet a sympathetic listener, he told him the story of his sorrow.

"My lady bright

Which I heve loved with all my might,

Is from me deed, and is agone ...

That was so fair, so fresh, so free."

Years of happiness he had spent with her, this sweet lady, who yet was so strong and helpful.

"When I hed wrong and she the right,

She wolde alwey so goodëly

Forgive me so débónnairly.

In alle my youth, in alle chance,

She took me in her governaunce.

Therewith she was alwày so trewe,

Our joys was ever y-liche newe."

And now she was dead. Words of comfort were of no avail. The poet could no longer intrude on grief so overwhelming. He could only silently sympathise, and then leave the mourning knight alone in his sorrow, with the parting words

"Is that your los? By God, hit is routhe."

Soon after he had written this touching tribute to the memory of a woman who had been his ideal of goodness and graciousness, Chaucer was sent on a mission to Genoa and Florence, a journey which left its influence upon him in a very marked manner, as he made the acquaintance of Francis Petrarch, the Italian poet, and through him he learned to know the works of Dante and the delightful stories of Boccaccio. A new world was opened out to him, and eagerly he wandered through it, eyes and mind open to every fresh vision that unfolded itself before him. From this time forward his works were tinged with Italian influence, and thereby became much the richer. For he lost none of his own sturdy individuality and fresh, pure style; he only added to this more warmth, more colouring, more romance.

On his return to England he was made Comptroller of the Customs of the Port of London, on the understanding that he did all the accounts himself, so important was it that this post should be filled by a man who was both shrewd and honest; and in addition to this both the king and John of Gaunt granted him certain allowances and privileges, so that in worldly affairs he prospered. Good fortune, however, did not cause him to become idle, and his poems followed each other in quick succession. There was the "Assembly of Fowles," of course an allegory, and written probably to celebrate the betrothal of young King Richard to the Princess Anne of Bohemia.

"Troilus and Cresside" was a much deeper poem, full of sadness, and Chaucer himself called it his "little Tragedie," adding the hope that one day God might send it to him to "write some Comedie." It is in this work that he refers to the great difficulty with which he, in common with the other writers of his day, had to contend—the unsettled state of the language. The struggle as to whether the French or English tongue should prevail had been a fierce one, but it was now in its last throes. Chaucer, through his works, helped more than any one else to develop our language as it is to-day, and strenuously avoided those "owre curyrows termes which could not be understood of comyn people, and which in every shire varied." But his own words show the difficulties which beset him.

"And for there is so great diversité

In English, and in writing of our tong,

So pray I God that none miswrite thee

Or thee mismetre for default of tong,

And red whereso thou be, or elles song,

That thou be understood, God I beseech."

And it is just because he wrote to be understood that the charm of Chaucer's style remains for ever fresh and entrancing.

In his "House of Fame" he had free scope for his pleasant wit, especially when he tells of all he saw and heard in the "House of Rumour," whither came shipmen, pilgrims, pardoners, couriers, and their like, each bringing scraps of news, which, whether true or false, were passed on, growing like a rolling snowball. He set fame at its true value, and for himself only desires that in life he might be able to "study and rite alway," while for the rest—

"It suffyceth me, as I were dedd,

That no wight have my name in honde,

I wot myself best how I stonde."

The "Legend of Good Women" was written in praise of all those maidens and wives who loved truly and unchangingly.

Hitherto Chaucer, whose married life was not an altogether happy one, had sung but little of love in its highest, purest form. But here, in a prologue sparkling and radiant as the morning he describes, he tells us how he went out to greet the daisy, the flower he loved, and would ever love anew till his heart did die.

"Kneeling alway, til it unclosèd was

Upon the swetë, softë, swotë gras

That was with flourës swote embroidered all.

In his dream there came to him the God of Love, with his queen, Alcestis, who, daisy-like, was clad in royal habits green—

"A fret of golde she hedde next her heer,

And upon that a white courone she beer."

She it was who made him swear that from henceforth he would "poetize of wommen trewe in lovying," "speke wel of love," and so make a glorious legend.

Chaucer had intended writing at least nineteen stories on the lines decreed by Alcestis, but his days of prosperity had come to an end for the time being, with the exile of John of Gaunt, and he became so poor after his dismissal from the Customs, that he had to raise money on his pension. And so the legend seems to have been laid aside.

When Henry of Lancaster became king five years later, he doubled the pension, remembering how his father, just dead, had loved the poet; and so the cloud, which had been heavy enough while it lasted, passed away. But it is to those dark days that we owe the greatest of all Chaucer's work—his "Canterbury Tales"—work, it must be remembered, which rings and re-rings with cheerfulness, courage, sympathy, and kindliness. We know so little of Chaucer as a man but this one fact stands out, that he never allowed his own troubles or anxieties, or even his pressing poverty, to overcloud his heart or his mind. For him the sun shone always, though he saw it not, and because of that sunshine no trace of bitterness or harshness is to be found in his work.

In the prologue to the "Tales" Chaucer explains his plot in the most natural and personal way. One day in the spring, he says, he was waiting at the Tabard Inn, to rest before continuing a pilgrimage he had set out to make to Canterbury, when twenty-nine other pilgrims, all bound for the same destination, arrived. He soon made friends with them, and, finding their company very entertaining, arranged to join this party. Then came the proposal that each one should tell two tales to enliven the journey; a good supper at the end to be the reward of the pilgrim whose story found most favour. The jovial host of the inn decided to join them, and one morning in early spring the procession set out. What a motley crowd they were! Yet Chaucer, with his happy knack of describing people just as they appeared, has made them all so real to us, that it is easy to picture each one of them, and in so doing to get a vivid glimpse of the men and women whom the poet was accustomed to meet every day of his life. But for Chaucer we should know next to nothing about the people of his day. First came the knight, who "lovede chyvalrye," who had ridden far afield in his master's wars; a great soldier, but tender as a woman, "a verrey parfyte gentil knight." With him was his son, acting as his squire, great of strength, able to make brave songs, and to sit well his horse, handsomely dressed, yet in his manners "curteys, lowly, and servysable." His attendant was a yeoman, sunburnt and sturdy, who carried the sheaf of arrows, which he could dress right yeomanly. It seems likely that for a short while Chaucer served as a soldier in France, and if so, how familiar these three must have been to him. Then came the prioress, very "pleasant and semely," adopting court manners, and impressing every one with the idea that she was so compassionate and charitable that even to see a mouse in a trap made her weep. She had her own attendant nuns and priests. The monk was only interested in riding, but the friar, who was licensed to hear confessions, raise money, and perform the offices of the Church in a certain district, was merry, the good friend of all rich women, and reported to "hear confession very sweetly," being easy with the penances he ordered. Sometimes he lisped, "to make his English sweet upon the tongue," and when he sang to his guitar, "his eyes shone like stars on a frosty night." The merchant sat high on his horse, and talked loudly of his increased wealth, a great contrast to the poor clerk of Oxford, who looked hollow, wore a threadbare cloak, and had not been worldly enough to get a benefice. The sergeant-at-law, the landholder, the haberdasher, carpenter, weaver, dyer, tapestry-maker, the cook, the sailor, and the doctor, all had their special characteristics, but of these there is not space to speak. The wife of Bath had a bold face and wore bright clothes; had buried five husbands, all of whom she had ruled, and was quite willing to try a sixth. The poor parson, who was "a shepherd holy and vertuous, never despising sinful men, but teaching them the law of Christ, which he faithfully followed," was, I think, the pilgrim whom Chaucer most reverenced. The religion of the monks and friars revolted him, but those poor priests, leading their simple lives of work and worship, were to his eyes in very truth the servants of Christ, who witnessed loyally to their Master, in spite of the contempt with which their very poverty caused them to be treated. His brother, the ploughman, was in his way as good a man as the priest, for he was a true and honest labourer, who lived in charity with all, loved God, and would, for Christ's sake, "thresh, dyke, or delve for the poor widow's hire." The miller; the manciple, who bought the food for an Inn of Court; the reeve or steward; the summoner to the ecclesiastical courts; and the pardoner, with his packets of relics which he always sold successfully, made up the party; and all having agreed to the host's proposals as to the tales to be told, they drew lots to decide who should begin, the choice falling on the knight, whereat all rejoiced. "Tell us merry things," was the injunction of the host, who was rejoicing in a spell of freedom from his wife's sharp eyes and sharper tongue, and—

"Speak ye so plain at this time, we you pray,

That we may understandë what you say."

Just as Chaucer gave to each pilgrim his own individuality, so in every case he fitted the story to its teller. The knight had a tale of love, romance, and adventure; the clerk chose for heroine the patient, much-suffering Griselda; the prioress told of a child-martyr, and the poor parson, in earnest words, drew their thoughts upward to "that parfyt glorious pilgrimage which each and all must make to celestial Jerusalem." Chaucer did not live to finish all the tales he had planned out. In the year 1399 he had taken on a long lease a house at Westminster, which stood where now is Henry VII.'s chapel, and here he spent the last few months of his life, reading and writing contentedly to the end, in high favour at the Palace hard by, and the centre of a little group who loved and revered him. Probably the poor priest's tale was his last bit of work, and that significantly ends with words concerning the pilgrimage of man to the Heavenly City, "To thilke life He bring us, that bought us with His precious blood. Amen."

Chaucer's wife had been dead many years, and of his children we know nothing, except that to his son Lewis he gave an astrolabe, an instrument for taking the height of the stars, and wrote for him a "little treatise" on the subject, in which he craves pardon for his "rude inditing and his superfluity of words," explaining that a child is best taught by simple words and much repetition. But we can never think of Chaucer as alone or solitary in his old age. Rather was the house at Westminster a pleasant haven of rest where he anchored surrounded by his many comrades and friends. So greatly honoured was he, that when he died it was at once decided to bury him in the Abbey. The verses with which I end have been called Chaucer's Creed, and some say he repeated them just before his death. Certain it is that they guided his conduct through life.

THE GOOD COUNSEL OF CHAUCER

Flee from the crowd and dwell with truthfulness,
Contented with thy good, though it be small.
Treasure breeds hate and climbing dizziness;
The world is envious, wealth beguiles us all.
Care not for loftier things than to thee fall,
Counsel thyself, who counsel'st others' need,
And Truth shall thee deliver without dread.

Pain thee not all the crooked to redress,
Trusting to her who turneth as a ball;
For little meddling wins much easiness.
Beware lest thou dost kick against an awl!
Strive not, as doth a clay pot with a wall.
Judge thou thyself, who judgest others' deeds,
And Truth shall thee deliver without dread.

All that is sent receive with cheerfulness:
To wrestle with this world inviteth fall.
Here is no home, here is but wilderness.
Forth! pilgrim, forth! Forth, beast, out of thy stall!
Look up on high, and thank thy God for all!
Cast by ambition, let thy soul thee lead,
And Truth shall thee deliver, without dread.

CHAUCER'S TOMB.

CHAPTER XV
SPENSER, ADDISON, AND THE POETS' CORNER

Chaucer was buried in the year 1400, and it was close upon two hundred years before another great poet, Edmund Spenser, "followed here the footing of his feet." During much of this interval England had been in a state of unrest and excitement. First the Wars of the Roses, then the Reformation, with the bitter persecutions that followed it, had stirred men to the very core. Their eyes had been dazzled by the sudden and vehement changes which had followed each other. English blood had flown freely, English life had been offered up on English soil, not only in the great battles of the Civil War, but on scaffolds and in fiery names. It had not been an age for poets or writers. Of the few who have left their mark on our literature during that time, John Wycliffe had not even been allowed to rest in peace after death, for his body was taken from its grave and burnt, and his ashes were thrown into the river Swift, while both Sir Thomas More and the Earl of Surrey had been executed at the command of Henry VIII. One important piece of work had indeed been commenced and carried on during those days of storm which affected both earlier and later writers, and which was distinctly connected with the Abbey. For in the year 1477, William Caxton had settled with his printing press in the Almonry at Westminster, and had issued his famous advertisement, in which he had made known the fact "that if it should plese ony man, spiritual or temporal, to bye ony pyes of two and three commemoracions of Salisbro's use, enpryntid after the forme of this present lettre, which been wel and truly correct, lete hym come to Westmonester into the Almonerye at the Red Pale, and he shal have them good chepe." He had learned his art in Cologne and Bruges, having lived for nearly thirty years in the latter place, where he traded as a merchant, and during those years he had translated a number of books into English. Why he settled on Westminster when at last he returned to England as a middle-aged man, we know not, unless it was that he fancied he should find quiet and security under the walls of the Abbey, or that the abbots and monks, as the patrons of learning, would prove themselves good friends to him. But here he came, and here from his study, "where lay many and diverse paunflettis and bookys," this wonderful man, who was master-printer, translator, corrector, and editor, worked and directed his apprentices. Over a hundred different books were issued from this press, among them being "The Canterbury Tales," the "fayre and ornate termes" of which gave Caxton "such greate playsir," that he desired to make them widely known. Many people, some friends, some strangers, found their way, full of curiosity and interest, to the quaint house, which was marked by a large white shield with a red bar, there to watch Master Caxton and his workmen at their strange new craft, and many shook their heads, declaring that "so many books could never find purchasers." But the wise printer heeded them not. He worked with a will from morn till eve, and marked his hours by the Abbey bells. It was not only Chaucer's writings that he gave to the public, but many other works which without him would long have remained unknown or forgotten, and more than any one else he helped to fix the language which Chaucer had used, by himself using the same in all his translations. His busy life came to an end in 1491, and he was buried in the Church of St. Margaret's, Westminster. But at the sign of the Red Pale his favourite apprentice, Wynken de Worde, carried on the master's work with the same extraordinary industry, producing no fewer than five hundred separate books up to the time of his death in 1535. This date brings us to within about twenty years of the time when Edmund Spenser, Walter Raleigh, and Philip Sidney, the singing birds and knightly spirits of the Elizabethan Court, were born. Like Chaucer, Spenser was a Londoner and he describes his birthplace as

"The merry London, my most kyndly nurse,

That to me gave this life's first active source."

He proudly declared that "he took his name from an ancient house," but we know little of his immediate family. His boyhood was spent at Smithfield, then within easy reach of woods and fields, and he has given us a glimpse of it in these words, which show that he was a boy very much like all other boys:—

"Whilome in youth, when flowed my joy full spring

Like swallow swift, I wandered here and there

for heat of headlesse lust me did so sting,

That I oft doubted daunger, had no fear:

I went the wastefull woodes and forrest wide

Withouten dread of wolves to bene espied.

"I wont to raunge amid the mazie thicket,

And gather nuttes to make my Christmas game,

And joyed oft to chase the trembling pricket,

Or hunt the hartlesse hare till she were tame.

What wrecked I of wintrie age's waste?

Tho' deemed I my spring would ever last.

"How often have I scaled the craggie oke,

All to dislodge the raven of her nest?

How have I wearied with many a stroke

The stately walnut tree, the while the rest

Under the tree fell all for nuttes at strife?

For like to me was libertye and life."

He was educated at the Merchant Taylors' School, and afterwards at Cambridge, where an old biographer declares "he mispent not his time, as the fruites of his labours doe manifest, for that he became an excellent scholar, especially most happy in English poetry." But no other memories remain to us of his university life except the names of his two great and lifelong friends, and all we know of him during the first few years after he left Cambridge is that he lived in the north, and that he fell violently in love with a certain Rosaline, "a gentlewoman both of nature and manners, worthy to be commended to immortalitie for her rare and singular virtues," but who apparently did not in any way return his ardent affections. He lamented her indifference so deeply that he left his home and made his way to London, "all weeping and disconsolate," and though he was by nature light-hearted and pleasure-loving, he treasured the memory of her many charms for fourteen years, until he met and married the Elizabeth whom he described as "my love, my life's last ornament." But if it was despair which drove Spenser to London, he had no cause ever to regret the move, for it led to his making the acquaintance of Sir Philip Sidney, who introduced him to his uncle, the all-powerful Earl of Leicester. Both received him cordially, and in a short time he was mixing in all the intellectual society of the day. England was at peace; Elizabeth's firm rule made for prosperity; the new learning had taken root; the spirit of adventure, of imagination, of chivalry had free scope; the spirit of growth, of progress, of enterprise pervaded the air. All was ready for the coming of a poet who could sing as Chaucer had done, and make sweet music with the national language. In the winter of 1579 Spenser published, not under his own name, his "Shepherdes Calendar," a series of shepherd tales, one for each of the twelve months of the year, and these he dedicated to "Maister Philip Sidney, that noble and vertuous gentleman, most worthy of all titles, both of learning and chevalrie." At once the "new poet" leapt into fame, though nothing could have been in greater contrast than Chaucer's Tales and Spenser's Calendar. The first faithfully pictured life as it was without romance or exaggeration; the second, according to the fashion of the day, was in the form of a masquerade: the heroes and heroines were all shepherds or shepherdesses; everything took place in the country, every one was a rustic, and the highest praise that could be given to Chaucer was to call him the "god of shepherds." So the Calendar had none of that simplicity and truthfulness which gave to Chaucer's work its great charm. Shepherds and shepherdesses, when put in all kinds of unnatural positions, could not fail to be unreal and artificial, especially when they were made to talk in the language of scholars. But Spenser's strength lay in the melody of his verse, in his sense of beauty and his power over language, and it has been truly said that though he is not the greatest of poets, his poetry is the most poetical of all poetry.

Fuller, who wrote on the "Worthies of England," tells us that Spenser was presented to Queen Elizabeth, who was so overcome by the beauties of his poem, that she ordered Lord Burleigh to give him a hundred pounds, to which the cautious Treasurer objected, saying it was too much. "Then give him what is reason," said the Queen. But it was evident that Burleigh had not a great liking for the new poet, probably because he was such a friend of Leicester's, and Spenser saw nothing of the money till he brought it to the Queen's remembrance in a little rhyme. He soon found that he could not live by his poetry, but he had no desire to exist on the favours of Leicester or Sidney, and preferred to earn his own daily bread in some honourable and independent way. An opening came unexpectedly. Ireland was causing much anxiety to the crown; one Lord Deputy after another sent from England had failed to restore to it order or good government, and had come home depressed and disheartened, if not actually disgraced. In 1579 the Government pressed Lord Grey de Wilton—the "good Lord Grey"—high-minded, religious, and fearless, to undertake the thankless task, and he, from a sense of duty, accepted the office of Lord Deputy. He invited Spenser to come with him, as his secretary, and the offer was at once accepted, though it must have cost the poet something to tear himself away from the centre of life and learning, from the society he so enjoyed, to bury himself in a country regarded as only half civilised, and which at that very time was in open rebellion. He left behind him Merrie England, with all that was pleasant to him, when he went to Ireland, which was then in a most turbulent and rebellious condition, and for the time being his writing had to be laid aside for sterner stuff. But all honour to him that he chose work rather than dependence.

Lord Grey de Wilton did not succeed any better than his predecessors had done. Naturally kind-hearted, he nevertheless deemed it his duty to carry out a policy of great severity, and himself almost a Puritan in his religious views, he saw no hope for the distressful country until Protestantism reigned there. Spenser adopted the same opinions as his master, and pitiless force was the only weapon used in the warfare. Of course it availed nothing, and Lord Grey was recalled, more or less under a cloud, for he had many enemies at home among those who found him too uncompromisingly straightforward and honourable, as well as among those who condemned his fanatical severity and his ruthlessly heavy hand. Spenser, who stayed behind in Ireland, always remained loyal to him, and sturdily defended that "most just and honourable personage, whose least virtues, of many most excellent, which abounded in his heroical spirit, they were never able to aspire to, who with evil tongues did most untruly and maliciously backbite and slander him."

For the next few years the poet held various clerkships and other posts, and at last he became the possessor of Kilcolman Castle, where he lived for some time, devoting his spare hours to the great work he so long had in contemplation, "The Faerie Queene." In 1590 he got permission to return for awhile to England that he might publish that part of his book which he had finished, a permission he owed to Raleigh, who had read much of the work when staying as his guest in Ireland, and who with generous sympathy longed to give to the poet the fame which was so justly his. Thanks to him, too, the Queen listened to some portions of the poem, and was greatly delighted with the many references made to herself. For Spenser had learnt how to flatter gracefully in his verse, and had realised that to find favour in the Queen's eyes he would do well

"To lyken her to a crowne of lillies

Upon a virgin bryde's adorned head,

With roses dight and goolds and daffadillies;

Or like the circlet of a Turtle true

In which alle colours of the rainbow bee.

Or like faire Phebes' garland shining new,

In which alle pure perfection one may see.

But vain it is to think by paragone

Of earthly things, to judge of things Divine."

He had dedicated his book to her, "The most High, Mightie, and Magnificent Empress, renowned for Pietie, Virtue, and alle gracious Government;" and at the end of the dedication expressed the humble hope that "thus his labours might live with the eternity of her fame." Elizabeth smiled graciously on one who added such glory to her court, and gave Spenser a pension of £50. "The Faerie Queene" was greeted with a chorus of enthusiastic praise, and the publisher, who in an introduction had begged gentle readers to "graciouslie entertain the new Poet," had no reason to complain of the warm welcome given to him.

Of course, the work was an allegory, a double allegory, so to speak; for besides having a general meaning to his story, he had a special one which referred to living people, such as the Queen, Sir Philip Sidney, Lord Grey, and so on. The whole poem, therefore, is rather complicated, and in great contrast to the well-arranged plots which Chaucer had woven into his stories. The general idea was that in a certain happy country there reigned a great Queen Gloriana, around whose presence had gathered a body of brave and fearless knights. The queen decided to hold a feast for twelve days, and on each day an adventure was to be undertaken by one of these knights for the purpose of righting some wrong, releasing some captive, or succouring some oppressed person. Spenser purposed to tell of these several adventures in twelve books, but only six were finished. Now if in "The Faerie Queene" we attempt to unravel the very knotted allegory, we shall soon get into difficulties, for Spenser's greatest gifts did not lie in his power of making a clear story, but in his perfectly chosen language, his lofty thoughts, and the never-failing music of his verse. So the wisest plan, I think, is to read the romances for their own beauty without trying to find a hidden meaning in every line, and even so, we shall everywhere discover rich gems.

It is strange that in spite of all the fame which "The Faerie Queene" gave the poet, it brought him neither wealth nor even work, and he "tourned back to his sheepe" in Ireland. He married, and poured out his joy in an exquisite song called "Epithalamion." Besides this, he wrote more books of his great work, many sonnets and hymns, and a treatise on Ireland. He was made Sheriff of Cork, and altogether his worldly affairs prospered; for Burleigh was dead, and it was Burleigh who had always checked the Queen's generosity towards him, "saying a song needed not such liberal payment." Suddenly a fresh and violent rebellion broke out in Ireland. Spenser's castle was attacked and set on fire; his little child was burned to death; and all his valued possessions were destroyed. He came back to London with his wife, homeless, penniless, broken-hearted. Over the next few months a veil is drawn; how it came to pass that his many friends and admirers knew nothing of his sufferings, or knowing did not raise a hand to help him, remains a mystery. This is certain, that he died of grief and for lack of bread in a street near Westminster. After his death, indeed, his friends came to the fore once more. The Earl of Essex paid all the expenses of his funeral, which took place in the Abbey. Poets and writers flocked to his grave-side, throwing on to his coffin their songs of woe. We may take it for granted that Shakespeare was among the mourners, and with him were all the brightest spirits of the day. Truly the broken-hearted poet was well honoured on that last event of his life. At some period of his career, probably near the end, he had written a poem on "Change and Mutabilitie." God grant that in those bitter closing days he found the ray of hope he thus did sing of:—

"Then gin I think on that which Nature sayd,

Of that same time when no more Change shall be,

But stedfast rest of all things firmly stayd,

Upon the Pillars of Eternitie,

That is contrayr to Mutabilitie.

For all that moveth does in change delight:

But thenceforth all shall rest eternally

With Him, that is the God of Sabbaoth hight:

O that great Sabbaoth God, grant me that Sabbaoth's sight."

True it is that Spenser, the herald of the Elizabethan day, gives to the Poets' Corner the reflected glory of that period, but we can never cease to regret that Shakespeare, its crown and its sun, lies so far away from Westminster. Only the Abbey seems a fitting monument to that great mind, our king of English literature.

"Thou art a monument without a tomb,

And art alive while still thy books doth live,

And we have wits to read, and praise to give."

So wrote Ben Jonson. With that thought, and the fact that, a hundred and twenty years after his death, a memorial to Shakespeare was put up in the Poets' Corner by public subscription, we must rest content. Ben Jonson himself was buried here, having in his imperious way demanded of the king "eighteen inches of ground in the Abbey," and so he remained in death "a child of Westminster." He had been educated at Westminster School, this turbulent, strong-spirited lad, with Border blood in him, who could never settle down to the trade of a builder, to which he had been apprenticed, and who was heard of among actors and playwriters. He was the friend of Shakespeare; indeed, it is said that the great man not only warmly praised his first play, "Every Man in his Humour," but acted in it himself at the Globe Theatre. Jonson produced a great number of plays and a still greater number of court masques. He was a master of plot, and everything he wrote was full of force and personality. Such a fiery character as his could hardly fail to lead him into a series of quarrels; but, in spite of this, he was held by his large circle of friends to be "the prince of good fellows," and the words, "O rare Ben Jonson," carved on his tomb by order of Sir John Young, "who, walking here when the grave was covering, gave the fellow eighteenpence to cut it," is an epitaph that came from the hearts of those who loved him and recognised his genius. Francis Beaumont, another Elizabethan playwriter, and the intimate friend of the whole group of dramatists, lies here; as does Michael Drayton, who wrote more than one hundred thousand lines of verse, and who, despite the fact that he was always quarrelling with his booksellers, whom he described as "a company of base knaves I scorn to kick," was known among his contemporaries as the "all-loved Drayton." Abraham Cowley, held in his day to be a great poet, had a magnificent funeral and a most flattering epitaph, but though one enthusiastic admirer went so far as to declare that the Great Fire left the Abbey untouched because Fate would that Cowley's tomb should be preserved, his works did not long survive him. Close to him was laid John Dryden, who as a boy had been well whipped by the great Doctor Busby. He says himself that he "endeavoured to write good English," and he produced several plays and some excellent political satires. He was not a great poet, but he had the knack of reasoning well in verse, of choosing apt words, and of writing vigorously. And we must remember that he lived in the days of the later Stuarts, when poets had well-nigh forgotten the sweet music of the Elizabethan age. Near to his tomb stands the bust of his bitter enemy, Shadwell, of whom he had written:—

"Shadwell alone of all my sons is he

Who stands confirmed in all stupidity.

The rest to some faint meaning made pretence,

But Shadwell never deviates into sense."

Even so did the Abbey unite these rival poets-laureate.

POETS' CORNER

Another satirist, Samuel Butler, has a monument, but not a tomb, in the Abbey. He also died in abject poverty, and of him these lines were written, which apply to more than one of those commemorated in the Poets' Corner:—

"When Butler, needy wretch, was yet alive,

No generous patron would a dinner give.

Behold him starved to death and turned to dust,

Presented with a monumental bust.

The poet's fate is here in emblem shown:

He asked for bread, and he received a stone."

Thomas May, the historian; Davenant, the Royalist poet-laureate; Sir John Denham, a Royalist versifier, and John Phillips, a devoted imitator of Milton, are little more than names to us; but then we must remember that, with few exceptions, neither the poets nor the poetry of that period which ended with the death of William III. have lived on through our literature. With the accession of Anne there came a burst of new life, and the next great name we come to in the Abbey is that of Joseph Addison, the most charming of our prose writers. To find his grave, however, we must leave the Poets' Corner and go to General Monk's vault in Henry VII.'s Chapel. For here, close to his friend Charles Montagu, Lord Keeper, he of "piercing wit, gentle irony, and sparkling humour," the regular contributor to our two earliest newspapers, the *Tattler* and the *Spectator*, was buried. His own words, from an article in the *Spectator* when it was about twelve days old, best describe both the man and his aims: "It is with much satisfaction that I hear this great city enquiring day by day after these my papers, and receiving my morning lectures with a becoming seriousness and attention. My publisher tells me that already three thousand of them are distributed every day, so that if I allow twenty readers to every paper, I may reckon about threescore thousand disciples in London and Westminster, who, I hope, will take care to distinguish themselves from the thoughtless herd of their ignorant and unattentive brethren. I shall spare no pains to make their instruction agreeable and their diversion useful. For which reason I shall endeavour to enliven morality with wit and to temper wit with morality.... I have resolved to refresh their memories from day to day, till I have recovered them from that desperate state of folly and vice into which the age is fallen. The mind that lies fallow but a single day sprouts up in follies that are only to be killed by assiduous culture. It was said of Socrates that he brought philosophy down from heaven to inhabit among men, and I shall be ambitious to have it said of me that I brought philosophy out of closets and libraries, schools and colleges, to dwell in clubs and assemblies, at tea-tables and in coffee-houses." Then, having given his general aim, he goes on to especially commend his paper to all well-regulated families; to those gentlemen of leisure who consider the world a theatre, and desire to form a right judgment of those who are the actors on it; and to those "poor souls called the blanks of society, who are altogether unfurnished with ideas, who ask the first men they meet if there is any news stirring, and who know not what to talk about till twelve o'clock in the morning, by which time they are pretty good judges of the weather, and know which way the wind sets;" while finally he appeals to the female world: "I have often thought," he says, "that there has not been sufficient pains taken to find out proper employments and diversions for the fair ones. Their amusements seem contrived for them rather as they are women than as they are reasonable creatures. The toilet is their great scene of business, and the right adjusting of their hair the principal employment of their lives. This, I say, is the state of ordinary women, though I know there are multitudes of those that move in an exalted sphere of knowledge and virtue, and that join all the beauties of mind to the ornaments of dress. I hope to increase the number of those by publishing this daily paper, which I shall always endeavour to make an innocent entertainment, and by that means at least divert the minds of my female readers from far greater trifles."

Faithfully and yet very pleasantly did Addison carry out his scheme. His humour was always kindly, his good sense was unvarying, his thoughts were always generous and true, and his easy unaffected language completed the charm. Instead of dropping to the level of his readers, he raised them to the much higher level on which he himself stood, and this without dull lecturing or violent denunciations. Religion, duty, love, honour, purity, truth, kindliness, and public-spiritedness were all real things to him, and he sought to make them everywhere realities too, gilding his little moral pills so cleverly, that until they were swallowed no one knew they were pills, and then they left nothing but a sweet taste behind.

"About an age ago," he writes, "it was the fashion in England for every one who would be thought religious to throw as much sanctity as possible into his face. The saint was of a sorrowful countenance, and generally was eaten up with melancholy. I do not presume to tax such characters with hypocrisy, as is done too frequently, that being a vice which, I think, none but He who knows the secrets of men's hearts should pretend to discover in another. But I think they would do well to consider whether such a behaviour does not deter men from religion.... In short, those who represent religion in so unamiable a light are like the spies sent out by Moses to make a discovery in the Land of Promise, when by their reports they discouraged the people from entering upon it. Those that show us the joys, the cheerfulness, the good-humour that naturally spring up in this happy state are like the spies bringing along with them clusters of grapes and delicious fruits that so invited their companions into the pleasant country which produced them."

Two of his articles have Westminster Abbey for their subject. On one occasion Addison, as the Spectator, goes there for a walk, and thus describes his feelings:—"I yesterday passed a whole afternoon in the Cloisters and the Church ... And I began to consider with myself what innumerable multitudes of people lay confused under the pavement of that ancient cathedral; how men and women, friends and enemies, priests and soldiers, monks and prebendaries were crumbled one against the other; how beauty, strength, and youth, with old age, weakness, and deformity, lay undistinguished in the same heap of matter.... Some of the monuments were covered with such extravagant epitaphs that, if it were possible for the dead person to be acquainted with them, he would blush at the praises which his friends bestowed on him. There were others so excessively modest that they deliver the character of the person departed in Greek or Hebrew so that they are not understood once in a twelvemonth. I found there were poets which had no monuments, and monuments which had no poets.... Sir Cloudesley Shovel's monument gave me great offence. Instead of the brave, rough English admiral, which was the distinguishing character of that plain gallant man, he is represented on his tomb by the figure of a beau, dressed in a long periwig, and reposing himself upon velvet cushions under a canopy of state. The Dutch, whom we are apt to despise for want of genius, show an infinitely greater taste.... The monuments of their admirals which have been erected at the public expense represent them like themselves, and are adorned with rostral crowns and naval ornaments, with beautiful festoons of seaweed, shells, and coral. When I look upon the tombs of the great, every emotion of envy dies in me; when I read the epitaphs of the beautiful, every inordinate desire goes out; when I meet with the grief of parents upon a tombstone, my heart melts with compassion; when I see the tombs of the parents themselves, I consider the vanity of grieving for those that we must quickly follow. When I see kings lying by those who deposed them, when I consider rival wits placed side by side, or the holy men that divided the world with their contests and disputes, I reflect with sorrow and astonishment on the little competitions, factions, and debates of mankind. When I read the several dates of the tombs, of some that died yesterday, and some six hundred years ago, I consider that great day when we shall all of us be contemporaries, and make our appearance together."

The next visit Spectator paid to the Abbey was in the company of Sir Roger de Coverley, his own creation, that gentleman of ancient descent, whose "singularities proceeded from his good sense, and were contradictions to the manners of the world only as he thought the world was in the wrong," and who was such a great lover of mankind, with such a mirthful cast in his behaviour, so cheerful, gay, and hearty, that "his tenants grew rich, his servants were satisfied, all young women professed love to him, and the young men were glad of his company." The squire was now spending one of his frequent visits to London, and informed the Spectator that having read his paper on Westminster Abbey, he should like to go there with him, never having visited the tombs since he read history.

"As we went up the body of the church, the knight pointed at the trophies on one of the new monuments, and cried out, 'A brave man! I warrant him!' Passing afterwards by Sir Cloudesley Shovel, he flung his head that way, and cried, 'Sir Cloudesley Shovel, a very gallant man!' As we stood before Busby's tomb the knight uttered himself again after the same manner. 'Doctor Busby, a great man! He whipped my grandfather; I should have gone to him myself, if I had not been a blockhead. A very great man!' Among several other figures he was very well pleased to see the statesman Cecil upon his knees.... Sir Roger, in the next place, laid his hand upon Edward III.'s sword, and leaning upon the pommel of it gave us the whole history of the Black Prince, concluding that, in Sir Richard Baker's opinion, Edward III. was one of the greatest princes that ever sat upon the English throne. We were then shown Edward the Confessor's tomb, upon which Sir Roger acquainted us that he was the first who touched for the evil, and afterwards Henry IV.'s, upon which he shook his head, and told us there was fine reading in the casualties of that reign. Our conductor then pointed to that monument where there is the figure of one of our English kings without a head, and upon giving us to know that the head, which was of beaten silver, had been stolen away years before, 'Some Whig, I warrant you!' says Sir Roger. 'You ought to lock your kings up better. They will carry off the body, too, if you don't take care!' The glorious names of Queen Elizabeth and Henry V. gave the knight great opportunities of shining. For my own part, I could not but be pleased to see the knight show such an honest passion for the glory of his country, and such a respectful gratitude to the memory of its princes."

Addison died when under fifty years of age, and the story goes that in his last moments he sent for young Lord Warwick, his stepson.

"Dear sir," said the lad, "any commands you may give me, I shall hold most sacred."

"See in what peace a Christian can die," answered the older man tenderly.

Years before, in his first letter as Spectator, he had written these honest words, "If I can in any way contribute to the improvement of the country in which I live, I shall leave it, when I am summoned out of it, with the secret satisfaction of thinking that I have not lived in vain." And the knowledge that he had been true to this pure ambition brought him a calm content in that hour when all the things of this life vanished into the dim background.

His funeral in the Abbey has been thus vividly described by Tickell, his friend:—

"Can I forget the dismal night that gave

My soul's best part for ever to the grave?

How silent did his old companions tread,

By midnight lamps, the mansions of the dead.

Through breathing statues, then unheeded things,

Through rows of warriors and through walks of kings!

What awe did the slow solemn march inspire,

The pealing organ and the pausing choir;

The duties by the lawn-robed prelate paid

And the last words that dust to dust conveyed!

While speechless o'er the closing grave we bend—

Accept those tears, thou dear departed friend!

Oh, gone for ever, take this last adieu,

And sleep in peace next thy loved Montagu."

CHAPTER XVI
GARRICK, JOHNSON, AND SHERIDAN

Near together and under the shadow of Shakespeare's monument lie three men whose lives brought them into close contact with each other: David Garrick, the actor and manager; Dr. Samuel Johnson, the critic and conversationalist; and Richard Brinsley Sheridan, prince of playwriters and parliamentary orators. Little Davy Garrick was the first of the trio on whom the curtain fell, and his funeral in the Abbey, which took place on the 1st of February 1779, was a most imposing one. The streets were crowded with people gathered to see the last of him they had so delighted in applauding. The procession extended far down into the Strand; players from Drury Lane and Covent Garden mourned the kindliest and most lovable of comrades; seven carriages were filled with the members of the Literary Club, and round the grave stood Edmund Burke, Charles James Fox, Sheridan, Dr. Johnson, with many another distinguished man. That was a day of triumph for the English stage. True, indeed, other players had been buried in Westminster—Anne Oldfield, who lies in the nave; Anne Bracegirdle and Mr. Cibber, whose graves are in the cloisters—but the death of David Garrick was accounted a national loss, and all desired to honour him, under whose wise guidance "the drama had risen from utter chaos into order, fine actors had been trained, fine plays had been written for the fine actors to act, and fine, never-failing audiences had assembled to see the fine plays which the fine actors had acted." It has often been said that even had he been neither an actor nor a public character his name would have gone down to future generations as a perfect English gentleman, so great was the spell of his charm and his influence. He was born in an inn at Hereford in the year 1716, the son of a penniless officer in the dragoons, who had married Miss Isabella Clough, the equally penniless daughter of the vicar-choral of Lichfield Cathedral. The lieutenant had to serve at Gibraltar, and little David, a bright lad, ever ready with a witty answer, got his early education in a free school at Lichfield, presided over by a master who used the rod freely, "to save his boys from the gallows," as he assured them for their comfort. An older boy at the same school was Samuel Johnson, the son of a highly respected bookseller in Lichfield. In spite of the great difference in their ages, he became David's friend, and together they used to patronise such plays as the companies of strolling players brought within their reach, the acting taking place in such barns as were available. David, full of enterprise, organised and drilled a little company of his own when he was barely eleven, which company performed a play called "The Recruiting Officer," to the admiration of a large and interested audience, composed mainly of parents. But funds did not allow of many such pastimes, and a year later David was sent out to Portugal to work in the office of an uncle, a prosperous wine merchant there. Never was boy more unfit for the daily routine of an office, a fact which, fortunately, his uncle soon recognised, for in a few months he was back again in Lichfield, slightly in disgrace, it is true, and was sent to his old school that "discipline might repair his deficiencies."

DR. SAMUEL JOHNSON.

Young Johnson, who by now had returned from Oxford, had, thanks to the assistance of a wealthy friend, Mr. Walmesley, set up a school of his own in the town, dignified by the name of "The Academy." At this seat of learning Garrick studied for a while, and years afterwards he wrote of his solemn ponderous master, "I honoured him, he endured me." But the academy did not prosper, and Johnson, who had already begun to write, determined to try his fate in London. Thither, too, young Garrick was bent, for it had been decided that he was to study law, and kind Mr. Walmesley had arranged to pay the expenses of the special instruction he would need, declaring him to be "of a good disposition, and as ingenious and promising a young man as ever I knew in my life." So together they set out, and together they lived for awhile, Johnson finding a scanty livelihood as a bookseller's assistant, David working as a student of Lincoln's Inn.

Soon afterwards Captain Garrick died, and at the same time died also the rich wine merchant uncle, who left a fair sum of money to his brother's children, with a special legacy to David, of whom he had been particularly fond. Then it was that for the first time the boy's ambition took definite shape: he knew there was only one life and one career for him, and that was summed up in the stage. His mother, though, shrank in horror from the idea, and to his eternal credit, rather than add to her sorrows, he set aside his own wishes, and made one more desperate effort to please his family by going into the wine business, as the London manager, with his brother Peter. Even in so doing, theatrical life pursued him, for his wines were so patronised by the coffee-houses and clubs to which the actors resorted, that he considered it part of his business to amuse and entertain his customers by "standing on the tables at the clubs to give his diverting and loudly applauded mimicries." To make a long story short, the genius that was in David would not allow him to settle down to a wine merchant's career; he became restless and dissatisfied, and one fine morning two letters fell like bombshells into the Garrick household at Lichfield: one from David, saying that his mind was so inclined to the stage that he could no longer resist it, and he hoped they would all forgive him when they found he had the genius of an actor; the other from an old friend, who hastened to assure the family how great a success Davy's first appearance had been, how the audience was in raptures, and how several men of judgment had wondered that he had kept off the stage so long. Richard II. was the ambitious part Garrick had undertaken. "I played the part to the surprise of every one," he wrote humbly to his furious brother. "It is what I doat upon, and I am resolved to pursue it." The *Daily Post* had an enthusiastic notice about this unknown gentleman who had never appeared before, "whose reception was the most extraordinary and great that was ever known, whose voice was clear, without monotony, drawling, affectation, bellowing, or grumbling; whose mien was neither strutting, slouching, stiff, nor mincing." Pope, most keen of critics, had watched him delightedly from a box. "That young man never had his equal, and never will have a rival," he remarked; adding, "I only fear lest he should become vain and ruined by applause."

But there was a simplicity of character and a fund of good sense in David which saved him from this latter fate, even though he quickly became the talk of the town, the man about whom the fashionable London world went mad. After acting with ever-increasing success in nineteen different parts, his London season came to an end for the time being, and in response to an urgent invitation he went over to Dublin, where the craze for him was so intense that, when a mild epidemic broke out, it was given the name of the Garrick fever. A second visit to that gay capital was even more successful, and Garrick finally returned to London with a clear £600 in his pocket.

It was then that various difficulties beset him, chiefly owing to the bad management of the theatres and the endless quarrels between the principal actors of the day; but at last, thanks to the many friends who firmly believed in him, and whose faith he never disappointed, he was able to invest £8000 in Drury Lane Theatre, and to become its manager as well as its leading actor. His determination was to "get together the best company in England," and it is characteristic of him that he let no past jealousies or quarrels interfere with his selection. Even Macklin, who had violently attacked him with tongue and pen, was engaged, as well as his wife, and he skilfully smoothed down the sensitive feelings of the various ladies. He insisted on rehearsals, which hitherto had seldom been enforced, and he also insisted that players should learn their parts, a very necessary proviso. On the opening night he remembered the friend with whom he had entered London, when triumphs such as this had been undreamt of, and it was Dr. Johnson whom he commissioned to write the prologue, which he himself gave with splendid effect. Later on he loyally did his best to make a success of Johnson's heavy and somewhat clumsy play "Irene," and thanks to his efforts and the money he freely spent on its staging, it ran for nine nights, so that the Doctor made the sum of £300. But with this the author was far from satisfied, and always declared that the actors had not done justice to their parts!

It would take too long to dwell on the many plays Garrick produced, the many parts he created, the wide range of writers new and old he explored, and the excellent standard he maintained. Whether it was a tragedy of Shakespeare's, or a comedy of Ben Jonson's, or a pantomime, he threw himself heartily into them all and never spared himself. He knew his public and catered for them, but at the same time he taught them to understand and applaud the best. His kindness to every one with whom he came in contact was proverbial; indeed, his greatest weakness lay in his good-nature. He could not bear to vex people by refusing them anything, and this trait often landed him into difficulties with the army of playwriters to whose entreaties that he would produce their works he seldom turned a deaf ear. And when these plays were too hopelessly bad to be dreamt of, David tried to soften the blow by a gift of money, sometimes actually a pension. As might have been expected, he had a wide circle of acquaintances from the highest in the land to the poorest Grub Street poets, and rarely was man so well liked. For in spite of his weaknesses—and he was restless and sensitive to the point of touchiness—he never allowed himself to be unjust or ungenerous to other people, and no thought of self ever interfered with the standard he had set up for his theatre and his own profession.

More than once he talked of retiring, for the strain of his life was heavy, and he looked forward to years of restful enjoyment with his "sweet wife," who had been before her marriage the celebrated dancer Mademoiselle Violette. But the very mention of such an idea raised a storm of excitement. Once even the king intervened when David had taken an unusually long holiday, and his Majesty requested Mr. Garrick to shortly appear again. The night when, thus commanded, he reappeared in "The Beggar's Opera," was one of his greatest triumphs; again "the town went half mad," and the theatre was crowded to an alarming extent. All ideas of retirement vanished from David's mind; the old magic had not lost its spell, and for more than ten years longer he went on with his work as vigorously as ever.

His fame became even more widespread, his public loved him even more dearly, and from far-away country places people journeyed to London so that they might boast of once having seen the great Mr. Garrick.

But in 1776, an illness, which he had long kept at bay, made itself felt, and he was the first to recognise that the time had nearly come for the curtain to fall. He gave a series of his greatest representations, ending with Richard II. "I gained my fame in Richard," he said, "and I mean to close with it."— Though he confessed to being in agonies of pain, in the eyes of his enraptured audience he was as great as he had ever been in his palmiest days of success, as graceful, as winsome, and as gay. His real farewell play, however, was "The Wonder," in which he took his favourite part, that of Don Felix, and "as his grand eyes wandered round the crowded house, he saw a sea of faces, friends, strangers, even foreigners, a boundless amphitheatre representing most affectionate sympathies and exalted admiration. He played as he had never played before. When the last note of applause had died away, the other actors left the stage and he stood there alone. The house listened in awe-struck silence. At first he tried in vain to speak; for once the ready words would not come for his calling. When at last he went on to thank his friends for their wonderful kindness to him, he broke down, and his tears fell fast. Sobs rang through the theatre. "Farewell! Farewell!" was cried in many a quivering voice. Mrs. Garrick wept bitterly in her box, and David slowly walked off the stage with one last wistful glance at the sea of faces all around him.

His interest in his theatre did not cease after he had left it, and he was disturbed at finding that the new manager, Sheridan, was sadly easy-going and unbusiness-like. But there was not much time left for such things to trouble him. Though he kept up his merry heart and his sprightly manner to the end, and though he delighted in the undisturbed companionship of his wife, the disease gained rapidly and he suffered much pain. Gradually a stupor crept over him, and though it sometimes lifted, so that with his old sweet smile he had a jest or a word of welcome for his friends, it never cleared, and he passed gently away in the early dawn of a January morning, 1779, "leaving that human stage where he had played with as much excellence and dignity as ever he had done on his own."

So ended a prosperous, pleasant life, and rarely was a man better liked by his fellows, or more genuinely mourned. Dr. Johnson, in this moment, forgot all his later coldness towards the Davy he had once so loved. He left a card on Mrs. Garrick, and "wished some endeavours of his could enable her to support a loss which the world cannot repair;" while he wrote those well-known words, which Mrs. Garrick had engraved on her husband's memorial monument in Lichfield Cathedral, and which form an inscription more appropriate than that on the Abbey tomb:—"I am disappointed by that stroke of death, which has eclipsed the gaiety of nations and impoverished the public stock of harmless pleasure."

David's devoted wife outlived him for over forty years, keenly interested to the last in all matters theatrical, and a well-known figure in the Abbey, where, little and bent, she often made her way to the tomb which held him she had so loved, and standing there would readily recount over and over again to willing listeners the triumphs of "her Davy."

Johnson, as we have seen, settled down in London with the intention of making literature pay. "No man but a blockhead," he said in his strongest manner, "ever wrote except for money." Perhaps it was for opinions such as these that his wife, more than twenty years older than himself, declared him to be the most sensible man that lived. A curious figure he must have seemed to those booksellers of whom he demanded work as a translator, mightily tall and broadly made, with a face which he twirled and twisted about in a strange fashion, features scarred by disease, eyes which were of little use to him, and a manner pompous and overbearing, though redeemed by a kindliness of heart not to be concealed. But he managed to struggle along, writing squibs or pamphlets, reporting speeches in Parliament, trying his hand at plays or poetry, and all the while working away at his Great Dictionary, for which when finished he was to receive £1500, he out of that sum paying his copyists and assistants. He founded a club at which he began to make his reputation as a talker, and out of those conversations with his special friends there came to him the idea of starting a newspaper on the lines of Addison's *Spectator*. But Johnson's heavy hand, his love of long discourses, and the natural melancholy of his nature, did not fit him for work such as this. His *Rambler* only lasted for two years, and certainly made him no fortune, though it may have helped him to exist during that time. His Dictionary, when it was at last completed, gave him a surer position in the literary world of London, and he was paid the sum of £100 for his story of "Rasselas," but most of this went in paying for the last illness and funeral of his mother, and Johnson seems to have been sadly in need of money. Through the influence of some friends, the king, George III. who declared that he was most anxious to offer "brighter prospects to men of literary merit," proposed to give Johnson a pension of £300 a year.

At first he would not hear of accepting it—indeed, there was a rather formidable difficulty in the way, for in his Dictionary he had defined the word pension as being "generally understood to mean pay given to a State hireling for treason to his country." However, the explanations and persuasions of his friends at last overcame the obstacle, and from that time forward he became one of the best known public characters. A favourite such as David Garrick he could never have aspired to be, and to fashionable folks, especially to ladies, he was an untidy, conceited, rugged old man, who ate enormous meals, drank sometimes twenty-five cups of tea at one sitting, wore slovenly and dirty clothes, half-burnt wigs, and slippers almost in tatters. Then he contradicted flatly, and his anger was of a very vehement kind; though he always declared himself to be a "most polite man," and was occasionally ceremonious to a wonderful degree. And yet as he discoursed, men listened to him with such pleasure that they forgot entirely his many monstrous failings. His power of argument was magnificent; never could man so slay an adversary by his words as could this vigorous, quarrelsome, brilliant talker, and though he hit hard, he did not hit cruelly. There was no venom in his words, and however violently he argued, he never seems to have lost a friend through it. On the contrary his circle of admirers constantly grew, and cheerfully submitted to whatever demands he made upon them. Chief among those friends, of course, stands the faithful Boswell, who idolised him with a worship that must have been very wearisome. If Johnson so much as opened his mouth Boswell bent forward wild with eagerness, terrified lest one precious word should escape him; he sat as close to him as he could get, he hung around him like a dog, and no amount of snubbing could damp his ardour. He delighted in asking his master a series of such questions as these:—"What would you do if you were shut up in a castle with a new-born baby?" Or, "Why is a cow's tail long?"

"I will not be baited with what and why," Johnson would answer impatiently. "You have only two subjects, yourself and me. I am sick of both. If your presence does not drive a man out of his house, nothing will."

Johnson's daily life seems to have been mapped out in this wise. He lay in bed late into the morning, surrounded by an admiring circle of men friends, who consulted him on every particular, and listened respectfully to all his opinions. He only rose in time for a late dinner at some tavern which occupied most of the afternoon, as other circles of friends came to listen to him. Then he would drink tea at some house, frequently spending the rest of the evening there, unless he was supping with other acquaintances. Except for his "Lives of the Poets," he wrote but little at this period of his life, and said in excuse, "that a man could do as much good by talking as by writing."

Johnson was generally melancholy, the result of his miserable health to a great extent. Yet his pessimism never affected his wonderfully tender heart. Of his pension he barely spent a third on himself. His house became, after the death of his wife, the haven for a variety of unfortunate and homeless people, and there lived in it Miss Williams, a blind lady, whose temper was not sweet; Levett, a waiter, who had become a quack doctor; Mrs. Desmoulins, and her daughter, old Lichfield acquaintances, and a certain Miss Carmichael. Needless to say there was very little peace in that household, and the poor old Doctor often dreaded going home. "Williams hates everybody," he wrote to his really good friends, the Thrales. "Levett hates Desmoulins, and does not love Williams; Desmoulins hates them both; Poll Carmichael loves none of them."

And yet this "rugged old giant," as he has been called, provided for them all, and for many others who came and went at their will, and who grumbled if everything was not exactly to their liking. As his bodily sufferings increased, he nerved himself to face the end with a touchingly childlike confidence. His thoughts wandered back to his wife. "We have been parted thirty years," he said. "Perhaps she is now praying for me. God help me. God, Thou art merciful, hear my prayers, and enable me to trust in Thee." Years before, when wandering about the dark aisles with Goldsmith, he had pointed to the sleeping figures around, saying, "And our names may perhaps be mixed with theirs." So now he was delighted when, in answer to his question, he was told that he would be buried in Westminster Abbey. "Do not give me any more physic," he asked the doctor at the very last; "I desire to render up my soul to God unclouded."

His funeral was a very quiet one, in great contrast to Garrick's, but his executors felt that "a cathedral service with lights and music" would have been too costly; as it was, the Dean and Chapter charged high fees, and the expenses came to more than two hundred pounds. But Boswell assures us that a "respectable number of his friends attended," and though the Abbey holds many a greater name than that of Samuel Johnson, few that sleep there carried a braver, kindlier heart throughout a life of constant suffering.

Richard Brinsley Sheridan was the son of an actor and manager who had been driven from Ireland, his native country, by a series of misfortunes, and forced to earn his living in England as a teacher of elocution. Want of money, endless debts, a wonderful power of spending freely with an entire absence of forethought, characterised the Sheridan family, and young Richard was brought up on those very happy-go-lucky principles. He was sent to Harrow, where his tutor said, "The sources of his infirmities were a scanty and precarious allowance from the father;" and when he left school, a handsome, brilliant, careless boy of seventeen the state of the family purse made any further education out of the question. His father had settled in

Bath, and here Richard made the acquaintance of that beautiful girl and wonderful singer, Elizabeth Lindley "the link between an angel and a woman," as an Irish bishop called her, whose father also taught music and gave concerts in Bath. She was very unhappy, as her relations wished to force her into a marriage with a rich but elderly gentleman whom she disliked, and in her despair she confided her troubles to Richard Sheridan, the one among her many admirers to whom she had given her heart. To make a long story short, the young couple fled together "on a matrimonial expedition," as the *London Chronicle* worded it; and in spite of all opposition they married, and took up their abode in London, near Portman Square. Though neither of them had any private fortune, Sheridan refused to allow his wife to sing in public. This action of his was warmly discussed by Dr. Johnson's friends, some of whom said that as the young gentleman had not a shilling in the world, he was foolishly delicate or foolishly proud. The Doctor, however, applauded him roundly. "He is a brave man. He resolved wisely and nobly. Would not a gentleman be disgraced by having his wife singing publicly for him? No, sir, there can be no doubt here." But Sheridan had another surprise in store for his friends, and suddenly it became known that he had written a play called "The Rivals," with which the manager of Covent Garden Theatre was entranced, a light, fresh comedy, bearing on fashionable life in Bath. It was produced, and in spite of its many faults, chiefly arising from its having been written in such hot haste, it made a reputation for its author, which prepared the way for his great triumph two years later, when he brought out "The School for Scandal," still the most popular of English comedies. With it he leapt into fame, and though barely twenty-five, he became the man whose name was in everybody's mouth. With characteristic airiness and vagueness in money matters, he took upon himself the responsible duties of manager to Drury Lane Theatre after Garrick retired, and brilliant though he was, his recklessness and want of any business habits, soon brought about a serious state of chaos and rebellion there. This, however, seemed to disturb him but little, and he turned his attention to politics; for at the Literary Club he had made many political friends, including Fox, and he proposed going into Parliament as an independent member, though he believed that "either ministry or opposition would be happy to engage him." He found a seat at Stafford, and freely promised employment in Drury Lane Theatre to those who voted for him; while the necessary money for the election, which of course Sheridan did not possess, was provided by a gentleman in return for a share in the Opera House. His first speech was not a success, but though disappointed he was not daunted.

"It is in me, however," he declared, "and it shall come out."

Within a very short time the House of Commons listened to him as it would listen to no one else. By constant practice he had trained himself to speak perfectly and true to his Irish blood, he had a rich store of language, a fund of wit and humour, and the power of handling every emotion. His great speech in the Warren Hastings case lasted six hours, during the whole of which time he held the House in the hollow of his hand, and when he continued his attack in Westminster Hall, people paid twenty guineas a day to hear him. "I cannot tell you," wrote his devoted wife to her sister, "the adoration that he has excited in the breasts of every class of people. Every party prejudice has been overcome by such a display of genius, eloquence, and goodness."

Sheridan indeed was at the height of his glory; but fame is a dangerous pinnacle for the strongest of men, and Sheridan had no foundation-stones of strength or stability. His wife's death was the beginning of his fall, debt and drink did the rest. All sense of honour seems to have left him where money was concerned. His actors could get no payments save in fair words; he kept the money which resulted from special benefits; he borrowed where he could, and then plunged the more deeply into debt, but he never curbed his extravagances, or went without anything he desired, no matter to what means he had to resort. His buoyancy never failed him. Even when his theatre was burnt to the ground with a loss to him of £200,000, his ready wit did not desert him. He sat drinking his wine in a coffee-house from where he could see the flames, merely remarking to a sympathetic friend, "A man likes to take a glass of wine by his own fireside." All the latter part of his life is painfully sad; debt, poverty, and dishonour hemmed him in, and excessive drinking brought on his last illness. A few days before his death he was discovered almost starving in an unfurnished room. Even then the bailiffs were about to carry him away to the debtors' gaol, and only the doctor, who stayed and nursed him to the end, prevented this last disgrace. The news of his destitution horrified those who remembered him in the days of his dazzling triumphs, and in one paper an eloquent appeal was made to the public generosity, "that we may prefer ministering in the chamber of sadness to ministering at the splendid sorrows which adorn the hearse." In response, crowds of people, royal dukes included, flocked to leave delicacies at his lodging. But it was too late; the fitful life with all its successes and failures was over, the shining eyes of which he had been so proud were closed for ever now, the man who had "done everything perfectly" was no more: the greatest orator of his day was silent.

He had always hoped to be buried in Westminster Abbey, "where there is very snug lying," and if possible next to Fox and Pitt. Moreover, he had desired that his passage to the grave should be quiet and simple. But his friend, Peter Moore, determined that he should have a splendid funeral;

every one was invited and every one came. The procession was of great length, and "such an array of rank, so great a number of distinguished persons" had never before assembled within the memory of the beholders. There was just room for a single grave near to where David Garrick lay, and here Sheridan was buried. While lest his name should be all too soon forgotten, a simply worded tablet was immediately prepared—the last tribute of Peter Moore.

CHAPTER XVII
THE MUSICIANS IN THE ABBEY

The Abbey which has its poets, its writers, and its actors, has also its musicians. Henry Purcell, who lies in the north aisle, spent his short life among Westminster precincts, for he was born in the year 1658 at "an ancient house of Westminster, next door to the public-house and skittle ground—the 'Bell and Fish.'" His father, a "master of musique, who could sing brave songs," was a gentleman of the Chapel Royal, a singing man of the Abbey, master of the choristers there, and, most important of all, the musical copyist. For under the Commonwealth, church choirs and music had been sternly repressed, organs had been broken up, singing books had been burned as superstitious and ungodly, so that when once more the old cathedral services were allowed to be held, but few of the old service books were left, and copyists had to make good the deficiency. The older Purcell died when his little boy was quite young, but Thomas Purcell, an uncle, also a gentleman of the Chapel Royal, took him in hand, and at six years old Henry became a chorister under that delightful old Master of the Children of the chapel, Captain Cook, a musician whose devotion to King Charles I. had led him to turn soldier during the Civil War, and who in his old age had returned to his first love. Purcell was under this original master for eight years, and the old soldier seems to have taken a special pride in the little chorister. But he did not live to see his favourite pupil become famous, for in 1672 the old master died and was buried in the Westminster cloisters, whither he was followed two years later by his successor Humphreys. Then John Blow, another pupil, became Master of the Children, and, as it is specially stated on his monument in the Abbey, at the same time "master to the famous Henry Purcell." It was everything to the boy to be under so rare a teacher, for not only was he an excellent musician, but also a man singularly sympathetic and pure-minded, generous to a degree and without a thought of self. He became organist of Westminster Abbey, but he resigned it because he thought it the very post Purcell could fill with advantage. He then accepted St. Paul's, but having another pupil, Clarke, whom he considered suited to it, he again set his own interests entirely on one side and retired in his favour.

GEORGE FREDERICK HANDEL.

GEORGE FREDERICK HANDEL.

Purcell became a copyist of Westminster, but he chiefly devoted his time to composing operas, as the managers of theatres offered him plenty of work. He also turned his attention to church music and anthems. The year 1680 saw Purcell organist of the Abbey at the age of twenty-two, and soon afterwards he modestly brought out a book of sonatas for two violins, a bass, and the harpsichord or organ, in the preface to which he said he had faithfully endeavoured a just imitation of the most famed Italian masters, and went on to explain that, lest the terms of art should puzzle his readers, *adagio* imported nothing but a very slow movement; *presto*, *largo*, and *vivace*, a very brisk, swift, or fast movement; and *piano* a soft one. Operas, anthems, and odes all seem to have flowed easily from his ready pen, and a list of them would only be tedious. Among his anthems, perhaps the best known is the one composed for the coronation of James II., "I was glad when they said unto me, we will go into the House of the Lord." The coronation of William and Mary, however, led to quite a stir in the inner circle of the Abbey, for Purcell allowed a number of persons to watch the ceremony from his organ-loft, charging them for admission. Now to this there was no objection, but when rumour related that the fees so obtained amounted to some hundreds of pounds, the Dean and Chapter, presuming that this was worth contending for, claimed the money as their dues. Purcell declared that he had a right to organ-loft fees; and the feeling must have run high, as in an old chapter note-book there runs the order that "Mr. Purcell, the *organ blower*, is to pay such money as was received by him for places in the organ-loft, in default thereof his place to be declared null and void." How the quarrel ended is not known. However, Purcell did not leave the Abbey, but went on with his flow of compositions, and won from the poet Dryden the statement that "here we have at length found an *Englishman* equal with the best abroad." It was to Purcell that Dryden turned for the music to his opera King Arthur, "for," he declared, "the artful hands of Mr. Purcell compose with so great a genius, that he has nothing to fear but an ignorant, ill-judging audience." Queen Mary seems to have had a liking for very popular music, and once seriously offended Purcell, when some of his compositions were being performed to her, by asking to have sung instead the old Scotch ballad, "Cold and raw." So when he next had to compose a birthday ode for her, he carefully introduced the air of "Cold and raw." When the Queen died he wrote two beautiful anthems for the funeral service in the Abbey, "Blessed is the man," and "Thou knowest, Lord, the secrets of our hearts," of which a singer in the choir writes, "I appeal to all who were present, to those who understood music as well as to those who did not, whether they ever heard anything so rapturously fine and solemn, so heavenly in the operation, drawing tears from all, and yet a plain natural composition, which shows the power of music when 'tis rightly fitted and adapted to devotional purposes." At many a great public funeral since, this touching music of Purcell's has been used, and nothing has taken its place.

Delicate from his boyhood, it was early evident that Henry Purcell's life as organist of the Abbey was to be a short one, and in the year 1695 a pathetic little note was added to his song, "Lovely Albinia," stating that, "This is the last song the author sett before his sickness." His illness was just a wasting away, "dangerously ill in the constitution, but in good and perfect minde and memory, thanks be to God," to quote his own words. A touching account has been given, in Dr. Cumming's "Life of Purcell" of the closing scene in this bright young life:—

"He lay in a house on the west side of Dean's Yard, Westminster, from whence he could probably hear some faint murmurs of the Evensong service wafted from the old Abbey close by, some well-remembered phrase, perhaps, of one of his own soul-stirring anthems. The Psalms for the day (the 21st) to be chanted at that evening service, concluded with words he had set to music which the world was not likely soon to forget, music which still remains unsurpassed in truthfulness and dignity. A more noble or more fitting death-chant for a child of son" it would be difficult to find—

"'Blessed be the Lord God of Israel

From everlasting, and world without end.

And let all the people say, Amen.'

"So his gentle spirit passed into the better world, there to continue his service of song and praise in fulness and perfection."

His own anthems were sung at his funeral; the organ he had so loved pealed out its rich farewell to him; and on his gravestone are these words in Latin—

"Dead? No, he lives, while yonder organ's sound,

And sacred echoes to the choir rebound."

Dr. Blow went back to his old post as Abbey organist on the death of his pupil, and devoted himself to church music. "To this," he said, "I have ever especially consecrated the thoughts of my whole life. All the rest I consider but as blossoms and leaves. With this I began my youthful raptures in this art, with this I hope calmly and comfortably to end my days." His best known anthem, "I beheld, and lo!" was written within a week for James II., who had asked him if he could do as well as the Italian composers, and the king, much pleased with it, sent Father Peter to congratulate Blow after service. The priest, however, took it upon himself to add that, "in his opinion, it was somewhat too long." "That," replied Blow scornfully, "is only one fool's opinion. I heed it not."

Blow, who died and was buried opposite to Purcell in 1708, was considered by his fellow-musicians "to be the greatest master in the world for the organ, especially in his voluntaries, which he played gravely and seriously." The inscription on his grave declares "that his musical compositions are a far nobler monument to his memory than any that can be raised to him," and on the open music-book below is given the *Gloria* from his fine Jubilate in C major.

William Croft succeeded Blow as organist, and most of his musical compositions were written for special occasions; as, for example, his anthem, "I will give thanks," which was produced after the famous

Blenheim victory. He, too, was of a lovable, kindly disposition, and the inscription on his monument ends thus quaintly: "He emigrated to the Heavenly Choir, with that Concert of Angels, for which he was better fitted, adding his Hallelujah. Awake up my glory! Awake lute and harp! I myself will awake right early."

Half a century later, that prince among musicians, George Frederick Handel, was buried in the Poets' Corner. Though not of English birth or upbringing, he had become an English subject, and had found a warm welcome in the hearts of the English people. From babyhood he had shown the bent of his mind. Even his toys were tiny trumpets, horns, and Jew's harps, much to the annoyance of his kind old father, the well-known doctor in the German town of Halle, who thought this craze of George Frederick's should be forcibly put a stop to, and who decreed therefore, that "there was to be no more jingling, neither was he to go into houses where music was practised."

The boy was outwardly submissive, but the longing within was too strong for him. Somehow he got possession of an old clavichord, one of those muffled instruments on which musical monks could practise without disturbing the brethren, and this he smuggled up to a garret in the roof of the house, where, with storks to bear him company, he played away to his soul's content. It was in utter ignorance of all this, that Dr. Handel took the little boy with him once, when summoned to attend the Court at Sache-Weisseufels, where the reigning duke delighted in learning, art, and music. Naturally, George Frederick found his way to the organ-loft, where the good-natured organist lifted him up, for he was but seven, that he might touch the notes. To his surprise, the child began to play with a practised hand, and with so much style, that the Grand Duke, who heard him, sent for the doctor and begged him not further to thwart such a genius. So from this time forward the boy was allowed to study seriously, under the enthusiastic organist of the Liebfrauen Kirche in Halle, who taught him to play the harpsichord, the organ, the violin, the hautboy, and other instruments, besides the art of counterpoint. When, after years of study, he came to England, where Purcell's death had made a blank not yet filled up, he was received with open arms, his fame having preceded him. At once he was engaged to write an opera for the Queen's Theatre, and having discovered a *libretto* which greatly pleased him, a stirring story of the Crusades, his ideas poured forth so fast and so easily, that in a fortnight he had completed the work, and his "Rinaldo" was soon the rage of the season. Although Handel held the post of Kapellmeister to the Elector of Hanover, and had only been given leave of absence for a "reasonable time," he could not tear himself away from London, so well did he like the place and the people.

From operatic music he turned to oratorio. The Duke of Chandos, who lived in almost regal state at his palace at Cannons, maintained an orchestra and choir, so that the musical services of his private chapel might be as nearly perfect as possible. To Handel he offered the post of musical director, and thus, in church music, the great composer's genius found a new outlet. The wonderful old Bible stories, with their vigour and dramatic force, and the stately Bible language, with its rich simplicity, strongly appealed to him, and it is because of his oratorios and cantatas rather than through his other works, that the name and the memory of Handel remain for ever fresh among us. "Esther" was his first great work in this new line, first performed in a private house at Westminster by the children of the Chapel Royal, assisted by the choristers of the Abbey. So pleased were the guests, that a few days later the performance was repeated at the Crown and Anchor tavern in the Strand, and would further have been given at the Opera House, had not the Bishop of London refused permission for any choristers to take part. Eventually, with a new band of singers, the oratorio was publicly given, by the king's command, in the Haymarket Theatre, "with a great number of voices and instruments," and it was specially announced that "there would be no acting on the stage, though the house would be fitted up in a decent manner for the audience." To this performance came all the royal family, while so great was the crowd, that hundreds were turned empty away, and six extra performances had to be at once arranged for.

"Deborah" and "Athaliah" soon followed, also "Acis and Galatea," which latter, though not sacred music, served to increase his popularity, his audiences numbering thousands. A great blow to him was the death of Queen Caroline, his kindest, most sympathetic friend, and in composing the anthem for her funeral in the Abbey he wrote from the depths of his sorrowing heart. Nothing could exceed the pathos or the sweetness of that music, with its undercurrent of desolate grief, and when, in the February of 1901, the Abbey was thronged with a great representative assembly, there to pay a last tribute of reverence to another queen, this anthem rang once more through the old walls.

Success to Handel was but a stepping-stone, leading him towards something higher. He was never satisfied with himself, but went on from strength to strength, conscious of his own power to produce music which should live for ever. His "Saul" and his "Israel in Egypt" showed how completely he could throw himself into the spirit of his subject, and through the pages of his music, Saul, Goliath and David, the Children of Israel, the Egyptians and Miriam, all spring into life for us. As we listen, the story takes new shape, and the events which surround it stand out with a new lurid light.

But the greatest work of all was not produced in London. Handel went on a visit to Dublin, where he found audiences "more numerous and polite than he had ever seen on like occasions," and the general enthusiasm "so put him in good spirits," that after completing a second series of concerts a special performance was announced, at which "Mr. Handel's new grand oratorio called 'The Messiah'" was to be given. Furthermore, as a great crowd was anticipated, ladies were begged to come without their hoops, and gentlemen without their swords, for in this way quite another hundred persons could be accommodated.

"The finest composition of musick that was ever heard," was the verdict of that "grand, polite, and crowded audience," and a liberal sum was received for the "relief of the prisoners in the gaols," to which charity Handel, with peculiar appropriateness, had offered to devote the profits. Strange to say, the new work did not at once take root in London, but with repeated performances its triumph became steady and lasting. The subject was a great one. The smallest mistake in dealing with it would have jarred painfully, and so little would have robbed that simple story of its majesty. But Handel gave to it a new glory, a new splendid dignity, and to many a heart those familiar words have struck home with a reality hitherto undreamt of, through the beauty and the force of his music. Reverently he touched the great mystery, and as the story took life before his awe-struck eyes, he translated it into harmonies worthy of so vast a theme.

"I did think I did see all heaven before me, and the great God Himself," said Handel reverently, as he spoke of the Hallelujah Chorus, which so deeply impressed the audience in the Covent Garden Theatre on the first night that, one and all, with the king setting the example, they sprang to their feet and stood to the end. The musician had led them into the very Presence of God.

Other oratorios followed—"Samson," "Judas Maccabeus," and "Jephtha"—but none of them equalled "The Messiah." To this great work Handel had given freely of his best, before that dark cloud arose which saddened all his later days. For gradually blindness crept over him, till at last his sight departed for ever. In spite of this he continued to conduct his own works, and to the last insisted on being led to the organ, that he might play the concertos and voluntaries between the parts of his oratorios. And we hear how, when the fine solo in "Samson"—

"Total eclipse—no sun, no moon:
All dark amid the blaze of noon,"

was sung with great feeling at one performance, the sight of the blind composer sitting at the organ was so indescribably touching, that many present were moved to tears.

On the 5th of April, 1759, a notice appeared in the *Public Advertiser* that "The Messiah" would be performed in Covent Garden on the 6th of April for the last time in the season.

Handel conducted his work, was carried fainting from the hall, and in less than a week had passed away. His own wish, when he knew how near the end loomed, was that he might die on Good Friday, "in hopes," he said, "of meeting my good God and sweet Saviour on the day of His resurrection." And in this trustful spirit he went to the God he had so worthily worshipped.

His funeral was intended to be private, but thousands came to it, and though no trace remains of the music sung on that occasion, I cannot help hoping that some boy's clear voice rang through the aisles as he sang "I know that my Redeemer liveth." Nothing would have been so fitting, and those are the words, nobler far than any epitaph, which the good taste of some friend caused to be inscribed on his monument in the Poets' Corner.

CHAPTER XVIII
WILBERFORCE AND HIS FELLOW-WORKERS

The desire of Abou Ben Adhem that his name might be handed on as one "who loved his fellow-men" would form a fitting epitaph not only to those great-hearted workers in the cause of humanity whom the Abbey has delighted to honour—William Wilberforce, the liberator of the slave, and David Livingstone, the missionary and explorer in Darkest Africa—but also to those others who toiled with them in the same great cause of freedom, and whose claims to the grateful recollection of the nation are recorded only by monuments—Granville Sharp, Jonas Hanway, Zachary Macaulay, Fowell Buxton, and Anthony Astley Cooper, Earl of Shaftesbury. A few words first about one of these latter, Granville Sharp, for he it was who became the pioneer of that noble band who never ceased from their labours till they had freed the slave on British territory.

He was only a linen-draper's assistant, afterwards becoming a clerk in the Ordnance Office; but the monotony of his work never allowed monotony or narrowness to enter his life. His heart was responsive to every high claim, and difficulties only meant to him obstacles to be overcome. Courage, energy, and determination were his watchwords. His brother was a doctor in Mincing Lane, who saw poor people free of charge, and among his patients was a negro called Jonathan Strong, who had been brought to London by his master, a lawyer, from Barbadoes, only to be turned out into the streets friendless and homeless when he fell ill. Dr. Sharp treated him so successfully that he became quite well, and Granville Sharp found him a situation with a chemist, which he kept for some years, until one day he was seen and recognised by his old employer, who finding him well and active had him seized, and kept in custody until he could be shipped off to the West Indies. Jonathan, in despair, thought of Granville Sharp, and appealed to him for protection. Sharp at once went to the Lord Mayor, who gave judgment that the man had been wrongfully seized and held without a warrant, and ordered him to be at once set at liberty. But then arose an unlooked-for difficulty. Jonathan's late master had sold him, and his new owner appeared with the bill of sale, claiming his property and declaring he had been robbed. Then came the question as to whether the traffic in slaves which went on openly, especially in London and Liverpool, was lawful or not. Was a slave free when he reached England, or could he be seized and compelled to go back? The lawyers declared that no English law protected the slave. Granville Sharp refused to believe it. During the next few years he spent every hour of his spare time in studying the law; in wading through masses of dry Acts; in sorting, sifting, verifying, and quoting, though more than one friendly lawyer assured him that all his work was a useless waste of time. But the result of his labours surprised them as much as it cheered the heart of Granville Sharp, for it proved that "there was nothing in any English law or statute which could justify the enslaving of others." He at once published a plain, clear pamphlet which he called "The Injustice of Tolerating Slavery in England;" and further than that, certain in the justice of his cause, he went down, armed with a writ of Habeas Corpus, to Gravesend, where he had been told of a captured negro who was being taken back by force. He found the wretched man chained to the mainmast, but after a fierce struggle he got possession of him and returned with him in triumph to London. He did much the same in the case of another negro called James Somerset, whose owner promptly brought the matter before Lord Chief-Justice Mansfield, who declared the question to be so important and doubtful a one that he must take the opinion of the judges upon it. A very lengthy trial followed. At last the court gave the opinion, that every man in England had a right to his liberty unless he had broken the law; that the power to seize or claim a slave in England had never been acknowledged by the law, and that therefore Somerset was free. It was the first great step towards a more far-reaching freedom, and it was mainly won by the careful, devoted study of Granville Sharp, whose pamphlet had made a great impression on the Lord Chief-Justice. The next step was to found a society for the Abolition of Slavery, and to this flocked a number of men, chiefly Quakers, who banded themselves together with most steadfast determination never to cease from their labours until Parliament had declared all traffic in slaves to be illegal in every part of the British Empire. This was a gigantic undertaking, for British merchants dealt largely in slaves, and they were so powerful a body that it was certain the Government would shrink from opposing them. But this little band of religious, earnest, chivalrous men had the strength which comes from the conviction that theirs was a righteous cause destined in the end to triumph over every obstacle. One of their number was William Wilberforce, a young and a delicate-looking man, who when only twenty years of age had been elected as member for Hull, with no powerful support except what he derived from his own personal influence and his independent character. In London he soon made his mark. Pitt became his greatest friend, and in society he was made much of, so full was he of wit and charm; while in addition to his many other gifts, he was an excellent singer. But fascinating and absorbing as was the life into which he was then thrown, it did not satisfy him. Even while he stood on a height, he caught the glimpse of the height that is higher, the which having once seen, no true man can rest until he has attained it. As the vision unfolded itself before his eyes Wilberforce became a changed man, so much so that for a time it was believed by his friends that he would leave public life and go quietly to the country. But his vision, instead of narrowing down his conception of duty, broadened it out. "To shut myself up," he said to his mother, "would merit no better name than desertion. It would be flying from the post in which I have been placed, and I could not look for the blessing of God upon my retirement."

Just at this crisis he came under the influence of two or three people who felt intensely on the slavery question, and in him they saw the very Parliamentary champion they needed. With his great influence, his powers of speech, his many friends, his independent character, and his high enthusiasms, Wilberforce seemed destined for this work, and he eagerly grasped it. Here was a direct call from God, and to him now every gift, every power he possessed was held as a sacred trust. Besides, he was respected by all parties in the House, and the hope of the Anti-Slavery party lay in their cause being non-political. Victory could only crown their efforts when the whole moral feeling of the nation was aroused, and much, very much hung on their choice of a leader. "Mr. Wilberforce," said Granville Sharp, "with his position as member for the largest county, the great influence of his personal connections, added to his unblemished character, will secure every advantage to the cause." So from the year 1787, William Wilberforce, chivalrous as any knight of old, gave up his life to the righting of a great wrong and to the deliverance of the oppressed.

For twenty years the fight went on, and though he was successfully opposed over and over again by the strong West Indian party, assisted by many of the Tories and the majority in the House of Lords, he was never baffled or disheartened.

"I am in no degree discouraged," he said after one defeat. "It is again my intention to move next year for the abolition, and though I dare not hope to carry the bill through both Houses, yet, if I do not deceive myself, this infamous and wicked traffic will not last out the century."

Both Pitt and Fox supported Wilberforce, but the opposition was solid and wealthy, and the bill above mentioned, brought in during the session of 1796, was again defeated by 78 votes to 61. The Revolution in France was causing much excitement and apprehension among all classes of Englishmen, and the opponents of Wilberforce attempted, among other things, to prove that he was at heart a revolutionist, and that his efforts to set free a class who had always been kept in slavery showed that he believed in the revolutionary "rights of men."

"There is no greater enemy to all such delusions," Pitt warmly and indignantly made reply.

But by 1804 a change had come about. All fears regarding a revolution in England were allayed; every year Wilberforce and his party, by their steady persistence, their moderation, and their powerful appeals to the highest motives, had gained converts to their cause both in and out of Parliament, and the Bill of May 30, 1804, was carried in the Commons by a majority of over 70. This was by far the greatest triumph Wilberforce had yet gained, but to his regret it was not proceeded with by the House of Lords, who had thrown out the two previous bills, though, in fairness be it said, the majorities with which they had come from the Commons had been very small. However, the Abolitionists were by now accustomed to possessing their souls in patience, and they knew the tide had turned in their favour. The death of Pitt put Fox, who of the two men was the more zealous supporter of their cause, into power; he prevailed upon a majority in the Cabinet to declare that the slave trade was contrary to the principles of justice, humanity, and sound policy, and should be abolished by the House with all practicable expediency. In 1807 the bill was again brought in, this time to be carried by a majority of 283 to 16. The Solicitor-General made a powerful speech, in which he contrasted the feelings of the Emperor of the French in all his greatness with those of that "honoured man who would soon lay his head on his pillow, knowing that the slave trade was no more." At this reference to Wilberforce the House burst into delighted applause. They had seen him during his many years of brave fighting, and now that victory was at hand, they cheered him with such cheers as had seldom before been given to any man sitting in his place in either House. Further opposition was useless, and the bill became law.

"God will bless this country," was Wilberforce's earnest declaration, in the gladdest, proudest moment of his life. His own share in the good work he counted as nothing.

Much was won, but not all. The slave trade was abolished—that is to say, slaves could not be taken to any British possession, or put on any British ships, and our warships were instructed to capture any vessels disobeying this order. Yet slaves were still held by British masters in the West Indies and on the American coast. Wilberforce, far from resting content with his victory, made ready for a second fight, having now for his lieutenant in the House of Commons, Fowell Buxton, called Elephant Buxton, on account of his great size, a man as energetic and indefatigable by nature as he was powerful in appearance. However sad the lot of the slaves, they had been bought and paid for under the old law by their masters, just as if they had been cattle or any other marketable produce, so that if they were to be set free by law, the money spent on them must in honour be returned to these masters, or otherwise they would be ruined, and a great injustice would be done. To compensate the owners, and thus honourably to free every slave, required a large sum of money, not less than £20,000,000; but so changed had become public opinion throughout England, and consequently in Parliament, that the money was voted in 1833. For the last few years Wilberforce had been in failing health, and his old place in the House of Commons knew him no more; but Buxton had valiantly carried on the work, in a spirit best illustrated by some words of his own:—

"The longer I live, the more certain I am that the great difference between men, between the feeble and the powerful, the great and the insignificant, is energy, *invincible determination*—a purpose once fixed, and then, death or victory! That quality will do anything that can be done in the world, and no talents, no circumstances, no opportunities, will make a two-legged creature a man without it."

Wilberforce just lived to hear the glorious news which crowned his life and work, and to realise that from that day forward there would not exist a slave in any British colony. It was the great triumph of righteousness, and humbly he thanked God that his had been the privilege of leading the little army which had gone on from strength to strength until its mission was accomplished. Two or three days later he passed peacefully away, and immediately after his death this letter, signed by all the leading members of both Houses of Parliament, was sent to his son:—

"We being anxious upon public grounds to show our respect for the memory of the late William Wilberforce, and being also satisfied that public honours cannot be more fitly bestowed than upon such benefactors of mankind, earnestly request that he may be buried in Westminster Abbey, and that we, with others who agree with us in these sentiments, may have permission to attend the funeral."

So to the Abbey he was brought. All public business was suspended, and public men of every rank followed him to the grave. Members of Parliament were there in numbers to show their reverence for one whose eloquence had ever been put to the noblest uses, and, fitly enough, his body was laid close to the tombs of Pitt and Fox.

"If you carry this point in your life, that life will be far better spent than in being prime minister many years," a much-loved friend had said to Wilberforce when he first resolved to devote himself to the cause of the slave, and to set aside all thought of his own career and ambition. The young enthusiast had counted the cost, but it had not changed him from his determination, and though he lived and died plain William Wilberforce, member of parliament, the Abbey roll of honour is made richer by his name, and he rests worthily in the Statesmen's Corner, great as any of those among whom he lies.

Just as Wilberforce was nearing the close of his life, a young spinner in some mills near Glasgow, glowing with enthusiasm, was resolving to offer himself as a medical missionary to China or Africa. David Livingstone, for he it was, came of homely Scottish stock.

"The only point of family tradition I feel proud of is this," he declared. "One of my forefathers, when on his death-bed, called his children round him and said, 'I have searched diligently throughout all the traditions of our family, and I never could find there was a dishonest man among them.... So I leave this precept with you, Be honest.'"

DAVID LIVINGSTONE.

And perfectly honest David Livingstone certainly was to the end of his days. Though he went to work in the mills when ten years old, his love of books made him learn eagerly in every spare moment and on so late into the night, that his mother, half in anger, half in pride, often went to him at midnight and carried off every available light. However David was a sturdy youth, or twelve hours' work each day in the factory added to six hours' reading would have ruined his health. He was twenty-five when he offered himself to the London Missionary Society, and he was sent for a three months' trial to a training-place in Essex. But when he had to deliver his first sermon, every idea fled from his brain. "I have forgotten all I had to say, friends," he announced frankly, and left the pulpit. But for his other sterling qualities, this would have put an end to his career. As it was, he was given another three months and came successfully out of the ordeal, after which he went for two years to a London hospital. Africa was to be his destination, "Don't go to an old station," Dr. Moffat, the veteran missionary, said to him on the eve of his ordination. "But push on to the vast unoccupied district to the north, where on a clear morning I have seen the smoke of a thousand villages no missionary has ever reached." Kuruman, an important station of the Missionary Society, more than seven hundred miles up country, was his first halting-place after leaving Cape Town, and he set himself with great energy to learn the language of the natives, acting at the same time as their doctor. In this last capacity he soon made his name famous, and patients came to him over enormous distances. Splendid patients they were too, he always declared, perfectly obedient and of extraordinary courage. When once he had mastered their language, which he did in a short while, he combined his missionary and medical work very happily.

In 1843 he left Kuruman to form a new station about two hundred miles to the north-east at Mabotsa, and whilst here he married a daughter of Dr. Moffat, a girl who had lived among missionaries for many years, and so was accustomed to the rough, solitary existence which would be her lot. "My time," wrote Livingstone to a friend, "is filled up with building, gardening, cobbling, doctoring, tinkering, carpentering, gun-mending, farriering, preaching, schooling, teaching, and lecturing, while my wife, in addition to her usual work, makes clothes, soap, and candles, and teaches classes of children."

Gradually it dawned upon Livingstone that a great work awaited him in the interior, but it was a work which he must face alone. "I must not be a more sorry soldier than those who serve an earthly sovereign," he wrote to the Directors of the Mission, to whose care he commended his family. "And so powerfully am I convinced it is the will of God, that I will go, no matter who opposes."

Therefore in 1852, having seen his wife and children off to England, he started in his Cape waggon and again made for Kuruman, after leaving which he was constantly harassed by parties of Boers, who believed he was teaching their slaves to rise in revolt. But he reached the land of Sebituan, a friendly chief, safely, and found the warmest welcome awaiting him. As doctor and missionary his hands were full, and seeing the field of work opening all around him, he grew more and more anxious to become the pioneer missioner to the very interior. Fever, he realised, would be his worst enemy. "I would like," he wrote in his journal, "to discover some remedy for that terrible disease. I must go to parts where it prevails most and try to discover if the natives have a remedy for it.... I mean to open up a path to the interior or perish. I never have had the shadow of a doubt. Cannot the love of Christ carry the missionary where the slave trade carries the trader?"

The travels of Livingstone through that unknown country which he practically discovered, would have to be closely followed on a map from point to point to be made clear. Otherwise they are a mere string of strange names. He set out in the November of 1853. "I had three muskets for my people and a double-barrelled gun for myself," he said. "My ammunition was distributed through the luggage, that we might not be left without a supply. Our chief hopes for food were in our guns. I carried twenty pounds of beads, a few pounds of tea, sugar, and coffee. One tin canister was filled with spare clothes, another was stored with medicines, a third with books, and a fourth with a magic lantern. A small tent, a sheep-skin, and a horse-rug completed my equipment, as an array of baggage would have excited the tribes." Four years later, worn out by frequent attacks of fever, but otherwise perfectly satisfied with the result of his journeyings into parts where as yet no other Englishman had penetrated, Livingstone sailed for England, having heard nothing of his family for three years. He at once became the hero of the hour; dinners were given, speeches were made in his honour, and he was asked to equip and command a government expedition for the exploration of that part of South-Eastern Africa through which the river Zambesi flows. After some consideration he decided to undertake this, though it meant that from henceforth he would cease to be a missionary pure and simple. But he looked at the question in its broadest aspect. "Wherever I go," he said, "I go as the servant of God, following the leadings of His Hand. My ideal of a missionary is not that of a dumpy man with a Bible under his arm. I feel I am not my own. I am serving Christ in labouring as well as in preaching, and having by His help got information which I hope will bring blessing to Africa, am I to hide the light under a bushel, because some will not consider it sufficiently or even at all missionary? I refrain from taking any salary from Missionary Societies, so no loss is sustained by any one."

In the March of 1858 he returned to his work, and Mrs. Livingstone started with him to go at least as far as Kuruman. This second Zambesi expedition lasted nearly six years, and as Livingstone stood on the shores of Lake Nyasa, he was able to feel that he stood where no white man had ever stood before him. Three years later, Bishop Mackenzie and six missionaries followed him here, but among the many sorrows which fell upon him about this time, was the death of the "good bishop" from fever, the death of his own wife, and the growing feeling that the extreme unhealthiness of the district would make anything like colonisation impossible. His third great journey, commenced in 1866, was his last, and when more than three years passed by without any tidings of him, owing to his long stay in the country of the cannibal Manyema, the editor of the *New York Herald* equipped an expedition to go in search of him the man in charge of it being Henry Stanley, whose orders were "to find Livingstone, living or dead." It was in 1871 that the two men met face to face at Tanganyika, and the relieving party found the object of their search almost alone, worn out, fever-stricken, cut off from all news of his children, and as near to despair as was possible to one of his strong faith and brave nature. But when Stanley, after many attacks of fever, returned to Europe, he could not persuade his companion to leave the country, which held him as a magnet. He was determined to find the sources of the Nile, and the determination cost him his life. The district through which he fought his way has been described as "one vast sponge," and was poisonous to the last degree. His strength failed, and though his faithful natives bore him along on a litter with the utmost tenderness, his sufferings were terrible. He died on the first of May 1873, alone save for his natives, "the greatest and best man who ever explored Africa." Believing that to labour is to pray, if the work be done for God's glory and not for self-advancement, David Livingstone's life had been one long prayer, and throughout those lonely dangerous journeyings the sense of God's Presence had been his stay and comfort. Around the last hours of the brave man a veil is drawn. But who can doubt that the love of God overshadowed him, and made even that desolate, marsh-like place a road of light, along which the worn-out traveller passed to Him, his one true goal?

His native servants behaved with beautiful devotion, and would not leave him alone in death. His heart they buried where he died, but as best they could they embalmed his body, and by slow stages made their way towards the coast with their precious burden, which they were determined somehow to get to England. At one time every one of them was stricken down by the terrible fever, but on they went for many a month, through swamp and desert and through hostile lands. Nothing could daunt them. Their master must lie in his home, far away, over the seas. When at last they reached Zanzibar and handed over the trust they had so loyally guarded, they barely received a word of thanks. But one friend of Livingstone's came forward just in time, and undertook to pay all expenses for two of their number to go to England and be present at the funeral. Susi and Chuma, two of the slaves the Doctor had freed, and his most devoted attendants, were chosen to go with their master till the end of his journey. It was almost a year after his death when the great traveller was borne into the Abbey, and those two stood there among the mourners, awe-struck but contented. Their task was accomplished; the white man who had been their deliverer lay among his own people.

A very simple inscription, ending with the words, "Other sheep I have which are not of this fold. Them also must I bring," marks the place in the nave where, with a curious significance, Livingstone, an architect of the Empire, lies close to other architects, Sir Charles Barry, Sir Gilbert Scott, and John Pearson, whose works are to be seen in the Houses of Parliament, Westminster Abbey, and Westminster Hall.

We cannot leave these lovers of humanity without one glance at the statue of the good Earl of Shaftesbury, the friend of little children and of all those who were desolate and oppressed. Possessed of all that could make life attractive to him, he devoted himself to his dying day to the service of his fellows, and his name will go down to history as the liberator of the white slaves in England. For, as Wilberforce championed the negro, Shaftesbury fought long and steadily in the cause of the women and children employed in factories and collieries, who worked sometimes for thirty-six hours at a time under the most appalling conditions. At last he forced Parliament to take action, and to pass the Ten Hours' Bill, besides insisting that factory inspectors were appointed to see that all workers were protected as the law intended they should be. That was his greatest work, but to tell of all that he did would fill a volume with a record of golden deeds. Ever ready to lead an unpopular cause; an enthusiast without being a fanatic; strong, clear-headed, steadfast, reliable, and single-hearted, he stands out a noble figure in the social history of the nineteenth century. Just before his death, in 1885, his friend, Dean Stanley, in writing to him, spoke of Westminster Abbey as the place where he should rest. But the old man shook his head and begged to be buried in his country home.

However, the Abbey could not altogether refrain from doing him honour, and through streets lined with people, many of them the poorest in the land, most of them wearing some outward sign of mourning, a bit of black ribbon or a scrap of crape, followed by deputations from almost every charitable association, the coffin was carried to Westminster. Around it stood high and low, rich and poor. The wreaths sent by royal princes lay Bide by side with the tributes from the flower-girls and the boys on the training-ships. A mighty volume of sound ascended to the vaulted roof, as the familiar hymn was sung—

"Let saints on earth in concert sing,

With those whose rest is won,

For all the servants of our King

In earth and heaven are one!"

Then the organ ceased, the Blessing was given, and the great procession left the Abbey to the march of the coster-mongers' band, to the tramp of thousands of feet, whose way in life he had made more easy and more blessed.

In the north aisle of the nave rest three great men, builders in another way, who have served the world by their thoughts—Newton, Herschel, and Darwin.

Sir Isaac Newton made one of the most wonderful discoveries in the world of science and nature, the law of gravitation, and also invented a method by which the whole course of a comet could be calculated. On his monument you will see a globe, covered with constellations and the path of a comet, while below are groups of children weighing the sun and the moon. The long Latin epitaph was one which greatly offended Dr. Johnson, who said that "none but philosophers could understand it."

Sir John Herschel was the son of a distinguished father, and from his boyhood he resolved to follow in his father's footsteps. "To put my shoulders to the wheel, and to leave the world a little better than I found it," was the ideal he set before himself whilst at Cambridge, and in this spirit he carried on the work of making a careful study of the stars in the southern hemisphere, which had never been done before.

Besides astronomy he was devoted to books, especially to poetry, and translated many of Schiller's poems, as well as parts of the "Iliad," into English. "Give a man," he said, "once the taste for reading good books, and you place him in contact with the best society in every period of history, with the wisest, the wittiest, the tenderest, the bravest, and the purest of characters who have adorned humanity. You make him a denizen of all nations, a contemporary of all ages."

His eyes were fixed on the stars; his heart was ever set on those things that are above. These are the beautiful words in which he has described the object and the end of all his study:—

"To spring even a little way aloft, to carol for awhile in bright and sunny regions—to open the doors of the human mind to let in light and knowledge, always sure that right will come right at last—to rise to the level of our strength, and if we must sink again, to sink not exhausted but exercised, not dulled in spirit, but cheered in heart—such may be the contented and happy lot of him who can repose with equal confidence on the bosom of the earth, or ride above the mists of earth into the empyrean day."

He died loaded with honours in 1871, though no man sought fame or honour less.

"Enough if cleansed at last from earthly stain,

My homeward step be firm, and pure my evening sky."

Thus had he written, and how could longing soar higher?

CHARLES DARWIN.

Charles Darwin was perhaps the greatest man of the three, for after long years of patient hard work, bravely carried on through bad health, he produced as the result of his experiments a wonderful book called "The Origin of Species," in which he explained how the world, instead of being created all at once as it is to-day, has grown slowly and very gradually, through many processes, just as we ourselves, our minds, and all our powers have developed from a state of savagery into our present state of civilisation. When first Darwin published his work explaining all this, some people were frightened and horrified, and declared that he wanted to upset all the old ideas about God and religion. But thus they had said whenever a new discovery had been made, and yet with each new discovery we have only learnt more and more how great God is, and how—

"He moves in a mysterious way

His wonders to perform."

So all such great discoverers as Newton, Herschel, and Darwin give us in reality the same message, which is never to be afraid of truth, for truth comes from God, and the only danger is when we doubt, even for a moment, that it must come triumphant out of every honest discussion.

CHAPTER XIX
PITT AND THE STATESMEN'S CORNER

When William Pitt, Earl of Chatham, was buried in the north transept at Westminster Abbey in the year 1778, Parliament having decreed that "he ought to be brought near to the dust of kings," and not lie in St. Paul's Cathedral, earnestly though the City of London begged for this favour, he drew to that part of the Abbey so many distinguished ministers of the Crown, that it soon received the name of the Statesmen's Corner, in distinction to the Poets' Corner which Chaucer had created. Pitt the elder and Pitt the younger, Fox, Canning, Palmerston, Castlereagh, Grattan, and Gladstone—these are the names which most closely belong to the Statesmen's Corner, and through their lives we can catch glimpses of English political life from the reign of George II. down to our own day.

William Pitt entered Parliament in 1735, and joined the party calling themselves the Patriots, rallying round the Prince of Wales, who was always at enmity with the King and Queen. This party naturally included any one opposed to Walpole, still the all-powerful minister at Court. The Patriots were young men, talented and vigorous, and their first signal victory was obtained when they forced Walpole into declaring war against Spain, that country, they insisted, having systematically hampered, injured, and insulted British traders, in spite of treaties and negotiations. Walpole was before all else a peace minister; but the Patriots, supported by the country, declared that war was necessary if England was to uphold her position and power on the seas, and Pitt, full of energy and eloquence, was one of the most powerful, though one of the youngest, among the Patriots. This war, as Walpole had foreseen, was but the prelude to a general disturbance; England became involved in Continental quarrels, and the Stuart party seized this opportunity of making a final, though unsuccessful attempt to place Prince Charles Edward on the throne. After nine years a treaty of peace was signed at Aix-la-Chapelle, and broadly speaking, the result of the war, so far as this country was concerned, was that we had been successful on the seas, in Canada, and in India, unsuccessful on the Continent. Walpole had resigned, Newcastle was a Prime Minister "who had neither judgment nor ability," and Pitt became more and more the ruling power. The year 1757 saw him virtually Prime Minister, and with his whole might he set himself to arouse a national spirit in England, to make the people see that our real future lay not in the Continent, but in the Colonies. "I can save this country, nobody else can," he said confidently at this time, and it was no vain boast. The years which followed were glorious years. In India,

France had joined with a powerful native prince to oust the British traders, and had been utterly defeated at Plassey by the genius of Clive, who had but a handful of troops as against seventy thousand. That victory made the British masters of the whole province of Bengal, and laid the foundations of our Indian Empire. From henceforward the French power in India rapidly declined. In America an equal triumph crowned Pitt's policy. In Wolfe he had found a man able to do in the West what Clive did in the East, and Canada became a British Colony. Wolfe himself fell in the great struggle for Quebec, as did Montcalm, his rival French general, and a monument stands in the north ambulatory of the Abbey to the memory of the gallant young leader, who died in the hour of his victory. "It is necessary to watch for a victory every morning for fear of missing one," was the remark of Walpole's son Horace. And the nation felt that it was Pitt whose policy and whose power had made all these things possible. Parliament was entirely in his hands, he swayed the Commons by his eloquence just as he impressed them by his strength; the King supported him, and the people adored him.

But in 1760 George II. died, and his second son George, who succeeded him (Frederick Prince of Wales having died), did not care for a minister so fearless and independent. Neither was Pitt without enemies. When he saw that his opponents, supported by the King, were determined to make a peace with France of which he could not approve, he resigned, after making a powerful speech though he was very ill at the time. His words concluded thus: "It is because I see in this treaty the seeds of a future war that it meets with my most hearty disapprobation. The peace is insecure, because it restores the enemy to his former greatness; the peace is inadequate, because the places gained are no equivalent for the places surrendered." Before a year was over, all that Pitt foretold had come to pass, and England was again at war with Spain. Bute, who had been virtually Prime Minister since Pitt gave up office, now resigned, leaving in power Grenville, the leader in the House of Commons, and in a very short time Grenville brought forward a measure concerning America, which was so short-sighted and so opposed to the colonial spirit, that it could only have a disastrous ending. Practically all North America was in British hands, and it was divided into thirteen different States, besides Canada. Those States had their own Colonial Assemblies, but the supreme power rested with the British Parliament. In 1765 Grenville brought in the Stamp Act, by which American colonists had to use legal paper stamped in England for all their agreements, and this was carried without the consent of the colonists, as they had no representatives in Parliament, so that besides imposing a tax on them, Parliament had really tampered with one of their most sacred rights as British subjects. The Act was very badly received in America, and relations became so strained that Pitt, to whom any matter affecting the Colonies was very dear, came out of his retirement to protest against the Act, and brought all his splendid fearless eloquence to bear on the subject. "This kingdom has no right to tax the Colonies," he argued, and he went on to declare—

"I rejoice that America has resisted. Three millions of people so dead to all feelings of liberty as voluntarily to submit to be slaves, would have been fit instruments to make slaves of the rest.... The Commons of America have ever been in possession of their constitutional right of giving and granting their own money. They would have been slaves if they had not enjoyed it.... A gentleman asks, 'When were the Colonies emancipated?' I desire to know when were they made slaves? ... I stand up for this kingdom. I maintain that our legislative power over the Colonies is sovereign and supreme in every circumstance of government and legislation. But taxation is no part of the governing or legislative power. Taxes are a voluntary gift and grant of the Commons alone. When therefore in this House we give and grant, we give and grant what is our own. But in an American tax what do we do? We, your Majesty's Commons for Great Britain, give and grant to your Majesty—what? Our own property? No; we give and grant to your Majesty the property of your Majesty's Commons of America. It is an absurdity in terms. I beg leave to move that the Stamp Act be repealed absolutely, totally, and immediately; that the reason for the repeal be assigned because it was founded on an erroneous principle. At the same time let the sovereign authority of this country over the Colonies be asserted in as strong terms as can be devised, that we exercise every power except that of taking their money out of their pockets without their consent."

Pitt still held his sway over the House of Commons, and the Act was repealed. A few months later he was again Prime Minister, but now no longer as William Pitt, the great Commoner. He had accepted a title, to the disappointment of many of his followers, who had revered him in the past for his entire independence; and after he sat in the Lords as Earl of Chatham, his influence never made itself felt in the same way. Besides, his health continually broke down, bravely though he struggled against it, and he was often laid aside for many months at a time. During one of these periods, another irritating Act was passed, taxing all the tea, glass, and paper imported into America, and as this occurred just when the sore feelings over the Stamp Act had been allayed, it was particularly unfortunate. The Colonists looked on it as an act of revenge for their victory and determined to resist it, while the King was unfortunately surrounded by a party, of which Lord North was the chief, who urged him, whatever the cost might be, to force America into submission. Lord North becoming Prime Minister was the signal for an outbreak of public feeling in America; riots occurred, and some tea-laden ships in Boston harbour were boarded, the tea being all thrown into the water. Again Chatham raised his voice on the side of consideration, of common sense, and of conciliation.

"My Lords," he said, after he had used one telling argument after another to prove how useless and irritating had been the action of the Government, driving these loyal sons of the old country into actions which were the result of despair, and which in cooler moments they would heartily regret, "I am an old man, and I plead for a gentle mode of governing America, for the day is not far distant when America may vie with these kingdoms, not only in arms, but in arts also.... If we take a transient view of those motives which induced the ancestors of our fellow-subjects in America to leave their native country to encounter the innumerable difficulties of the unexplored regions of the western world, our astonishment at the present conduct of their descendants will naturally subside. There was no corner of the world into which men of their free and enterprising spirit would not fly with alacrity rather than submit to the slavish and tyrannical principles which prevailed at that period in their native country. And shall we wonder, my Lords, if the descendants of such illustrious characters spurn with contempt the hand of unconstitutional power, that would snatch from them the dearly-bought privilege they now contend for? My Lords, proceed like a kind and affectionate parent over a child whom he tenderly loves. Instead of these harsh and severe proceedings, pass an amnesty on their youthful errors; clasp them once more in fond, affectionate arms, and I venture to affirm you will find them children worthy of their sire."

But his powerful pleading fell on deaf ears. All in vain did he urge that though the Government might be revenged on America, no Government could conquer it. In 1775 war, terrible as a civil war, broke out between the old country and the new. The Congress raised an army, and set at the head of it George Washington. "The man first in war, first in peace, first in the hearts of his countrymen," solemnly declared that from henceforth the United Colonies would be free and independent States, and carried on the campaign with the utmost success, assisted by France. Dismayed at last and astonished, Lord North and his ministers began to talk of conciliation. But it was too late. Two British forces, each of about four thousand men, had been forced to surrender to the American troops. No longer was it possible for England to make terms.

At home there was consternation, irresolution, and a sense of deep resentment against the Government which had so blundered. Chatham was a dying man, but he yet had something to say. Weakness, irresolution, or fear were unknown words to him, even though now he admitted—

"I tremble for this country; I am almost led to despair that we shall ever be able to extricate ourselves."

On the 7th of April 1778 he lifted up his voice for the last time, this time against an ignominious surrender, which the discomfited Government, terrified by the action of France, were all too ready to accept. Conscious himself of his fast-ebbing strength, Chatham, the Imperialist minister of the eighteenth century, summoned all his old fire and eloquence to his aid, and spoke with intense feeling, rejoicing, he said, "that the grave had not yet closed on him, pressed down as he was by the hand of infirmity."

Panic-stricken, the Government were inclined to offer absolute independence to all the Colonies. Chatham vigorously opposed the idea.

"His Majesty," he declared, "succeeded to an empire as great in extent as its reputation was unsullied. Shall we tarnish the lustre of this nation by an ignominious surrender of its rights and fairest possessions? Shall this great kingdom, that has survived whole and entire the Danish degradations, the Scottish invasion, the Norman Conquest, that has stood the threatened invasion of the Spanish Armada, now fall prostrate before the house of Bourbon? Shall a people that seventeen years ago was the terror of the world, now stoop so low as to tell its ancient and insatiate enemy, 'Take all we have: only give us peace.' In God's name, if it be absolutely necessary to declare for peace or war, and the former cannot be preserved with honour, why is not the latter commenced without hesitation? My Lords, any state is better than despair. Let us at least make an effort; and if we must fall, let us fall like men!"

With this brave appeal Chatham sat down exhausted. A few moments later he was carried fainting out of the House, which at once adjourned. And within a month, he who has been described as "the first Englishman of his time," had passed from the troubled arena of politics.

WILLIAM PITT
FIRST EARL OF CHATHAM.

WILLIAM PITT FIRST EARL OF CHATHAM.

His monument in the Abbey shows him to us as he must often have looked when, wearing his Parliamentary robes, he addressed the House in that clear, sweet voice of his, which he could use with such wonderful effect, and the sculptor has well caught the expression of his fearless strength. Near him stand Prudence and Fortitude; below is Britannia, Mistress of the Seas; and the inscription tells how, under his administration, Great Britain was exalted to a height of prosperity and glory, unknown in any former age.

His second son, William, was born in 1759, the year that was perhaps the most successful in his father's life, and as he was too delicate to go to school, the older man personally supervised the early education of this his favourite child. When quite small, Chatham began to give him lessons in public speaking, making him stand on a platform to recite poetry or speeches, and later on teaching him to argue their points. With such a teacher and such a ready pupil, it is not surprising to hear of excellent progress made.

Little Willy Pitt, as he was called, soon showed in which direction his inclinations lay. "I am glad I am not the eldest son," he remarked, when he was seven, "as I want to speak in the House of Commons like papa."

He was only nineteen when his father died, but it was he who had helped the old statesman to his place in the House of Lords on the last day of his life, he who assisted to carry him out, and he who stood as chief mourner at that impressive funeral in the Abbey, his elder brother being abroad. The thought of any life but a political and a public one, never entered his mind, and two years later he became a member of Parliament. The first step up the ladder was taken. Already a trained speaker, his gifts were at once recognised by the House. Members of both parties generously praised him, and prophesied that his would be a great career. "I doubt not," said honest William Wilberforce, "but that I shall one day see him the first man in the country." His likeness to his father was remarkable. "Language, gesture, and manner were all the same," wrote his delighted tutor. "All the old members recognised him instantly, and most of the young ones said this was the very man they had so often heard described."

But it was not on his father's merits that William Pitt sprang into immediate fame; his own personality was his passport.

Thirteen years before, another young man had entered Parliament, Charles James Fox, the brilliant, excitement-loving son of Lord Holland. After Eton and Oxford he had been sent abroad to complete his education, but so great were his follies and extravagances, that his father had to firmly summon him home. This mandate, we are told, "he obeyed with great reluctance," and he seems to have gone back with an extensive wardrobe of clothes in the latest and most costly fashions, leaving behind him enormous debts in every town he had visited.

Lord Holland, who flattered himself that he had studied the world and human nature with great attention and success, decided that a seat in the House of Commons would best steady this irrepressible young man, and provide him with occupation and ambition, so, though he was only nineteen, and therefore legally not entitled to become a member, he was duly elected, the Speaker, by wilful or accidental oversight, offering no opposition. He too from the first delighted the House as a speaker, for he was fresh, forcible, and graceful, with a great personal charm of manner and an entire absence of conceit, and no one gave a more cordial welcome to Pitt than he did, little dreaming in how short a time this young man would be his lifelong and his successful rival. Rockingham, who had succeeded North as Prime Minister, died suddenly in 1782, and from every point of view Fox appeared to be the man who ought to have succeeded him. But the King cordially disliked Fox, and sent instead for Lord Shelburne. Fox, ever impetuous and hasty, refused to serve under him, and Shelburne turned to Pitt, who thus at the age of twenty-three became Chancellor of the Exchequer and leader of the House of Commons. A year later Lord Shelburne resigned, and the Premiership was offered to Pitt, an honour greater perhaps than any honour ever offered to a young man of twenty-four. He declined it; the Duke of Portland accepted it; and Fox became leader in the House of Commons, with what seemed to be a strong coalition Government at the back of him. For the moment the Whigs were all-powerful, and against them stood Pitt, who refused to be a member of any coalition, with a handful of men who had belonged to the old Chatham party. No one hated the present arrangement more than the King, and before long he saw an opportunity of crushing it. Fox, chiefly by his own magnetic influence, had carried a bill concerning India through the Commons, but the Lords, influenced by the King, threw it out, whereupon he dismissed the Government, and persuaded Pitt to accept the office of Prime Minister. Never before had such a state of things prevailed. The Premier was a youth of twenty-four, with a majority of two to one against him in the House of Commons! Whatever he brought forward was defeated. Fox used all his eloquence against him, and over and over again he was put in an impossible position. Pitt, Lord Rosebery has told us, was never young. Certainly, at this crisis, his patience, his caution, his firmness, and his cool judgment would have done credit to a statesman of half a century's experience. He did not make a mistake, and gradually he won the country to his side. Before many months were over, Parliament was dissolved; an election had taken place; and Pitt came back into power with a large majority. For seventeen years he remained in office. Nothing could have been greater than the contrast between him and his strenuous opponent Fox, who was the most impulsive, genial, and lovable of men; extravagant in every direction, in his likes, his hates, and his sympathies; easily stirred and able to pour forth a torrent of passionate eloquence; living always in the excitement and impulses of the moment, with never a thought for the morrow. Pitt, on the contrary, was cool and thoughtful. He stood, as it were, aloof from all the world, though on the rare occasions when he unbent, he was full of charm. "Smiles were not natural to him," said a contemporary. "He is," said Wilberforce, who unfeignedly admired him, even though he could not always follow him, "one of the most public-spirited and upright men I ever knew." And he was called upon to guide the ship of State through troubled waters. It was his task to raise the money in payment of the American war bill, for a debt of about twenty millions stared him in the face. Then he had to face more than the usual amount of difficulty with Ireland, where the celebrated Dublin Parliament which Henry Grattan, its brilliant leader, had forced Fox to agree to, proved itself so unable to cope with the task undertaken, that riots and disturbances broke out in every quarter. Pitt believed that only one solution was possible, namely, that instead of a separate Parliament at Dublin, the Irish members with the Scotch should sit at Westminster, and in the year 1799 he brought in the Act of Union, which was carried during the next session, in spite of a strong speech against it by Grattan, who was dragged from his sick-room for the occasion. Pitt had also to contend with a restless wave which swept over England, the result of the French Revolution. But though the young minister was always ready for reform, he would have nothing to do with violent changes or with revolution, neither was he afraid to bring in such measures as seemed likely to repress the revolutionary spirits in England. The French leaders, not content with having executed their king and queen, and having waged war on Austria, when that country moved to rescue the luckless Austrian princess, now Queen Marie Antoinette, went to the further length of declaring that every country not agreeing with the doctrines of the Revolution was to be regarded as an enemy, and was to be forced into war. For some while Pitt managed to hold the English people from plunging into the conflict. He was altogether a peace minister. But public opinion was too strong for him; the old hatred of France was there, and the events of the last few years had fanned it into life. Pitt had to bow to the will of the nation, though it was the French who finally declared war in 1793 by an attack on Holland, after which England could no longer stand aloof, though Fox, in his hot-headed way, declared that in his opinion we had no right to demand the withdrawal of French troops from the Netherlands. From that time until the day of victory at Waterloo in 1815, the fight between England and France continued with more or less intensity.

And the final issue was due in no small degree to Pitt, who, though he hated the war, had during his long ministry of peace freely spent millions of pounds on the British navy, recognising that so long as England was mistress of the seas she was safe. From the moment, too, that war was declared, he threw himself heart and soul into every measure for carrying it through successfully; never for a moment did he show a weak front, or fail to be the leader in every sense of the word. When Napoleon, elated by his series of triumphs on the Continent, prepared to invade England, it was Pitt who gave an impetus to the volunteer movement by himself raising a force of 3000 men, and placing himself at their head. "His spirit will lead him to be foremost in the battle, and I am uneasy at it," said Wilberforce; "yet it is his proper post, and I can say nothing against it." In an incredibly short time a volunteer force of 300,000 was enrolled, "their good sense and firmness supplying their want of experience." But though his spirit was as strong as ever, his delicate frame was giving way under the high pressure at which he had lived. True to his promise to Wilberforce, he had pushed forward the Abolition of Slavery Bill, and he did not relax an effort as regards his war policy, though on the Continent Napoleon was still all victorious. Wellesley, a young soldier, had just come back from India with a good reputation, and Pitt, then a dying man, sent for him. He knew that what England wanted now was a great soldier to lead her armies; her navy was safe under such commanders as St. Vincent, Collingwood, and Nelson. For hours he talked to Wellesley, only ceasing when he fainted from exhaustion. "The greatest minister that has ever ruled England," was the verdict of the soldier statesman. Then came the news of the victory at Trafalgar, saddened only by the death of the heroic Nelson. But Pitt was drifting far away from all these things. His mind wandered as his life flickered out; only just at the end there was a rally. "Oh my country!" he cried; "how I leave my country!" That was his last thought and his last speech.

When the usual proposal was brought forward that he should be buried at Westminster at the expense of Parliament, and that a monument should be erected, Fox characteristically felt bound to oppose it. "He could not honestly," he said, "call a man an excellent statesman who had consistently supported so bad a system." But when it was further suggested that Parliament should pay the debts he had left and provide for his nearest relations, no one agreed so cordially or so readily as Fox. Wrong-headed he often was; wrong-hearted never.

Into the same grave as his father William Pitt was laid in the presence of all the distinguished people of the day, his pall-bearers being six men each of whom had been, or was to be, a Prime Minister of England. "The figure of the first William Pitt," wrote Wilberforce, "seemed to be looking down with consternation into the grave of his favourite son, the last perpetuator of the name he had ennobled. It was an affecting ceremony."

Pitt was still a young man, only forty-seven, yet into those years he had crowded a glorious life, and it was with truth that the herald proclaimed over his grave, "He lived not for himself, but for his country."

Eight months later, Fox, who did not live to enjoy the power his rival's death had placed within his reach, was buried close to him in the Abbey. During his short spell of office, he had carried Wilberforce's Slave Bill, and had frequently said he could retire happily when once that bill was made safe. He disdainfully refused a Peerage. "I will not close my politics in that foolish way," was his remark. Near together too, though not in the Statesmen's Corner, are the monuments of these two whose lives were throughout so interwoven. Pitt towers in lonely state over the west door, standing there as if he were about to pour forth his magnificent eloquence on the statues below and charm them back into life for one brief moment. Fox lies surrounded by weeping figures, one of whom represents the negro whose cause he had so powerfully championed. And so the great Mother Church gathers them both to herself, claiming each as a noble son of England.

Henry Grattan, the Irishman, is buried close to Fox, his friend and hero. He had often told his followers that he wished to lie in a quiet churchyard of his loved Ireland, but they had other ideas. "Well then," he said resignedly, "Westminster Abbey!" His funeral had a very distinctive touch, for it was attended by hundreds of Irish children from various charitable institutions, all of whom wore dresses of bright green.

Next to the imposing monument of Chatham is a statue to Lord Palmerston, that most English of statesmen. He went into political life more from a sense of duty than from any particular liking for it, or from any feelings of ambition. But into every office that he held he carried with him a sturdy independence, a dogged tenacity of purpose, a fund of common sense, and a very clear idea of what he meant to attain. Add to this that he was the essence of good-nature, the most genial of friends, simple and straight, manly and cheery, and we have some idea of the man whom the nation insisted on having for Prime Minister, when he was over seventy years of age, at a critical moment when it was felt that only a strong, fearless, popular statesman could guide the ship out of the storm.

And then, in contrast to the kindly, contented Palmerston, comes the tomb of Lord Castlereagh, a statesman as much out of touch with the people as "Pam" was their hero. He was Secretary of State for War in those days when the struggle with France was beginning, and because at first things went badly he was made the scapegoat. It was he who planned that combination of forces which at last broke down the French resistance, but that was not realised till long afterwards; in those early days his policy was not successful, so it was unpopular. He stood aloof from all men; he was cold, indifferent, wanting in tact, with no gifts as a speaker, and yet, looking back now on his work, it is easy to see how well he faced a period of unexampled difficulty. Nevertheless, he was invariably misunderstood, and therefore unjustly disliked, so that at last his mind gave way under the storm of hatred and abuse levelled against him, and, in a dark moment, he put an end to his life. Even at his funeral in the Abbey, the crowds could not forget their dislike of him, and shouted exultantly as the coffin was carried inside the doors. But the Abbey gave him a welcome and a resting-place.

On the opposite side stand the statues of the three Cannings: George Canning, the statesman; his youngest son, Lord Canning, first Viceroy of India; and their cousin, Lord Stratford de Radcliffe, "the wise old man of the East," who was our ambassador at Constantinople during those years which led up to the Crimean War, and whose influence, supported by the Government at home and France, made it possible for Turkey to hold Russia at bay. The verse on the statue:

"Thou third great Canning, stand among our best

And noblest, now thy long day's work hath ceased;

Here silent, in our Minster of the West,

Who wert the voice of England in the East,"

is the work of Tennyson, who has only written one other epitaph in the Abbey. Close together are the monuments of Sir Robert Peel and Benjamin Disraeli, Earl of Beaconsfield. Peel was the Minister who, in the face of violent opposition, caused the tax on imported corn to be repealed, thereby making bread cheaper; and Disraeli, who first won his reputation by the persistent manner in which he fought this policy of Peel's, doggedly forged his way to the front against much prejudice, until he, though not an Englishman by race, held the proud position of being the loved and trusted Prime Minister of Queen Victoria. The statue of Beaconsfield—for by his own desire he was buried next to his wife in the country churchyard at Hughenden—casts its shadow over the grave of William Ewart Gladstone, whose family only consented to his being laid there on the condition that Mrs. Gladstone should eventually rest beside him, even as Lady Palmerston lay by her husband's side. The coffin which contained this old statesman, who was better loved and better hated perhaps than any public man of our generation, was placed for some time in Westminster Hall, and nearly a quarter of a million people passed through to pay their last token of respect. The time has not yet come when his place in English history as a statesman can be fairly judged, but friend and foe alike can bear tribute to his brilliant intellect; his talents as a financier; his excellent learning; his wonderful personality; his rich eloquence; his generous sympathies; his stainless private life; and to those other qualities which his political opponent Lord Salisbury so finely described as making him "a great Christian." "God bless you, and this place, and the land you love," had been his last public utterance, and in the spirit of that message we leave him, who in life stirred up such sharp dissensions, sleeping peacefully in the Abbey.

CHAPTER XX
INDIAN STATESMEN AND SOLDIERS: LAWRENCE AND THE HEROES OF THE MUTINY

The Indian Mutiny, which produced "such a breed of warlike men," the equals of whom have rarely, if ever, been found awaiting their country's need of them, is especially commemorated in the Abbey, which holds the graves of Lord Lawrence; Colin Campbell, Lord Clyde; and Sir James Outram. Only a monument does honour to Warren Hastings, whose name is so indissolubly linked with Westminster and with India, for it was at Westminster School that he was educated, the favourite pupil of the headmaster Dr. Nichols, who found him "a hard student, bold, full of fire, ambitious in no ordinary degree;" and it was to India that he went, when eighteen, into the service of the East India Company. To the building up of the British Empire in India he gave his life, working with unfaltering courage under a thousand difficulties, sometimes no doubt making errors of judgment, more often the victim of other men's intrigues and treachery, but always the dauntless, enthusiastic servant of the State. And his reward was disgrace, confiscation, and impeachment. He was used by Ministers at home as a cat's-paw in the game of politics. Burke and Fox charged him in Parliament with cruelty, extortion, and corruption, while Sheridan's brilliant eloquence so dazzled the Commons as to obscure all their calm judgment, and they impeached Warren Hastings at the bar of the House of Lords for "high crimes and misdemeanours." In the February of 1788 this most famous of trials commenced in Westminster Hall, and it took Burke two days to get through his list of charges. All the force of his great powers as an orator was brought to bear against the accused, who "stood there small, spare, and upright, his bearing a mixture of deference and dignity, his soft sad eyes flashing defiance on his accusers; the lines of his mouth and chin firm, his face very pale but calm."

The trial lingered on and on; it was seven years before the verdict was given, a verdict which practically cleared Hastings, and proved that, if on occasions he had been unnecessarily ruthless or hard in his rule, he had not so acted from any selfish or unworthy motive, but because he believed that thereby he was best serving the interests both of England and of India. Though he was acquitted, he was practically a ruined man. The trial had cost him more than £70,000, and he was not rich, neither could he hope for any employment under Fox or Pitt. The East India Company voted him a pension for twenty-eight years, but refused him when he asked that it might be continued during the lifetime of his wife, "the dearest object of all his concerns." And so he died a bitterly disappointed man.

RT. HON. WARREN HASTINGS.

John Lawrence was the son of a soldier, and from boyhood he had chosen the army for his profession, as a matter of course. Three of his brothers had already gone to India, two into the cavalry, and one into the artillery, and John was hoping to enter the service of the East India Company in the same way, when to his disgust he was offered an appointment, not in their army, but in the Civil Service. There could be no question as to which of the two branches offered the better opening to any hard-working, ambitious young man, but John would hear none of this. "A soldier I was born, a soldier I will be," he said firmly. And he was only moved in his resolution by the simple, sensible arguments of his invalid sister Letitia, to whom he was entirely devoted. So to the East India College at Haileybury he went, and sailed for India at the age of eighteen, considered by his elders to be a reliable, intelligent lad, but nothing more. The old longing for a soldier's life came back to him on landing, and for the first few weeks he was so entirely miserable, that, as he said afterwards, "the offer of £100 a year would have taken me straight home again." Then he firmly pulled himself together and resolved that there should be no turning back now; he would go forward, and do the work which came to him with all his might. Delhi was his first destination, and soon he found himself in charge of a district, so good a reputation had he made for being both self-reliant and cautious. It was a turbulent, unsettled piece of country that he was given to bring into order, but his firmness, justice, and conscientious hard work accomplished wonders, and prepared him for greater things. Without a single soldier he kept perfect order among his people through the great drought, which filled his district with starving men and with bands of robbers, but at last his health gave way under the strain of eleven years' work, and he came home to England on sick leave. Two years later he returned to his post, now a married man, and was soon brought into close contact with that sturdy soldier, Sir Henry Hardinge, who was in command of the fierce campaign then being waged against the Sikhs. Hardinge entirely depended on being able to get sufficient supplies, guns, and ammunition from the base at Delhi, and it was to the civilian magistrate there, John Lawrence, that he appealed for help. Splendidly that help was given. Lawrence organised a system of carts, each to be driven by his owner; and in an incredibly short time a long train of guns, ammunition, and food of all sorts, reached the camp, as much to the delight as to the astonishment of the General. A few days after the arrival of these welcome supplies, the battle which ended the campaign was fought and won. Hardinge did not forget the man who had made this victory possible, and gave him for reward a most responsible piece of work, the charge of the newly won Sikh province of Jalandhar.

A second Sikh war, which ended in the complete submission of the Sikh army, gave the whole province of the Punjab into the hands of the Viceroy.

"What shall we do with it?" he asked of Lawrence.

"Annex it at once," was the answer; and when Lord Dalhousie pointed out the difficulties, Lawrence, who had known and realised them all, met every objection with the words: "Action, action, action!"

So the Punjab was annexed, and it was decided to govern it by a Board, which included Henry Lawrence and John Lawrence. Frankly, let us admit at once that the arrangement was not a happy one. Both brothers were men of strong character and great ability, but they saw things from very different points of view. Henry was enthusiastic, imaginative, and easily moved; John was entirely practical and clear-headed. Each loved and respected the other, but neither would give way on what seemed to each vital questions of importance. Finally, both sent in their resignations, and Lord Dalhousie, wisely recognising that John Lawrence was specially fitted for the special work required at the moment in the Punjab, made him the Chief Commissioner, and moved Henry to another field. It was a great province to reduce to law and order, even when it was divided into seven districts, ruled over by picked men. But Lawrence was a born organiser. Not only could he work himself indefatigably, but he knew how to choose other men for the posts that had to be filled, and having chosen them, he trusted them and supported them loyally. He had only to recognise "grit," or "metal," in a subordinate, and there was nothing he would not do to help him on. "Human nature is human nature," he would say, and "A strong horse if held with a tight hand will do more than a weak horse to whom you may give his head." So he managed to keep his brilliant colleagues all in one team; he smoothed over their disagreements, he dealt with them all quite frankly, criticising where he held it needful, praising generously whenever it was possible, and thus he gathered around him that band of men, including Nicholson, Chamberlain, and Edwardes, who came to the fore so vigorously a little later in the hour of the crisis. But Lawrence was to do still greater things in the near future.

A year later saw the outbreak of the Mutiny, which came as a thunderbolt to the British Government in India. The first rising, terrible in its suddenness, was at Meerut, where a maddened crowd of sepoys, thirsting for the blood of all Europeans, seized the arms and ammunition, released their prisoners, murdered whoever resisted them, and then made for Delhi, at which place all the rebels from the country round were assembling. Within Delhi, the native regiments joined the mutineers; Europeans were ruthlessly massacred, and though the tiny garrison made a magnificent defence, expecting every hour to be relieved by a strong British force, they at last had to realise that resistance was useless and that each one must escape for his life as best he could.

To Lawrence, just starting for his holiday, came the well-known message from Delhi, "The sepoys have come in from Meerut, and are burning everything. We must shut up," followed by a second telegram which told that Delhi was in the hands of the rebels. Strange to say nothing was being done from Meerut, where there was a fairly large force of British troops, to avenge the murderous outbreak.

John Lawrence, however, was a man of action, and his younger colleagues were not a whit less determined. At all costs Delhi must be regained—that was the first move unanimously agreed on; but every hour's delay meant danger, for each day brought recruits to the rebels, and the disarming of the doubtful native troops must be carried out at once if it were not to be too late. Lawrence had a twofold task. He must make safe and hold secure for England the Punjab, that vast inflammable province containing more than thirty thousand sepoys, for which work he knew he could rely on Chamberlain, Nicholson, and Edwardes; but more than this, he must put forth every power to assist in the retaking of Delhi. When at last an army of about three thousand men took up their stand on a ridge outside Delhi, they knew that within the walls of the city at least a hundred thousand foes awaited them, with numbers of guns and an unlimited supply of ammunition. Overwhelming indeed were the odds against them. But one fact gave them confidence. Behind them lay the road leading to the Punjab and to the man whom they knew would send along it, to their help, his best officers, his best troops, ample supplies and ammunition, who would never cease watching, working, and urging until once more the British flag waved over Delhi.

For twelve weary weeks the struggle waged, and Lawrence strained every nerve. The position in the Punjab was highly critical; only the ceaseless vigour of its Chief Commissioner, and his strong, fearless policy, held in check the rebellion all ready to break out. Had the Punjab failed, nothing but disaster could have overtaken the Delhi Field Force. But John Lawrence never doubted, never despaired, even when there reached him the appalling news of the Cawnpore massacre, followed by the tidings from beleaguered Lucknow, where Henry Lawrence had fallen at his post with the dying request that on his tomb might be recorded the words: "He tried to do his duty."

At last the tide turned. Delhi was saved, and though all was not yet won, Lawrence knew that the crisis was over. But that moment was clouded, for the man who, above all others, had brought about the capture of Delhi, was no more. John Nicholson had fallen in the proudest hour of his life, and when the news came to Lawrence he completely broke down.

"He was a glorious soldier," he said. "He seems to have been specially raised up for this juncture, and so long as British rule shall endure in India his fame shall never perish; without him, Delhi could not have fallen."

It was a generous tribute and a just one. But we must never forget that behind John Nicholson was John Lawrence.

"Not a bayonet or a rupee has reached Delhi from Calcutta or England," wrote Edwardes. "It has been recovered by Lawrence and his resources. Honour, all honour to Coachman John, and honour, too, to the team that pulled the coach. He alone was at the helm, and bore all the responsibility on his own shoulders"!

The district of which Delhi was the capital was at once handed over to the Punjab Government, and Lawrence hurried thither in a mail-cart, that law and order might be restored without delay. His policy was just what might have been expected of him—a generous combination of strength, mercy, and justice; and within six months he was able to report that "perfect order reigned throughout the Delhi territory."

It was just at this juncture that Colin Campbell arrived in India as Commander-in-Chief.

"When will you be ready to start?" Lord Palmerston had asked him in offering the command.

"To-morrow!" said the soldier promptly. And on the morrow he started.

He had distinguished himself in the Crimea. There he had held the command of the Highland Brigade, a post of all others for which he was fitted. A Highlander himself, he perfectly understood how to handle the men of his own race, and the advance on the Alma was splendidly made by his troops, who exhibited such rare courage combined with perfect coolness that when Lord Raglan rode up to compliment their commander, "his eyes filled with tears and his countenance quivered."

"The army is watching you, make me proud of the Highland Brigade," Campbell said to his men on the day of Balaclava. "Remember," he added, "there is no retreat from here! You die where you stand."

"Aye, aye, Sir Colin; we'll do that!" was the answer.

Rarely has a more touching farewell order been issued than that from Campbell to his men, when at the end of the campaign he was about to return to England. Part of it ran thus:—

"A long farewell! I am now old, and shall not be called to serve any more; and nothing will remain to me but the memory of my campaigns, and the memory too of the enduring, hardy, generous soldiers with whom I have been associated.... When you go home you will tell the story of your immortal advance up the heights of Alma, and you may speak of the old brigadier who led you and who loved you so well.... And the bagpipes will never sound near me without carrying me back to those bright days when I was at your head and wore the bonnet you gained for me, and the honourable decorations on my breast, many of which I owe to your conduct. Brave soldiers, kind comrades, farewell!"

But the old soldier had not done yet, and he promptly left England for India, where he arrived at the darkest hour, before the fall of Delhi, and when Havelock had been foiled in his brave attempt to relieve Lucknow.

Sir Colin and John Lawrence were old friends, and the Commander-in-Chief at once wrote: "It will be a matter of real gratification to me if we exchange our plans and ideas from time to time.... I am thankful you were in the Punjab to face the storm."

The chief concentrated all his energy on bringing order and organisation out of chaos at Calcutta, so that efficient reinforcements, properly equipped, might be speedily got together, and meanwhile Outram went to the assistance of Havelock. "Outram is a fine soldier and a fine man," Lawrence had written of him affectionately, and this "Bayard of India, who had served that country for forty years in war and council," as it is recorded in the Abbey, showed himself full worthy of the highest praises that could be bestowed on him. When he reached Cawnpore with reinforcements which would make possible the relief of Lucknow, he refused, though the senior officer, to take the command. Havelock had borne the heat and burden of the day, Havelock must be the hero when the hour of victory was at hand. "I cheerfully waive my rank and accompany the force to Lucknow, tendering my services to Brigadier-General Havelock as a volunteer," he said, with a fine chivalry which was characteristic of one "who ever esteemed others better than himself, who was valiant, self-denying, and magnanimous—in all the true knight!" The column forced its way into Lucknow, but even so, it was impossible to fully relieve the garrison. Once inside the walls Outram took over the command, and made the best of the position directly he realised that for the present he could only reinforce, not relieve. But Colin Campbell was on his way with the army of about five thousand men which he had collected after great efforts. A miscellaneous force indeed it was: Lancers, Sikhs, Punjab infantry, the Queen's, and the 93rd Highlanders, which the Commander-in-Chief had formed up, so that he might address them, and the Highlanders burst into cheers at the sight of their beloved General.

"You are my own lads," he said to them; "I rely on you to do yourselves and me credit."

"Aye, aye! Sir Colin," answered a voice from the ranks; "ye ken us, and we ken you. We'll bring the women and bairnies out of Lucknow, or we'll leave our ain banes there!"

Magnificently they kept their word. When it came to the last assault, Sikhs and Highlanders positively raced with each other to be first through the breach, and seemed impervious alike to the heavy fire poured on them, or the desperate hand-to-hand struggle. Over five hundred killed and wounded made up their casualty list; but the women and the bairnies were saved. And though Sir Colin longed to make a second decisive attack on the enemy, he held back with great self-control, deeming it his first duty to withdraw all the sick with the women and children in safety to Alumbagh, a feat difficult enough under any circumstances, and requiring all his available troops. Hardly had he accomplished this than news came that Cawnpore, with its tiny garrison, was once more surrounded by the enemy, and was, so the message said, "at its last gasp."

"How dare you say of her Majesty's troops that they are at their last gasp," thundered the chief. And forthwith made for the entrenchments, where his very presence saved the situation.

WEST TRANSEPT.

All this while John Lawrence had not relaxed his efforts, and just at this moment he sent the welcome intelligence to Sir Colin that he had three thousand cavalry and twelve guns waiting for him. With those and other welcome reinforcements the chief was able to make his final attack on Lucknow, which continued fiercely during nineteen days, but which ended in complete victory for the British troops, though they were but a force of 30,000 against 120,000 of the rebels. With the fall of Lucknow the burning flames of the Mutiny may be said to have been extinguished; what remained was the smouldering of the fire. To Sir Colin the Queen wrote an autograph letter which thrilled him with pride, part of which ran thus:—

"The Queen has had many proofs already of Sir Colin Campbell's devotion to his Sovereign and his country, and he has now greatly added to the debt of gratitude which both owe him. But Sir Colin must bear one reproof from his Queen, and this is, that he exposes himself too much. His life is most precious, and she entreats that he will neither put himself where his noble spirit would urge him to be—foremost in danger—nor fatigue himself so as to injure his health."

A little later her Majesty signified her intention of conferring on him a peerage.

"We dinna ken hoo tae address ye, Sir Colin, now that the Queen has made ye a lord!" said one of the Highlanders sadly.

"Just call me Sir Colin, John, the same as in the old times: I like the old name best," was the answer.

Although Lucknow was taken in the March of 1858, it was more than two years before Sir Colin Campbell was able to return to England, having finished his work; and then after three years spent at home, surrounded by "honour, love, and troops of friends," the old warrior passed away from the battle-field of life.

Lawrence, now a baronet, and greatly worn out by the heavy strain he had been through, had reached England in 1859, where he found the British public eager to shower honours on one whom they held to be the saviour of India. His great modesty led him to shrink from it all.

"If I was placed in a position of extreme danger and difficulty," he declared, "I was also fortunate in having around me some of the ablest civil and military officers in India. And I hope that some rewards will be extended to those who so nobly shared with me the perils of the struggle, and by whose aid my efforts were crowned with success."

He settled down to work as a member of the Council of India, and Lord Derby, then at the India Office, was deeply impressed not only by his great ability but by his "heroic simplicity." "Even if his opportunity had never come," he declared, "you would always have felt that you were in the presence of a man capable of accomplishing great things, and capable also of leaving the credit of them to any one who chose to take it."

The death of Outram was a great sorrow to Lawrence, and he it was who went to the Dean to beg that his old friend should be buried in the Abbey, as the one place worthy of him. He too made all the arrangements for the funeral, and it was at his suggestion that the sergeants of Outram's old regiment carried their beloved leader to his grave.

Quite unexpectedly the Government called on him to return to India as Viceroy, and though he would far rather have remained in England, he felt that he ought to go. To him the call of duty was ever the one call to which the heart of every true man must unfailingly respond. His appointment was for five years, and during this time he remained at his post, carrying out the policy of his life, by which he desired "to avoid complications, to consolidate our power in India, to give to its people the best government we can, to organise our administration in every department on a system which will combine economy with efficiency, and so to make our Government strong and respected."

"I do not wish to shorten my term of office, nor do I wish to prolong it," he said in answer to the question as to what his feelings were now that he was about to deliver over the government of the country.

"It was a proud moment for me," he added, "when I walked up the steps of this house, feeling that without political interest or influence I had been chosen to fill the highest office under the Crown, the Viceroy of the Queen. But it will be a happier moment for me when I walk down the steps with the feeling that I have tried to do my duty."

On his return home he was made a peer, and for some years he devoted himself untiringly to public and philanthropic work, acting as Chairman to the London School Board until his failing eyesight and his broken health put an end to his public life. "It is overpowering to see him thus laid low and worn out," wrote one who saw him daily. "But to us he seems grander than ever in his affliction, and we realise the truth that 'he who ruleth his spirit is greater than he who taketh a city.'"

Ten years after he had left India the end came, and Honest John, as he was affectionately called, was carried to the Abbey, to be buried there with all the honour that was his due.

CHAPTER XXI
DICKENS, BROWNING, AND TENNYSON

It is impossible to wander round the Poets' Corner without a longing that the Abbey could claim as her own all the great singers and seers who have made the literature of our country. Chaucer and Spenser indeed we have, with other writers of the Elizabethan and Stuart periods; but many familiar names are missing altogether, or marked only by a bust or slab. John Philips, Matthew Prior, John Gay, and Thomas Campbell—these were the last poets buried in Westminster for many a long day. Shakespeare, Milton, Goldsmith, Coleridge, Burns, Keble, Wordsworth, Thackeray, Matthew Arnold, Kingsley, Ruskin, have monuments, and so we have their names; but how many a one is there for whom we look in vain in this national temple of honour. Langland, Herrick, Herbert, Sidney, Pope, Byron, Shelley, Keats, Bunyan, Sir Thomas More, Defoe, and Swift are unknown English writers so far as the Abbey is concerned.

Towards the latter end of the nineteenth century, however, there came a change. Macaulay and Grote, historians, were both buried within its walls, and when Charles Dickens died in 1870, Dean Stanley at once suggested Westminster to his family, who declined the offer. Then there appeared an article in the *Times* declaring that the Abbey was the one place worthy to receive so distinguished a writer. Still his family hesitated, and at last only consented on the condition that the ceremony should be entirely private. So it came to pass that, one evening after dark, when the Abbey was closed, a grave was dug in the Poets' Corner close to Thackeray's bust, and in the early summer morning the funeral took place in solitary simplicity. But in a few hours the news had spread, and before the day was over thousands of persons had been to take a last look at the grave of the writer they loved, many of them the very poorest people, who yet brought with them a few flowers or some other humble token of remembrance.

There was no aspect of their life he had not understood and sympathised with, for his boyhood's days had been spent in their midst. His father, unable to pay his debts, had been cast into prison at Marshalsea, so the Dickens family had settled in the neighbourhood, little Charles supporting himself by pasting labels on to blacking-pots, and making the acquaintance of all those queer people and odd characters with whom his writings have taught us to be familiar. "David Copperfield" is to a great extent an autobiography of Charles Dickens himself, who started life "a prey to the cruel chances of the London streets, and who, for all the care that was taken of him, might easily have become a little robber or vagabond, but for the mercy of God," to use his own words. However, brighter days were in store for him, for the elder Dickens managed to get clear of his debts and became Parliamentary reporter to the *Morning Herald*; and Charles, after a few years at school, during which he had managed to learn as much as was possible, decided to take up newspaper work, though in many ways stage life was what attracted him most. "I was always an actor and a writer from a mere baby," he said.

Fortunately regular work was offered him on the staff of the *Morning Chronicle*, and before long he had made his name as the "best Parliamentary reporter in the Peers' Gallery." From henceforward he determined that writing should be his career, and under the name of Boz he launched a book of Sketches, "illustrating everyday life and everyday people," into the world. The sketches were just what they claimed to be, but it was a masterhand that had drawn them, and these everyday people were described with such a perfect touch that the general public, delighted and greatly entertained, at once set the young author on a pedestal of popularity.

The "Pickwick Papers," which followed shortly afterwards, increased his reputation and established his position. Here was a writer bubbling over with a fresh, keen sense of humour, and in every page of his book the humour came out, never strained or forced, always natural, kindly, and infectious. From "Pickwick" he turned to quite a different style, for in "Oliver Twist" he gave to the world a brilliant picture of the "dregs of life." The subject was sad enough, and Dickens, before all things a truthful writer, did not seek to conceal anything, and yet so wonderful was his sympathy with all humanity, even the most degraded, that he never failed to recognise goodness and nobleness however deep down they might be hidden away. He saw below the surface, and in all that he wrote he forced his readers to think the better of mankind. Dickens went on from one success to another; he thoroughly understood his public and his own line, and his great heart was so full, so responsive, so in tune with the tender emotions which belong to all men and women in common, that he never grew stale or dull. Master alike of pathos and of humour, he appealed direct to the hearts of his readers. "Nicholas Nickleby," "The Old Curiosity Shop," "Martin Chuzzlewit," "The Christmas Books," "Dombey & Son," "David Copperfield," "Bleak House," and "The Tale of Two Cities," in their turn won for him countless friends and admirers from every class of life in England and in America, for all his characters were living people, and though he never moralised or lectured, he always purified and uplifted.

"Do not harden your hearts," was his message to the world. "Sympathise, pity, help, understand, love. Laugh if you will, so long as you laugh not in scorn; but love always, love everywhere."

A gravestone in Westminster is his only monument there, but that was by his own desire. To a great crowd assembled in the Abbey on the Sunday after his funeral, Dean Stanley read aloud these words from his will, "sacred words," he said, "which come with a new meaning and a deeper force, because they come from the lips of a lost friend, because they are the most solemn utterance of lips now for ever closed in the grave":—

"'I direct that my name be inscribed in plain English letters on my tomb.... I conjure my friends on no account to make me the subject of any monument, memorial, or testimonial whatever. I rest my claims to be remembered of my country upon my published works, and to be remembered of my friends upon their experience of me in addition thereto.... And I exhort my dear children humbly to try to guide themselves by the teaching of the New Testament in its broad spirit, and to put no faith in any man's narrow construction of its letter here or there.'"

It was in this "broad spirit" of Christ's Teaching that Dickens lived and wrote. He tore down the veil that hid the lives of the poor and suffering from the lives of the rich and prosperous. The remembrance of those dark sights and scenes of his boyhood never passed away from him. "They pierce through my happiness, they haunt me day and night," he said. He could never rest till he had lifted up his voice in the cause of those "little ones" whom he loved and in whom he could recognise so much that was beautiful and true. Kindness, tenderness, sympathy, generosity, and divine pity, these were the stones with which he built up his monument, and they are stones which shall endure through the ages to come, a glorious memorial of him "who loved, with a rare and touching love, his friends, his country, and his fellow-men."

Robert Browning and Alfred Tennyson, the greatest poets of our generation, lie side by side, underneath Chaucer's monument, and to both of them was given a stately public funeral, which showed how honoured a place they held in the hearts of their countrymen. For more than fifty years Browning had been writing, and only very slowly, very gradually had he made his way in the public favour. He was not, except on occasions, a sweet singer; his rhymes did not flow gracefully and easily; his thoughts were great, but his words were clumsy; to himself what he taught was as clear as the day, but to his readers it was often sadly confused and hard to understand. Nor did he ever aim at winning popularity or success. He wrote more for the future than for the present, and he was quite content to wait.

"Were you never discouraged," a friend asked him once, "at the indifference of the public, and the enmity of the critics?"

"*Never*," was his emphatic answer.

And his reward came while he was still there to appreciate and rejoice, not after death as is so often the guerdon of him who sees what is hidden from his fellows. He set up a standard of thought and feeling, and slowly but steadily he saw the public coming up to that standard, and marching onward more hopefully, more bravely, more confidently. His life story is simply told. He was born in Camberwell, and most of his education was obtained at the London University. His father was a bank clerk, who hated the routine of office work, and had a perfect passion for books. He read in season and out of season, he was a familiar figure at all the old book-stalls, he knew many languages, and had a mind literally stored with treasures of culture and learning. Robert soon showed he had inherited the same love of books, and when he was fourteen coaxed his mother till, after some difficulty, she got him copies of the poems written by Keats and Shelley. "Those two poets came to me as two nightingales," he has told us, and from henceforward his mind was practically made up. He, too, would be a poet, and as if to begin a suitable course of training, he set himself to read and master the whole of Dr. Johnson's Dictionary. His father put no hindrances in his way, on the contrary he promised him every assistance, and an aunt came forward with offers of money, so firmly did she believe in the talents of her nephew. It was at her expense that his first book, "Pauline," was published anonymously, and though a very small public appreciated the work, here and there a friendly critic was found brave enough to say that the author, whoever he was, though he must not look for popularity or expect to make a sensation, was certainly a poet. "Paracelsus" followed, the story of a man who desired knowledge above all else, and who in the search for knowledge forgot to seek for love, hope, fear, and faith, those nobler qualities that give to life its true note and character; but at the time this shared the same fate as "Pauline," and was little appreciated. Then he tried his hand at dramatic writing, producing first "Stafford" and afterwards "The Blot in the Scutcheon," and though Dickens wrote enthusiastically concerning the latter, "This play has thrown me into a perfect passion of sorrow.... It is full of genius, natural and great thoughts, profound yet simple, and beautiful in its vigour," Browning contented himself with saying, "A pitfull of good-natured people applauded it." Then, with the buoyant hopefulness which was part of him, he added, "Failure will not discourage me from another effort: experience is yet to come, and earnest endeavour may yet remove many disadvantages."

And he continued to write. In 1844, being then thirty-two, he met Elizabeth Barrett, the invalid poetess with whose work he was already familiar, and from the first his heart went out to her. For some time she steadily refused to listen when he talked of marriage, on account of her ill health. But his persistence wore down her half-hearted resistance, especially as her happiness in the knowledge of his love proved a good doctor, and she showed signs of growing stronger. Her father, who seems to have objected to any of his daughters marrying, had made up his mind that Elizabeth would never leave home, and it was certain he would never have given his consent. So with some misgivings Miss Barrett consented to her lover's entreaties. They were married privately; he took her abroad, and in her newly found joy she rallied surprisingly. To the end of her life she was fragile, and it was never possible for her to stand side by side with him through all the daily ups and downs, but the sympathy between them was as complete as their love for each other was beautiful, and in spite of the many new responsibilities it laid upon him, his marriage with this rare mind brought a daily increasing happiness to the poet. From this time forward much of his time was spent in Italy, for the sake of his wife; but when in 1861, with her death, "the light of his life went out," he returned to London and lived here till the end, always working, always genial, drawn more and more into an ever-widening circle of friends, as the greatness of his mind and genius became known and appreciated. Active to the last, he died in 1889, while on a visit to Venice. But England claimed him as her own, and so strong was the feeling as to the Poets' Corner being the only place where he could be buried, that his son consented, in spite of the fact that Mrs. Browning slept under the blue skies of Italy.

It would be quite impossible now to talk of Robert Browning's poems by name; they are too many in number and too deep in thought to be lightly dealt with. But we can try to understand what it is that has made him so great a figure in English literature, why it is that he has left so powerful an influence on his age.

First of all he was a great teacher, he was a seer, as every true poet must be if his work is to live.

"To know the heart of all things was his duty;

All things did speak to him to make him wise,

And with a sorrowful and conquering beauty,

The soul of all looked grandly from his eyes.

He gazed on all within him and without him,

He watched the flowing of Time's steady tide,

And shapes of glory floated all about him,

And whispered to him, and he prophesied."

He looked on life as a great whole, part to be lived here, part to be lived beyond the grave, but each part belonging to the other. He believed that over all, guiding all and through all, was the Divine Power.

"God's in His Heaven:

All's well in the world."

He knew that human nature must work its way upwards by struggling bravely on through the darkness, certain of victory at last, because good and not evil was the all-conquering force. And so, while he was full of hope and full of confidence, his understanding and his sympathies were boundless.

Courage! unfailing, confident courage! is the refrain of which he never wearies. Aspire towards the highest; be your best; love for love's sake and not for reward; work your hardest; fight valiantly to the end; never listen to despair; never lessen your efforts. It is the struggle and the striving that makes life worth living, for—

"Life is probation, and this earth no goal

But starting-point of men."

Nor is there such a thing as failure to those who aspire rightly.

"A man's reach should exceed his grasp,

Or what's a Heaven for?"

And again—

"Then welcome each rebuff

That turns earth's smoothness rough,

Each sting that bids nor sit, nor stand, but go!

Be our joys three parts pain,

Strive, and hold cheap the strain;

Learn, nor account the pang: dare, never grudge the throe."

The power and the love of God, the possibilities within the reach of every man, and the unalterable certainty of the life beyond, these beliefs made it impossible for Browning to sing in any but a hopeful strain, and it is for this that we owe him our deepest debt of gratitude. For he always encourages us, he always inspires us, he always sends us on our way cheered by his own strong faith.

Sometimes, it is true, his verse is rough and rugged, often he is so absorbed in the sense of what he says that he cares very little how he says it, but every poem he wrote holds so many precious things that it is worth while wading through difficult places to get at them. And as he himself once said, "With care for a man or a book, most obstacles can be overcome."

Many a poem could I give to show you that Browning could pour out sweet music when he wrote of certain subjects. Here is one of his most charming songs—"Home Thoughts from Abroad":—

"Oh to be in England now that April's there,

And whoever wakes in England sees, some morning unaware,

That the lowest boughs and the brushwood sheaf

Round the elm-tree bole are in tiny leaf,

While the chaffinch sings on the orchard bough

In England—now!

And after April, when May follows,

And the white-throat builds, and all the swallows!

Hark, where my blossomed pear-tree in the hedge

Leans to the field and scatters on the clover

Blossoms and dewdrops—at the bent spray's edge,—

That's the wise thrush; he sings each song twice over,

Lest you think he never could recapture

The first, fine, careless rapture!"

On the day of his death there was published the last volume of his poems, and it had been a great pleasure to him to hear with how much interest they were expected. For more than fifty years he had waited, and at last his message to his generation was being understood. He had been "ever a fighter," and now, as he stood facing that "one fight more, the best and the last," which was at hand, he had still one fine marching song to send back to his fellow-men.

"Never say of me that I am *dead*," he had asked of a friend not long before.

"No work begun shall ever pause for death!

Love will be helpful to me more and more

In the coming course, the new path I must tread."

So when those who loved him read the words that told how Robert Browning had died at Venice, having lived more than his threescore years and ten, they turned for their comfort to his last stirring message, and remembered him as he had wished to be remembered—

"At the midnight, in the silence of the sleep time,

When you set your fancies free,

Will they pass to where—by death, fools think, imprisoned—

Low he lies, who once so loved you, whom you loved so.

Pity me?

Oh to love so, be so loved, yet so mistaken!

What had I on earth to do

With the slothful, with the mawkish, the unmanly?

Like the aimless, hopeless, did I drivel

Being who?

One who never turned his back, but marched breast forward,

Never doubted clouds would break,

Never dreamed though right were worsted wrong could triumph.

Held we fall to rise, are baffled to fight better,

Sleep to wake!

No, at noonday, in the bustle of men's work time,
Greet the unseen with a cheer.
Bid him forward, breast and back, as either should be.
'Strive and strive!' cry Speed—fight on, fare ever
There as here."

Three years after Browning's death a crowd of over eleven thousand persons filled Westminster to every corner, on the day when our other great poet, Alfred Tennyson, was borne here, to remain for ever "a citizen of the Abbey." His coffin, fitly draped with the Union Jack, because some of his finest lines had been called out by the thought of Empire, Flag, and Queen, was surrounded by all the most noteworthy men of the day as it was carried slowly through the aisles, "down the avenue of those men, princes and peers by right of intellect divine." Tennyson, like Browning, had written a last message to the world, but his was not a marching song. Instead it breathes of perfect peace, of the joy which came to him, "who throughout the night had trusted all to Him that held the helm, and then saw face to face, full flushed and glorious with the new morning's glow, the Pilot whom he had trusted."

"Twilight and evening bell,
And after that the dark!
And may there be no sadness of farewell
When I embark;
For though from out our bourne of Time and Place
The flood may bear me far,
I hope to see my Pilot face to face
When I have crost the bar."

These thoughts of his filled the Abbey with a sense of their restfulness; then there thundered out from thousands of voices the familiar hymn—

"Holy, holy, holy, Lord God Almighty!"

and the words recalled to many a mind that Vision of which the clear-souled poet had sung, the Gleam he had so faithfully followed, until now it had surely led him right up to the presence of God.

LORD TENNYSON.

Alfred Tennyson had been born at a country vicarage in Lincolnshire in the year 1809, and had begun to scribble verse almost as soon as he could write. When he was eight he produced such lines as—

"With slaughterous sons of thunder rolled the flood,"

which he thought "very grand" at the time; at twelve he wrote a poem of six thousand lines, and at fourteen a drama. He was not the sort of boy likely to be very happy at school, and he had, as he described it, "to shout his verses to the skies." But to his brother he was wont to say many a time, "Well, Arthur, I mean to be famous." He went to Cambridge, and when Thompson, that shrewd observer, afterwards Master of Trinity, saw him walk into the hall, "six feet high, broad-chested, strong-limbed, his face Shakespearean and with deep eyelids, his forehead ample, crowned with dark wavy hair, his head firmly poised," he remarked, "That man must be a poet!"

In 1829 he won the University Prize Poem on the not very inspiring subject of Timbuctoo, and soon afterwards published a volume of short poems, which was warmly welcomed and admired by his friends, one of whom, Arthur Hallam, remarked, "Tennyson will be the greatest poet of our generation." But the general public cared little for poetry, and preferred novels, so that Tennyson was thought to have scored quite a success when three hundred copies of his book had been sold.

In 1833 there fell on him a stunning blow. Arthur Hallam, the friend whom he had loved with an intense love, who was so full of exceptional promise that every one with whom he came in contact believed the greatest future was in store for him, died quite suddenly, and to Tennyson it seemed as if from henceforth the very light of his life had been snatched from him. Dark were the years that followed, rendered more so by the fact that the young poet was very poor and saw no chance of being able to marry the woman he loved. But gradually, as he "faced the need of going forward and braving the struggle of life" (to use his own words), a fuller understanding and a wider view opened out before him. Sorrow and work together led him out of the valley. He produced several volumes of short poems, each one showing more certainly his great poetic sense, his gift of using musical and beautiful language, and each one, too, making it clear from the subjects he chose, and his way of dealing with them, that he himself, like the poet of whom he wrote—

"Saw thro' life and death, thro' good and ill,

... Thro' his own soul,

The marvel of the Everlasting Will

An open scroll,

Before him lay."

Then came "The Princess," a longer work and a most delightful one, in which Tennyson, many years in advance of public opinion, pleaded the cause of women's education, and showed that "Woman's cause is man's; they rise or sink together;" and though "distinct in individualities," they must be "self-reverent each, and reverencing each," if they would in all their powers dispense the harvest, "sowing the To-be."

In 1850 he published his greatest work, "In Memoriam," the poem which came straight from his own heart, and went as straight to the hearts of all who ached under some crushing, desolating blow. It told of his love for his dead friend, and how this very love led him onwards and upwards, away from his own selfish sorrow, away from despair and darkness, till with this larger hope there came faith in God and faith in man; the certainty that good must be the final goal of ill; the conviction that Love was the great power working in all and through all, destined in the end to conquer all. "In Memoriam" has been rightly called "the triumph of a great love." The work brought him fame if not fortune, and at last he was able to marry her "who brought into his life," he said, "the peace of God." A year later he was made Poet Laureate, and settled down to a quiet country life at Farringford. "Maud," and some of his war poems, "The Ode to the Duke of Wellington," and "The Charge of the Light Brigade," were included in his work of the next few years, and then came what he considered the most ambitious thing he had attempted, "The Idylls of the King." The old mysterious story of King Arthur and his knights had fascinated many a poet before him, and the romance of it all laid full hold on his imagination. Nay, more than this, for he saw beyond the fragmentary story, and each one of the characters, under his hand, stands out in a new light. Arthur, Galahad, Percival, Bedivere, Lancelot, Guinevere, Enid, and Elaine—how real they all become to us! How intensely vivid are the scenes unfolded before our eyes, how great and noble are the ideals of the true chivalry as distinguished from the false, towards which Tennyson leads us, reverence for conscience, faithfulness to duty, pure-heartedness, love of truth, fear of sin, courtesy, gentleness, courage, pity, and forgiveness.

"A poet must teach, but not preach," Tennyson once said, and I think it is in these legendary stories of "The Idylls," told in the beautiful language of which he was master, that the poet has given some of his greatest lessons, and has held up his loftiest ideals to the age in which he lived. After "The Idylls" came some dramas, and many short poems, "Enoch Arden," perhaps, being the one best liked by the large public Tennyson could now command. But even to touch on the short poems is impossible here, so many and so varied are they; some, soul-stirring and patriotic, as "The Defence of Lucknow" or "The Revenge;" some, poems of nature; some, coloured with the quaint, north-country humour he knew so well; some, exquisite little word-pictures. His last volume of all was published in 1889, and it included "Merlin and the Gleam," an allegory of the ideals he had set before himself as a poet. He, as the old man, talks to the young mariners just about to set out. He tells of the Gleam which shines for every one who will see it; which calls, which beckons on through wilderness, desolate hollows, and wraiths of the mountain; past warbles of water and cataract music of falling torrents; by rolling of dragons and over the level of pasture and ploughland. Onwards, ever onwards, it leads. To follow it is to live, to die in the search for it is happiness, for the Gleam can never fail.

"Through the magic

Of Him that is mighty,

Who taught me in childhood,

There on the border

Of boundless Ocean

And all but in Heaven

Hovers the Gleam."

So to the young mariners, he, the old magician, gives his parting word of counsel—

"Down to the haven,

Launch your vessel

And crowd your canvas,

And, ere it vanishes

Over the margin,

After it, follow it,

Follow the Gleam."

"I want to go down to posterity," Tennyson once said, "as a poet who uttered nothing base." And the criticism which he declared was "the best and tenderest praise that came to cheer his old age," was the remark of a girl who said, "When I read his poems, I always rise determined to be better."

Much might be said about the perfect music of his poetry; the richness of his imagination; the faultless ear he had for words; the crystal clearness of his style; his power to see beauty and, having seen it, to shape it; his sympathy, his sensitive understanding, and his lofty ideals. His claim to greatness is based on all that and still more. Out of the depths of his pure soul he gazed on all things lovely, just, true, pure, and of good report; and translating these into language easy to be understood, he led those who listened to him along the Road Beautiful, till they too stood with him on

"The heights of life, with a glimpse of a height that is higher."

CHAPTER XXII
A LAST WANDER AROUND

There are still many monuments and memorials in the Abbey which do not come in under the broad headings we have made, and to some few of these I must take you in this our last wander round the aisles and chapels.

As we come in by the great north entrance and pass between the row of statesmen, we must stop for a moment by the Canning group and notice the monument to the "loyall Duke of Newcastle," who lost a large fortune and became an exile from England on account of his devoted faithfulness to Charles I. The Duchess, who came of a family in which "all the brothers were valiant and all the sisters virtuous," was, in the Duke's eyes at least, a very "wise, witty, and learned lady," though every one did not deem her so. Pepys, when he made her acquaintance, wrote: "She is a good, comely woman, but her dress is so antick, and her deportment so ordinary, that I did not like her at all. Nor did I hear her say anything that was worth hearing." It was curiosity, I suppose, that caused Pepys to stay at home one day "to read the history of my Lord of Newcastle, written by his wife." Certainly his criticisms were not favourable. "It shows her to be a mad, conceited, ridiculous woman," he said. "And he is an ass to suffer her to write what she writes to him and of him."

Perhaps the "loyall Duke" found his learned lady not always quite easy to restrain, for he is reported once to have declared to a friend, "Sir, a very wise woman may be a very foolish thing."

But she had better claims than her wit or wisdom to his love, as the inscription on her monument tells, for she proved herself to be "a louving carefull wife, who was with her lord all the time of his banishment and miseries, and when he came home, never parted from him in all his solitary retirements."

Round the west door, and underneath the statue of the younger Pitt, are a number of memorial monuments to men, many of whom lived and laboured in our own times. There is Lord John Russell, the great statesman, who throughout his life was true to the emblem and the motto of his house, which you will see on the pedestal—a mountain goat wending its way through dangerous precipices, but never losing its footing. And there is General Gordon, true type of the happy warrior, who lived for the poor, the needy, and the oppressed, and who fell at his post in far Khartoum, faithful unto death. On the one side is a spot sometimes called the Little Poets' Corner, and here, under a window given by an American to the memory of George Herbert and Cowper, "both Westminster scholars, and both religious poets," we find statues or busts of Wordsworth; of the two Arnolds, Dr. Arnold, the schoolmaster, and his son Matthew Arnold, the poet, whose beautiful verses about his father, telling of his radiant vigour, his buoyant cheerfulness, his strong soul, have inspired many a one struggling to be a leader, not a laggard, in the march of life. Here also is Keble, another religious poet, some of whose hymns, "Sun of my Soul" and "New every morning is the Love," are as well known to all of us as any poems in our language; and close by we find Maurice, the teacher and preacher who influenced so many young men to become knights of their own day; to war against all that was mean, or base, or false; to fight in the foremost rank for the wronged or the oppressed; to champion the unpopular cause, and defend the truth well-nigh forgotten. By those who loved him he was called the Prophet, because he stood, as it were, between God and man, because he looked beyond the present and the things that are seen, right into the hidden glories of the things eternal. Kingsley, too, lies here, the most famous of Maurice's disciples—the man who was scholar, poet, novelist, thinker, teacher, enthusiast, and leader all in one; who roused his listeners to a sense of the duty that lay at their door; who taught them to love the beautiful things in nature even as they loved nature's God; who made them enthusiastic for all that was chivalrous and soul-stirring; who himself so loved all humanity that round his grave the highest in the land, gipsies from the country lanes, and white-faced, sweated toilers from the great cities, mourned side by side, this their great-hearted friend.

Fittingly in this group comes Henry Fawcett, the most knightly figure in modern politics. For though he became blind through an accident when he was twenty-five, he refused to let that turn him aside from his purpose, and threw himself all the more earnestly into public life. At first when he tried to go into Parliament he was beaten, the electors actually being afraid of a blind candidate, but gradually his speeches, which showed how much he thought and cared, and how intensely alive he was to the needs of the working classes, broke down this foolish prejudice, and once in the House he was loved as he was trusted by men of both parties. His monument is quite one of the most beautiful among the modern monuments, and one great authority has declared that "the exquisite little figures which adorn it are the best of their kind since the little angels were placed on the tomb of Queen Philippa."

In the south aisle of the choir is the monument of Sir Cloudesley Shovel, which so annoyed Addison. And indeed it is rather hard on this British sailor, who worked his way up from the lowest rank till he became Commander-in-Chief of the Fleet, and was drowned in a shipwreck off the

Isle of Stilly, to be handed down to posterity, dressed, not in the uniform he loved and wore so honourably, but in the armour of a Roman general!

Monuments to Doctor Isaac Watts the hymn writer and to John and Charles Wesley are here, and very appropriate is the Wesley inscription, "The whole world is my Parish," breathing as it does the great-hearted spirit of the Abbey.

Sir Godfrey Kneller, the only painter who has a monument in the Abbey, refused to be buried here, declaring he would not lie among fools, and he left money for a memorial to himself which was to be put up in Twickenham Church. But the place he had chosen had already been appropriated by Pope, who refused to give way, so that after all the monument had to be put up in Westminster, and Pope, by way of compensation, undertook to write the inscription, in which he declared that "Kneller was by Heaven, not by master taught."

Gilbert Thornburgh, a courtier, has a delightful Latin epitaph which states that

> "He was always faithful
> To his God, his Prince, and his Friends.
> Formerly an earthly, now an Heavenly Courtier,
> It shall be no more said in the Age to come,
> Who must be good must leave the Court,
> When such shining Piety as his shall appear there."

Some epitaphs are humorous, as when we read of one Francis Newman, a Fellow of All Souls College in Oxford, who in 1649, "divested of Body was received among the seats of the Blessed Souls, and became truly a New-Man;" or of Sir John Fullerton, a courtier, who died "Fuller of Faith than of Feare, Fuller of Resolution than of Paines, Fuller of Honour than of Dayes."

Unconsciously humorous are the words on the tombstone of James Fox, who at the age of twelve fell ill of smallpox and took his flight to heaven. "He was a man even when a child, and a Hercules from his cradle; favoured with Beauty, Wisdom, and all Endowments of Mind and Body no less than were Adonis, Venus, and Apollo; a child of singular dutifulness and great sincerity."

"Oh parents! pity his parents.

Oh posterity! reflect upon your loss!"

It was smallpox which caused the death both of Richard Boothey—who was "of manly judgment even in his youth, of so happy a memory as to be envied, a flower, more beautiful than the rest, cut off in the spring of life"—and of Mr. Thomas Smith, buried in the little cloisters, "who through the spotted veil of smallpox rendered a pure unspotted soul to God, expecting but never fearing death."

More pathetic perhaps than any other is the little tablet in the cloisters which marks the grave of "Jane Lister, dear child," though almost as touching is the inscription which tells us of "Mary, daughter of William Green, more adorned with virtue than with high birth, who married William Bulmer, Gentleman, to whom she was no occasion of trouble except by leaving him at her death. She bore him one son, William, a youth of great genius, who was snatched away by too hasty death. His most tender mother chose to be buried near him, that she, though dead, might be united in death with him she so entirely loved while living." Right at the other end of the Abbey, in the Chapel of St. Erasmus, is the tomb of Mrs. Mary Kendall, which has these words for inscription:—

> "She had great virtues, and as great a desire of concealing them.
> Was of a severe life, but of an easy conversation.
> Courteous to all, yet strictly sincere.
> Humble without meanness. Beneficent without ostentation.
> Devout without superstition.
> Those admirable qualities,
> In which she was equalled by few of her sex, surpassed by none,
> Rendered her in every way worthy of that close union and friendship
> In which she lived with the Lady Katherine Jones."

And in the adjoining Chapel of St. Andrew is the heart-broken tribute of the Earl of Kerry, "to his affectionately beloved wife, Anastatia, the dearest, most loved, most faithful companion that ever blessed man, who for thirty-one years rendered him the happiest of mankind."

The last of our epitaphs must be that of Archbishop Boulter, who pulled a great many political strings in Ireland, and lived a very eventful life. But his inscription reveals us none of these things, and only describes a series of promotions, for it relates that "He was born January the 4th, 1671: he was consecrated Bishop of Bristol 1718: he was translated to the Archbishoprick of Armagh in 1723, and from thence to Heaven, on Sep. 27, 1742."

Over Abbot Islip's Chapel is a chantry, now used for keeping the few wax effigies which remain. For, as you remember, it used to be the custom at royal funerals, or indeed at any important funerals, to carry the likeness of the dead man or woman before the coffin; these painted effigies being made of boiled leather, wood, or wax, dressed up in the clothes of the person they represented. Only eleven of these remain, though at one time there must have been quite a collection of royal figures in the Abbey which were open to the public, gaze, and evidently left to the mercy of the public. Queen Elizabeth can still be seen, gorgeously dressed, but weary and sad-looking; Charles II. is there, and the beautiful Duchess of Richmond of the Stuart race, whose monument, with that of her husband, is in Henry VII.'s Chapel. Then there is the Duchess of Buckinghamshire, proud and pomp-loving, who insisted on seeing the canopy for her funeral hearse, that she might be sure it was magnificent enough, and who made her attendants promise that even when she became unconscious they would still stand in her presence. By her is her little son, and near her, her eldest son, who also died young. Queen Anne beams on us; William and Mary have the crown set between them, and he stands on a stool so as not to appear smaller than his wife. General Monk's armour is there, much the worse for wear; and Pitt, Earl of Chatham, is splendid in his Parliamentary robes. Nelson was put here from a very worldly point of view, for when he was buried in St. Paul's, such crowds went to see his grave, that Westminster Abbey was neglected, and as the pence of the sightseers were too valuable to be lost, it was decided that some memorial of the great hero must be placed in the Abbey to attract people back again. All the clothes except the coat, and certainly the hat, belonged to Nelson, but a waxwork effigy hardly seems a worthy monument to him in the place which he must have loved and honoured, nay, must have dreamt of, when he cried to his men as he led them to attack, "Westminster Abbey, or glorious victory."

And now, leaving monuments, sleeping figures, epitaphs, inscriptions, and effigies, come and stand for a moment on the steps leading up to the High Altar, that we may take our last look at the Abbey from what is perhaps the most interesting spot in it. For, as you will remember, it is in this part of the Church that the coronation service takes place, it is here that every sovereign of England has been crowned from the days of Harold onwards.

THE HIGH ALTAR. (SHEWING ABBOT WARE'S PAVEMENT.)

THE HIGH ALTAR. (SHEWING ABBOT WARE'S PAVEMENT.)

The pavement inside the rails is made of the mosaics brought back from Rome by Abbot Ware in 1267, where he went to be duly confirmed in his office by the Pope; the pillars near the altar are on the very bases which were put there when Edward the Confessor built his church. Here are the tombs of Aymer de Valence, of Edmund Crouchback, Earl of Lancaster, and of Aveline his young wife, who as a bride had stood in front of the altar but a few months before her death in the year 1269. Opposite, King Sebert is said to lie; under the pavement rests Abbot Ware, with other of his successors, and Richard the Second's sad helpless face looks at us from his portrait with its fine background of tapestry. The altar and the reredos which we see are both new, and just as the old frieze through in the Confessor's Chapel depicts scenes in the life of Edward, so the modern reredos gives us glimpses of Him in whose honour the Saxon king first raised these walls. From among the gold, four white figures stand out, "the four living creatures which have been thought worthy to stand round the central figure of our departing Master," as Dean Stanley described them when they were erected. On the right stands St. Peter, patron saint of the Abbey, holding in one hand the keys, and in the other a book, on which is written the great truth, "God is no respecter of persons," and next to him is Moses, the first statesman and lawgiver, looking towards the buried statesmen in the Abbey.

On the left stands St. Paul, grasping in his hand that Sword of the Spirit which he had named as the weapon of the Christian warrior, and by him is David, the sweet singer of Israel, whose face is turned towards the Poets' Corner as though he would claim those sleeping there for his brethren.

Through the glass we catch a glimpse of the Chapel of the Kings, and all around is a network of slender arches fashioned by master-hands into forms of stately but perfect beauty. High above are the three Eastern Windows, though in the course of the years these have been so constantly repaired with any scraps of glass available, that the effect is rather confusing. But the figure of a thorn-crowned Christ stands out, and near to Him are Edward the Confessor and St. John the Evangelist.

Now turn to the west, look at the glade of arches stretching down the nave, at the Statesmen's Corner on the right, where under the Rose Window Chatham's fine figure stands out almost with an air of proud satisfaction, and then towards the left to the monument of Oliver Goldsmith, and the more imposing memorial to the great Duke of Argyll, "an honest man, a constant friend, a general and an orator." Two commanding statues of Campbell and Addison loom out in the half light, Campbell casting a shadow over the graves of Abbot Litlington, Owen Tudor, and Dean Benson, and hiding from our view the dignified, thoughtful figure of William Shakespeare, who holds in his hands a scroll on which are those lines of his from the "Tempest":—

"The cloud-capt towers,

The gorgeous palaces,

The solemn temples,

The great globe itself,

Yea, all which it inherit

Shall dissolve,

And like the baseless fabric of a vision

Leave not a wreck behind."

Burns and Sir Walter Scott greet us from their niches; Grote and Thirlwall, the truth-loving writers of history; Camden, the Westminster master and antiquarian; Garrick the actor, Handel the musician, all cluster around us as we look down the southern aisle; and we can just see at the end the newest addition to the building, a bronze memorial to John Ruskin, a great teacher and writer of our own day. Some words of his come to my mind at this moment, as applying in a very special sense to the Abbey: "The greatest glory of a building is not in its stones, nor in its gold. The glory is in its age, and in that deep sense of voicefulness, of stern watching, of mysterious sympathy, nay, even of approval or condemnation, which we feel in walls that have long been washed by the passing waves of humanity.... It is in the golden stain of time that we are to look for the real light, and colour, and preciousness of architecture; and it is not until a building has assumed this character, till it has been entrusted with the fame and hallowed by the deeds of men, till its walls have been witnesses of suffering, and its pillars rise out of the shadows of death, that its existence, more lasting as it is than the natural objects of the world around it, can be gifted with even so much as those possess of language and of life. Therefore, when we build, let us think that we build for ever.... God has lent us the earth for our life; it is a great entail. It belongs as much to those who are to come after us, and whose names are already written in the Book of Creation, as to us."

And surely, too, the Abbey leads our thoughts towards other temples, which it is ours to guard, to honour, and to make honourable, temples not fashioned by human hands. Those old builders often worked in the dark; some corner, some piece was allotted to them, and into this they put all their skill, all their genius, caring little for fame or reward, knowing nothing of the whole plan which they would never live to see accomplished. Only this was their task, to beautify the little part entrusted to them. And because they were faithful to this ideal, we, who gaze on their completed work, do grateful homage to those nameless craftsmen, long since dead and forgotten. Nay more, we will make it our aim to labour as they laboured; to live not basely and selfishly in the Present, but nobly and truly, with the Future ever before our eyes; so that in days to come Englishmen shall still be able to say, "See! This our fathers did for us!" and generations, yet unborn, will deem that we were faithful to ourselves and to them.

THE END

Milton Keynes UK
Ingram Content Group UK Ltd.
UKHW030905151124
451262UK00006B/1003